Praise for *The Secret Psychic*

"This book spells out possibilities, assuring each of us that IT IS NOT WEIRD to expect signs and blessings from the Universe. It should be expected."

—Pam Grout, #1 *New York Times* bestselling author of *E-Squared*

"This book will make you realize something: each of us is psychic in our own way. Not *a little psychic*—psychic, period. By the last page, you'll not only believe in your own power, but you'll have the tools to begin using it."

—Amanda Lovelace, author of *Shine Your Icy Crown*

"A 'must-have' for those awakening to their inherent divine gifts…I highly recommend this book."

—Raven Keyes, author of *Medical Reiki*

"This excellent book gives you the insights, understanding, and perhaps even the permission needed to fully embrace your innate gift."

—Margaret Ann Lembo, author of *Chakra Awakening*

"An incredible resource and guide for anyone on an intuitive and psychic journey—secret or not."

—Tammy Mastroberte, bestselling author of the award-winning book *The Universe Is Talking to You*

"An exciting book—one that encourages readers to both acknowledge and develop their own inherent psychic abilities…Well written, interesting, and enlightening."

—Kenneth J. Doka, PhD, author of *When We Die*

"[Angela] knows what she's talking about and you can trust the process that this great book will take you through."

—Echo Bodine, bestselling author of *The Gift*

"*The Secret Psychic* will help you go from hidden spiritual life to one where you can finally embrace, expand, and share your gifts."

—Amy B. Scher, author of *How to Heal Yourself When No One Else Can*

"A book which we all need…Read *The Secret Psychic* to become aware of your hidden potential, accept the truth and validity of what you experience, and learn ways to enhance your life and that of others."
—Bernie Siegel, MD, *New York Times* bestselling author of
Love, Medicine & Miracles

"Angela masterfully lays out all the pitfalls of budding intuition and helps readers successfully and confidently reveal their talents to the world with grace and humility."
—Shelley A. Kaehr, PhD, author of *Blast from the Past*

"[A] wise, inspiring, down-to-earth guide. It will help you bridge the gap between logic and intuition, form and spirit, known and unknown, so you can wield your intuitive abilities with confidence, mastery, and joy."
—Tess Whitehurst, author of *The Self-Love Superpower*

"A compelling guide to the hidden superpower we all possess: intuition. With characteristic warmth and wonder, Angela Wix explores the natural yet marvelous ability we all have to tune in to the unseen and reveal the mysteries of the unknown."
—Dr. Clare Johnson, author of *The Art of Lucid Dreaming*

"You'll find hands-on practices to magnify and perfect your natural psychic skills. [This book is] overflowing with practical information and techniques."
—Nicholas Pearson, author of *Crystal Basics* & *Foundations of Reiki Ryoho*

"A much-needed handbook…Its pages contain practical advice for embracing intuitive gifts and gently integrating them into daily life at a comfortable pace."
—Natalie Fowler, award-winning author of *The Spirit's Way Home*

"A beautiful tome about the realities of 'coming out' as a psychic and the discoveries therein. A very real and honest look at psychic development."
—Tiffany Johnson, author of *Picture Yourself Developing Your Psychic Abilities*

"Anyone who is wrestling with their own awesome inner magic needs to read *The Secret Psychic*."
—Raymond Moody, *New York Times* bestselling author of *Life After Life*

the
secret
psychic

About the Author

Angela A. Wix has acquired body-mind-spirit titles for Llewellyn Worldwide. Her writing has been featured in *The Edge, Elephant Journal, The Mighty, Gone Dogs,* and *Llewellyn's Complete Book of Mindful Living.* She is also the author of *Llewellyn's Little Book of Unicorns* (a guide to finding your inner magic so you can shine, even through dark times) and *Your Pain Is Real: The Warrior's Guide to Endo* (a resource for understanding and surviving endometriosis and its related conditions).

Angela is a lifelong intuitive medium-in-training and has studied in various programs to help hone her skills, including at the Center for Spiritual Development with Echo Bodine, Arthur Findlay College, The Journey Within Spiritualists' National Union Church, and Oakbridge Institute.

Angela is a Certified Massage Therapist (CMT), a Certified Medical Reiki Master (CMRM), and an ordained interfaith minister of spiritual healing, following a three-year program in energy-based medicine. She has professionally practiced massage therapy and energy medicine and continues to be a passionate student of holistic practices. Her artwork has also appeared in hospitals and healing clinics as part of the Phipps Center for the Arts healing arts program.

Angela is based in the greater Twin Cities area with her favorite person and their fur-babies. For more on her writing, art, and healing endeavors (and many pictures of her dogs) or to reach out to her directly, visit her at www.AngelaAnn.Wix.com/arts or Facebook and Instagram @AngelaAWix.

Angela A. Wix

Foreword by Echo Bodine,
bestselling author of *The Gift*

the secret psychic

EMBRACE THE MAGIC
OF SUBTLE INTUITION,
NATURAL SPIRIT COMMUNICATION,
AND YOUR HIDDEN SPIRITUAL LIFE

Llewellyn Publications • Woodbury, Minnesota

FIRST EDITION
First Printing, 2022

Cover art by Angela A. Wix
Cover design by Shira Atakpu
Interior chakra figure on page 39 by Mary Ann Zapalac
Interior contributor photo credits on page 293
Interior flower and leaves icons by Angela A. Wix

Llewellyn Publications is a registered trademark of Llewellyn Worldwide Ltd.

Library of Congress Cataloging-in-Publication Data
Names: Wix, Angela A., author.
Title: The secret psychic : embrace the magic of subtle intuition, natural
    spirit communication, and your hidden spiritual life / by Angela A.
    Wix.
Description: First edition. | Woodbury, Minnesota : Llewellyn Worldwide,
    [2022] | Includes bibliographical references and index. | Summary: "In
    this book you will learn to understand your subtle intuitive abilities,
    recognize the natural occurrence of spirit communication, and find the
    support you need to discover and share your hidden spiritual life"—
    Provided by publisher.
Identifiers: LCCN 2021040289 (print) | LCCN 2021040290 (ebook) | ISBN
    9780738766089 (paperback) | ISBN 9780738766362 (ebook)
Subjects: LCSH: Psychic ability. | Intuition—Miscellanea. | Spiritualism.
Classification: LCC BF1031 .W74 2022 (print) | LCC BF1031 (ebook) | DDC
    133.8—dc23
LC record available at https://lccn.loc.gov/2021040289
LC ebook record available at https://lccn.loc.gov/2021040290

Llewellyn Publications
A Division of Llewellyn Worldwide Ltd.
2143 Wooddale Drive
Woodbury, MN 55125-2989
www.llewellyn.com

Printed in the United States of America

Other Books by Angela A. Wix

Llewellyn's Little Book of Unicorns
(Llewellyn, 2019)

Gone Dogs: Tales of Dogs We've Loved
(contributor, Thomas Woodland, 2019)

Llewellyn's Complete Book of Mindful Living
(contributor, Llewellyn, 2016)

Forthcoming Books by Angela A. Wix

Your Pain Is Real: The Warrior's Guide to Endo;
Understand Endometriosis & Its Related Conditions
So You Can Be a Fierce Advocate for Yourself,
Find the Support You Need &
Change the World Along the Way
(anticipated 2023)

Disclaimer

The information in this book is not intended to be used to diagnose, treat, or prevent any condition. The material in this book is not a substitute for trained medical, psychological, or legal advice. Readers are advised to consult their personal healthcare professionals regarding health concerns, conditions, and treatment. The publisher and the author assume no liability for any damage or injuries to person or property that may result from the reader's use of the content contained herein and recommend common sense when contemplating the practices described in the work.

For Pam,
my friend with all the questions,
without whom this book would not exist.
I hope it provides you (and all of the other secret psychics out there)
with answers you seek.

And again for Amanda, aka Amy.
You always said we would write a book together one day.
I know now *this* is that book.

Contents

Part 2: Answers from Secret Psychic Mentors

Practices

Chapter 5

Part 2

Stories

There are a lot of stories woven throughout the theory, explanation, and practice in part 1. If stories are what you're most interested in and you want to jump to those at any point, this list will help you do that. The stories detailed here don't have their own subheads calling them out in the text, but you'll be able to find them on the pages indicated below.

Foreword

I love this book. I wish a family member would read every child this very important book before they ever hit preschool. Growing up as a "sensitive" little girl, being me was not easy, and I don't say that with a "feel bad for me" attitude. I knew I was very sensitive to everything around me, and I also knew it really bugged my dad. He would ask my mom if there was something she could do to make me less sensitive about everything, and poor Mom didn't know what to do.

I knew if classmates were sick even before they knew it themselves. I could "hear" animals when they were afraid. I would end up crying because I didn't know how I knew, and I didn't know what to do with the information. What was I supposed to say? "Excuse me, Mr. Nelson, but your dog told me he's afraid of you." I would touch people and could feel what they were feeling, although I didn't know at the time that that's what was happening. My mom had a very sensitive stomach, and when I was around her, I would always get a stomachache. Fortunately, that stopped when I moved out of the house at age twenty-three!

I could go on and on with story after story of being a very "sensitive child and teenager," but I know that if you are reading this book, you know exactly what I'm talking about.

I'm so glad Angela took the time to write this very well-written book about intuition and psychic development. She took painstaking measures to lay it all out for you step-by-step, first in recognizing your spiritual gifts, but also in developing them. She has featured numerous stories from different gifted psychics so that you can see we're not all alike in how our gifts present themselves. In one example of my own, early on in a psychic development class I took that had eight people in it, each of us had different talents and ways of expressing our gifts. Some people read auras, while others communicate with the deceased. Some have visions, while others communicate through mental telepathy with their guides. Some see past lives, and others see the future.

Angela has also taken the time to describe how tough this way of life can become. Just about every psychic I know has kept their abilities a secret for a very long time. It was twelve years from the time I discovered what psychic abilities were to the time I came out of the psychic closet. I was terrified of people finding out that I had these gifts, and in the beginning I wasn't sure if they were a gift or a curse.

I've never met a psychic who fully embraced their gifts upon realizing they had them. We all go through a process of back and forth, wondering if they're real versus imagined, and then wondering what to do with them. As a professional psychic myself, I know that using our intuitive gifts is a tremendous responsibility, and that's why I'm so grateful that Angela laid it all out so well. She knows what she's talking about and you can trust the process that this great book will take you through.

I wish you the best on your journey.

Echo Bodine
Psychic, healer, and spiritual teacher
Founder of the Healing Pen Pal Program
Bestselling author of *The Gift*

Introduction

One afternoon in early fall I found myself in a small tea shop that a friend and I had claimed as our meeting grounds. As other people bustled in and out, the jangle of the doorbell tinkled in the background, mixing with a symphony of other conversations inside the tiny space. Sitting on a lumpy old couch, we pretended no one else existed and tried not to care if we were overheard. Sometimes this was no small feat, as we were in tight quarters and our conversations frequently meandered into what many people would view as strange and unusual. But as Lydia Deetz from Tim Burton's movie *Beetlejuice* says, "I myself *am* strange and unusual."[1] We knew it of ourselves and each other, and we just tried to own it. When it came to our secret psychic selves, we knew we had found a safe space to bring up virtually anything, at least in each other's company. We were assured that the other would always provide an open mind. And more often than not, when we finally confided something that we thought had been our own unusual secret, we found that the other had also experienced similar things. We were living the unusual, side by side. Or maybe, just maybe, *the unusual wasn't as unusual as we'd originally thought.*

On this day with a chill in the air and leaves starting to turn their lovely shades of orange and yellow just outside the window, I held my warm cup of tea and listened to my friend, Pam. She was bursting with newfound personal insights and questions. At the end of a breathless telling, she sighed and asked, "How do I exist in what feels like two separate places?

----

1. *Beetlejuice*, directed by Tim Burton (Warner Brothers, 1988).

Bringing them together feels like trying to push two magnets together the wrong way."

I knew these questions. I'd asked them myself as much as twenty years prior. I recognized that the shift I'd gone through back then was the same transition she was going through now. She sought validation, practice, community, and support. She was looking for guidance in how to go about sorting through instilled beliefs that were acting as barriers to the direction she was being called in. And she was looking for answers to questions on how to emerge from her safe and secretive space in order to live fully as who she authentically felt she was meant to be.

Her progression through many of the same steps and hurdles I'd experienced myself was chillingly familiar. From the outside in, I could see she was in the mode of "secret psychic," and I soon recognized that our shared experience was one that's common for those who embark on this path. I wanted to provide her with all the answers I'd gathered over the years that I hadn't had when I was in the same place. And so this book was born.

What You'll Find Here

Within these pages you'll be exploring how to practice your subtle energetic abilities and live within your new spiritual reality, even while feeling like you can't be open about it with those around you. You'll learn what it means to be a secret psychic, how to start out practicing on your own, common hurdles to be aware of, how to even begin revealing this part of yourself to others, and how to integrate your experience so you don't feel like you're caught between two worlds. This initial sense of disassociation, as though you're trying to live two different lives, can be unsettling. Here you'll begin to learn how to bring both sides of your experience together as a whole, because wholeness is exactly what you're exploring. By embracing these skills, you're connecting with your authentic self and being true to who you really are.

This material can be broken down into three core topics:

- Understanding your subtle intuitive abilities
- Recognizing the natural occurrence of spirit communication

- Finding the support you need in order to discover and share your hidden spiritual life

Part 1 is the heart of the book and is a deep dive into the magic of your inner world. Here you'll discover what it means to be a secret psychic and why you even feel the need to remain "secret" to begin with. This process is a form of transformation, and you'll be learning how to move through it with intention.

As we begin, we'll lay the groundwork for a variety of psychic communication methods. You'll explore the foundational details of your intuition, how subtle energy translates into information, and how you naturally go about using that information. Practices will guide you with tuning in and sensing subtle energy. As you begin to learn more about consciously making use of your subtle energetic abilities, you'll also learn the importance of your personal symbolic language and how to determine whether you've interpreted intuitive messages correctly.

Recognizing the natural occurrence of spirit communication is a practical next step, as this process makes use of so many of our subtle abilities. You'll learn about who it is that might be contacting you from Spirit, as well as what that contact might look like, whether it is perceived through sight, sound, feeling, disturbances, dreams, or some other form. Even if you desire to connect with someone, you might find that you're actually resisting that connection. You'll learn why this might be and what you can do about it.

Our subtle abilities and connection to Spirit can have fuzzy boundaries, and sometimes our intuitive senses seep into everyday life. This can seem amazing, disturbing, or both! No matter the case, we'll look at the various ways this might occur, whether you're hearing others' thoughts, feeling others' feelings, seeing spontaneous visions, sensing unexpected energy, recalling past trauma, or some other unanticipated connection. We'll also address what you can do to resolve these types of issues, especially if they're unsettling to you.

Finally, you'll glean insight into how you can go about honoring and integrating your spiritual experience so you don't feel so much like you're living two different lives between your public self and private self. Pinning down the passion or desire that's driving you toward growth and change is an important step, and one that you'll be led through in a practice in chapter 5 called "Define Your Underlying Desire." Continuing to practice your subtle intuitive abilities is also key, especially in ways that bring them into your everyday life as something that is simply a natural occurrence. Through that practice, asking for those abilities to prove themselves to you will help build up confidence in your skills. With that confidence, you might eventually find that you're comfortable enough to share this side of yourself with a trusted confidant. As you continue to develop your abilities, you'll also be asked to consider your long-held beliefs versus your new spiritual experience to see what still holds meaning for you and fits with the direction in which you're growing. With this continued exploration, hopefully you'll eventually feel like you're truly living to your full potential as your genuine self.

This whole experience is likely to leave you burning with questions. If part 1 doesn't provide all the answers you seek, you're likely to find them in part 2, where I interviewed other professional psychics, mediums, and subtle energy intuitives so that I could present a broad range of perspectives. Seeing this gathered wisdom from such an array of well-known and respected spiritual leaders is exciting! You'll have the chance to review the responses to the Secret Psychic Questionnaire (which can be found in appendix 3) from these Secret Psychic Mentors, all of whom at one time found themselves at the starting point you may find yourself at right now.

In appendix 2 you'll find some common symbols that you may encounter and their potential meanings. This information might prove helpful as you begin interpreting intuitive messages, but my advice is to wait to look at it until after you've completed the practice in chapter 2 on personally intuiting the meanings of those symbols yourself.

Be sure to check out the recommended resources section at the end of the book. The lists there can provide insight on where to go next once you get through this book and are looking for additional outlets for exploration.

Throughout the book there are practices for you to pause and engage with. When I was first starting out on this secret psychic journey, the books I read sometimes talked about practicing with a friend, which was frustrating because at that point in my life I didn't have anyone to ask who I thought would be on board. With this in mind, the practices in this book focus on things that you can do to cultivate your abilities independently. Some of them do talk about working with a partner, but in those instances it's only mentioned as a secondary option, and the primary point of the practice will guide you in working on your own.

I recommend that you follow the practices in order when you're starting out, as some of them build on past practice. However, you'll find some instances in the text where I call out certain practices that you might find helpful for a particular situation. In those instances you might consider jumping around to the suggested exercises as extra support. There's a list of exercises following the main table of contents of this book to help you find what you need.

There are a few ways to work through the meditation and visualization practices. You could first read aloud and record the practice, then play it back in order to do it. You could read through the practice several times until you commit the basics to memory, then organically guide yourself through the practice and allow it to unfold for you. Or you could read as you practice and kind of suspend yourself between your physical space and your inner imagination. Some people find they don't have success when they try to guide themselves through a practice, and they absolutely need a recording of it. Others won't do the exercise if they have to take time to record it first, and they find the dual-world approach works just fine for them. Do what works for you.

Language

Here are a few language clarifications before we dive in.

I use *Spirit* (capitalized) when I'm referring to the broader reference, as in God, the universe, or the collective of angels + deceased loved ones +

ascended beings, etc. Example: "the call of Spirit." If you have other language that feels more authentic to you, please mentally insert that when
you come across this use. I use *spirit* (lowercase) when I'm referring to specific instances, like the spirit of a deceased loved one or the reader's spirit.
Example: "I heard a spirit."

While spirit communication is a big part of what I discuss in this book, if
the afterlife or the idea of spirits is not something that aligns with your beliefs,
it's fine to think of it in a way that feels natural to you. When we get into that
part of the material, you can think of instances of this type of communication in terms of energy. I perceive this communication as coming from spirit
guides or deceased loved ones. You may perceive the connection as coming
from a more general universal energy or collective consciousness.

Weirdos and Regular People Welcome

As you dive into the material, you might ask who I am that I would have
any answers to share as insight for the secret psychic. I'm a secret psychic
myself, and I've come to these answers on the seemingly random scaven-
ger hunt of life, moved to find them through my own curiosity and pas-
sion-driven life. In unearthing these answers, I found my authentic self. I
hope to help others do the same, no matter if they've been attuned to their
innate abilities from the time they were a kid or come to them with new
awareness as an adult. While I don't currently practice as a professional
psychic in terms of giving readings to people, I do make use of my subtle
and intuitive skills in my daily life, as all of us naturally do. While I believe
I'm more aware of my use of these abilities than the average person, I also
believe everyone has the potential to develop these skills, so long as they
have the interest.

This is all my way of saying that I'm a regular person. I'm not a celebrity
hugely known for this topic, I haven't been a professional psychic, and my
intuitive abilities didn't come about mysteriously during a spiritual pilgrim-
age or after an astonishing event like a near death experience. I'm not living
my life in a mystifying way or at a different level than you are. Instead, the
skills and abilities I have are actually something I consider to be the norm,

which means this material is something that's accessible *to all of us*. Some people might come to their abilities more naturally than others, but if you have the interest, you can hone them, like learning a language or playing an instrument.

I've used these subtle skills as a massage therapist and energy worker, where I would intuit what people were feeling and tap into where they needed attention for healing. Often subtle messages would also arise while I was connected with their energy. Eventually I determined at that point in my life giving readings wasn't really my interest, but these skills did make their way into my professional work. My understanding has provided a foundation where I can be helpful to other people in writing their own books on various metaphysical topics. I've worked with hundreds of authors in a symbiotic relationship where, through my own experience, I've been able to help them effectively share their messages as I also learned from their wisdom.

While I've gathered a wealth of knowledge over the years on mind-body-spirit topics and the use of our subtle abilities, it all began in my dark candlelit bedroom as a weird kid with my nose in book after book and my mind on the practices that I gleaned from them. Eventually I would move on to train with others in energy medicine, psychic development, and more. But sometimes I imagine myself back at the beginning of my journey and finding this book on a shelf at the library, devouring its contents, and feeling a little less alone within this secret space. No matter where you are on your journey, I hope you'll find a similar sense of comfort and support.

PART 1
Explore the Magic of Your Secret Inner World

Exploration of your subtle abilities and spiritual nature begins in part 1, which is the heart of the book. In chapters 1 and 2 you'll learn about what it means to be a secret psychic, how your intuition works, and how you can become more aware of and skilled at working with these abilities. In chapter 3 you'll discover how spirit communication happens naturally on a regular basis and the various ways you might experience it in your life. Understanding how these forms of energetic perception might crop up as you go about your daily life will be addressed in chapter 4. This is especially important when you're starting out, so that you have a better understanding of what's going on when it happens and you have the tools to manage those types of occurrences. Finally, in chapter 5 you'll get insight and tips on how you can begin to integrate this newly awakened side of yourself into the rest of your life. Let's begin!

CHAPTER 1
What It Means to Be a Secret Psychic

Do you feel as though you need to keep a huge part of yourself hidden from others? Do you feel like you're in the midst of deep personal transformation that has left you burning with questions about your subtle abilities and spiritual nature? Do you have a desire to share these amazing insights with those around you, yet you don't know how or with whom it's safe to share? If so, welcome! You, my friend, are a secret psychic. And you've come to the right place.

If you find yourself reading these pages, it's likely that you're still testing the waters of your intuitive abilities and exploring new realms of your personal spirituality. Perhaps you feel caught between two worlds—internal versus external, private versus public, physical versus energetic—and are trying to figure out how to maneuver while living in this gap. While the very title of this book includes the word *psychic*, that doesn't necessarily mean you're seeking to eventually do psychic readings for other people. Perhaps that *is* your interest, and if so, that's fine. You'll learn plenty here to help you with that goal. On the other hand, it may be that you've come here because you're on a personal spiritual journey in which psychic ability plays a big role. If any of this rings a bell for you, then it's probably also likely that you're feeling very alone in your experience. Believe me, I did too. My hope is that by the end of this book, you'll feel far less alone than you do right now.

One of the first steps in alleviating that sense of isolation is to realize that what you're going through is actually a common experience that tells the story of the human spirit's potential. And while you may be going through this in secret, so are many others, just as I and others have before you, and just as many more will after us. This means there is already existing wisdom about this natural process from those who have come before you that's available to you. You'll find some of that wisdom right here within these pages.

In this chapter we'll cover exactly what is meant by the word *psychic*, how it compares to the more commonly used term *intuitive* (or *intuition*), and why you might have a preference for one of these terms over the other. We'll dig into various reasons why you might feel as though you're caught between two worlds, along with reasons why you may sense the need to keep this side of yourself secret. Tips for ethical and safe practice will also be shared, as well as some notes of caution to ensure your experience remains a positive one as you increasingly open yourself up to subtle energy.

Your Abilities Are a Natural Phenomenon

Let's make this point clear up front: your subtle abilities are a very natural phenomenon. One of my favorite examples of someone making this point comes from the movie *Phenomenon*, where the main character, George Malley, is an average, hardworking man and a loved member of his small community. After seeing flashing lights one night, he begins to develop sensitivity to energy and extraordinary abilities such as telekinesis (the psychic ability to move objects without touching them), clairsentience (psychic feeling), and heightened intelligence. As his abilities grow, an increasing number of people begin to be wary and distance themselves from him. Only a select few remain faithful. In the end (spoiler alert!), it's revealed that the flashing lights and his phenomenal abilities were all due to a tumor that was growing in and stimulating his brain.

When he's questioned by a doctor, George declares, "I think I'm what everybody can be.... Anybody can get here. I'm the possibility."[2] He clarifies that given the choice between his abilities arising from a tumor or from something like an alien encounter (as some people had suspected), he would choose the tumor, because it shows that the capability is innate and part of the human spirit that's already within us. It's not alien or unknown. It's here, now, part of everyone's potential. It's within our grasp.

That's also my perspective on psychic ability. Think of how animals are born with instincts that help them naturally know how to do things like migrate and stay protected. We, as beings that come from nature and this universe, also have natural senses that are part of our makeup. Our way of life, distanced and protected from the dangers of the natural world, has simply made those instinctual abilities less obvious. They now run in the background and are often entirely unacknowledged. But just because we may be unaware of these abilities doesn't mean we aren't all using them to some degree. We are. These are things that you (and everyone else in the world) have been using your whole life. These abilities are real. They are a part of us. And if we so choose, we can learn how to strengthen and make more conscious use of them. And for some of us, this mindful approach to the development and use of our subtle abilities equates to an inner spiritual experience. The emergence of our intuition is the call of Spirit, an awakening to our authentic self and the divine within.

Psychic vs. Intuition

While I refer to us as secret psychics, I know that many will feel a bit squeamish at the use of the word *psychic*, preferring to call themselves *intuitive* instead. To understand why this is, we need to break down the use of these two words.

You may be surprised to find out that these two terms are often communicating the same exact thing. Many people, including myself, use them interchangeably. While they're often used to mean the same thing, they're

---

2. *Phenomenon*, directed by Jon Turteltaub (Touchstone Pictures, 1996).

sometimes used in different ways. When people speak of having intuition, they're usually talking about a gut instinct or following a hunch. A humorous definition of intuition that I originally found attributed to Minds Journal sums it up perfectly: "*Intuition* (n.): when you have a keen sense of feely feels that feel feely and you feel like you know things that you don't know, but you *do* know because you're feeling them."[3] Intuition is subtle and often intangible or indescribable. You just *feel* it and *know* it. And you either trust and go along with it or you don't.

While I do use these two words interchangeably, I view intuition as energy communicating a message to you via your psychic abilities. I think of the two terms in this way:

- *intuition* = your subtle inner guidance
- *psychic* = the senses and abilities that intuition uses to gather information and communicate that guidance

Another way to think of it is like this: if *intuition* is the body as a whole, then *psychic* is the eyes, ears, tongue, nose, and fingers that gather subtle sensory information for the body to interpret and make sense of. Both have the aim of guiding us safely through life by gathering and sharing subtle nformation. To me, the use of one term over the other is more a distinction of language and not so much about ability. Intuition is the use of psychic ability. Psychic ability *is* intuition, broken down into our individual subtle senses, many of which correspond to our physical senses (i.e., psychic hearing, psychic seeing, psychic feeling, etc.). Intuition is the umbrella term for the use of those abilities.

Among the psychics I interviewed for this book, I found that our interpretations of these terms were very alike, with slight variations. For example, subtle energy expert Cyndi Dale breaks it down with even more distinction, saying, "I consider the psychic ability to be the foundation of intuition. To me, we are naturally psychic when born. Being psychic is the instinctive capability of receiving, interpreting, and sending subtle energy

---

3. America's Best Pics & Videos, "Intuition," October 12, 2021, https://americasbestpics.com /picture/intuition-n-when-you-have-a-keen-sense-of-feely-lcmRIUG38.

or data. At baseline, psychic activity promotes survival and our safety. Intuition is a more grown-up version of being psychic. It involves learning how to mindfully manage our psychic aptitude, or the subtle energy we are constantly exchanging between ourselves and the outside world. It takes more understanding and conscious training to function intuitively rather than only psychically."

Psychic and medium Sherrie Dillard's explanation beautifully states that "although intuition and psychic ability are essentially the same thing, there is a subtle difference. Psychic ability is a more focused and developed form of intuition. You can call on it when you want specific information and use specific skills such as clairvoyance and clairaudience to access energy information. Intuition for me is more free-flowing inner awareness that comes and goes. It, too, can be expressed in various different ways. However, we don't have as much control over how it surfaces."

In yet another example, psychic medium Kristy Robinett thinks of the two terms this way: "The Greek definition of the word *psychic* means 'soul.' The psychic information comes from the gift of clairvoyance and clairaudience. The definition of *intuition* is a hunch or feeling, and intuition comes from the gift of clairsentience and claircognizance. The gifts all come from the soul."

No matter how you define these two words, our subtle guidance is natural and a very practical form of inner guidance. As psychic medium Jodi Livon states, "Intuition is a free and natural resource and something to be celebrated, not shamefully hidden away."

Resistance to the Word Psychic

While the word *intuition* has a lightness about it, the term *psychic* is a loaded one for many people. In our culture, *psychic* has a somewhat negative connotation; it carries a lot of baggage, with set stereotypes and negative assumptions, and can feel scary due to the ingrained beliefs that many of us have picked up without even really being conscious of where they came from. But when you strip away those assumptions and understand the true meaning of the word, it starts to remove that fear.

While I was talking with a secret psychic friend of mine, she shared, "I don't yet identify with the word *psychic*. While I have a more logical understanding of what that word is, for many it might conjure images of fortune-tellers, crystal balls, strange people, and trying to predict the future." As a result of these kinds of historical assumptions, and the judgment (or even persecution) that has come along with them, identifying yourself with the word *psychic* simply may not feel natural because it's still bound with fear.

Another reason you might have reservations about the use of the word *psychic* is because it can feel like such a definitive claim. Saying you're psychic can feel very black-and-white, as though you're saying that *you know it all,* when in truth we're always learning. If you're reading this book, you likely are not trying to claim that you have a professional level of psychic ability. On the other hand, claiming yourself as *intuitive* probably feels like there's more forgiveness there, more room for error. If you tell others you're intuitive, they probably won't assume that you have all the answers. There's immediately more understanding around the subtle nature of your perception.

Which Word Should You Use?

In my first intuitive development class, the instructor gave us all buttons that read "Psychic in training" because of the expectation of perfection or sense of burden that can come with using the word *psychic*. When you're starting out, if the word *psychic* feels too heavy, then stick with *intuition* or regularly remind yourself that you're still a psychic in training.

While I do make a distinction between the terms *intuition* and *psychic*, they are truly tangled threads making up the same web, and I use them as interchangeable terms that are basically communicating the same thing. When I'm talking with someone whom I don't know for sure is "in my world," I'll use the more widely accepted term of intuition, but when I'm speaking with others who are more understanding of what these terms and abilities are all about, I naturally switch between both words. There really isn't a need to overcomplicate things. If you feel more drawn to one term over the other, go with it.

Keep in mind that words can make a difference in the way we think about things. When you're starting out, it can be helpful to stick with *intuition*, because the use of that term is less likely to sway you toward the ego mind. If you refer to yourself or your abilities as *psychic* and you feel like it puts you in the mindset of wanting to get attention for being special or of having extraordinary powers that others don't, it might be beneficial to use the word *intuition* instead, at least initially. This is because intuition is generally recognized as being something that everyone has to some degree. You're less likely to get swept away by your ego when referring to your intuition.

PRACTICE
Understanding Your Discomfort with the Word *Psychic*

Pause for a second now and think about the words *psychic* and *intuition* and the charge you feel with each. Notice if either term triggers you in a negative way. If so, note whether that's true for one word or for both. Sit in the feeling that you get and try to define what it feels like. Maybe it just feels icky, or maybe there is a specific emotion that you can attach to it. Try to trace the negative feeling in order to define where exactly it comes from. Determine whether the origin is something you find to be based in truth or whether it's something you now find to be not so true. If the belief is not true, do you feel that you can start to let go of it?

Moving forward, use the language that feels natural to you. As you continue on this journey, if using the word *psychic* to describe yourself feels loaded, know that we'll be unpacking why that may be. By the end of this book you may find that it no longer carries such weight.

Why All the Secrets?

You're not alone in living out this part of your life in a secret fashion, but it can sometimes be a mystery as to why it feels like this experience needs a secret safe space to evolve and bloom. There are various reasons why that may be.

When you are beginning a new project, some people believe that you shouldn't share about it, but instead should wait at least until you've developed it into something more substantial. Otherwise, in sharing, you divide up the energy and may end up expending what otherwise would have been put to use in *creating*. Sometimes when we overshare and talk about things too early on, we find that the initial spark of inspiration dwindles and fades. When we hold our inspiration close, letting it warm us from within, we feed that flame until it's a roaring fire that can then sustain its energy to warm others as well. Right now, your secret psychic experience may be that inner spark that you need to keep for yourself. At a later point you'll begin to sense if and when the time is right to share your inner world with others.

Another key reason why you probably feel the need to keep things secret is because you don't want others to think there is something mentally wrong with you. If you start telling people you're hearing voices or seeing visions, it's easy for others who don't get it to assume that you're just hallucinating. They may suspect that you have a psychological or neurological issue, like schizophrenia. For some people this is in fact the case, but in instances of hearing or seeing via our intuitive senses, that's not what's going on. It's not a disorder; it's a healthy and natural experience of the subtle senses.

Throughout time and all around the world, people have shared their subtle skills and were even celebrated for them, playing important roles in society in ways that made use of their gifts. Even in the Bible there's mention of such skills. For example, in the book of Daniel, the king of Babylon called on people with these skills to interpret his dreams. In one instance, the king was unwilling to give out the details of the dream he'd had. But even without any details, a man named Daniel still had the ability to interpret the dream for the king after receiving the information and meaning from Spirit.

Daniel became known as someone who was able to interpret visions and dreams.[4]

Another example can be found in the book of Genesis. In this story, Pharaoh had a dream that he called on diviners to interpret. Eventually, a man named Joseph (who had demonstrated an ability to interpret dreams successfully before) was able to interpret it for him after the meaning was revealed to him from Spirit.[5]

Psychic and spiritual teacher Echo Bodine shares in her book *The Gift* that in the Bible there is a plethora of positive references to prophets/seers and subtle abilities, as well as explanation for the "Gifts of the Spirit," or special abilities (including prophecy, which comes about from psychic abilities), that have been imparted *to all of us* by the Holy Spirit.[6]

In more recent history, the pendulum swung the other way, especially in the Western world. Instead of openness and appreciation for subtle abilities, there was suspicion and contempt. These abilities aligned with accusations of witchcraft and the persecution that came along with it. Psychic abilities and spiritual wisdom that was gained outside the boundaries of religion began to be associated with working with the devil. Laws were passed making the practice illegal in many places. As a result, the use of subtle abilities was lost, or what remained largely went underground and was practiced in secret.

When the Spiritualist movement began in the mid-1800s, appreciation for psychic skills grew. People participated in demonstrations of various skills, including readings by mediums, which opened up discussion about afterlife possibilities. But once again, the movement declined as magicians and scientists sought to explain away these experiences by claiming that people were being duped. While in some instances this was surely true, as one person puts it, "This is akin to saying that now that we can duplicate diamonds, all diamonds must be fake."[7]

··

4. Daniel 2: 1–49 (New International Version).

5. Genesis 41:1–57 (New International Version).

6. Echo Bodine, *The Gift: Understand and Develop Your Psychic Abilities* (Novato, CA: New World Library, 2003), 36–42.

7. Andy Jackson, "The Persecution of Psychics Throughout History," Psychics Directory, accessed Aug. 31, 2021, https://www.psychicsdirectory.com/articles/persecution-psychics-history/.

Movies and TV shows have perpetuated images of psychics as stereo-typical outcasts, oddballs, and even dangerous individuals living on the fringes of society, sometimes proving to be liars working their magic to hustle people out of money. And while over time this representation has improved to some extent, like a steady drip of advertising, these kinds of beliefs are so ingrained that they have continued from one generation to the next without us even consciously being aware of it.

In light of all this, it's understandable that you might want to keep your inner world a secret. Of course you don't want to be seen as a liar, as mentally unwell, or as dangerous just for being who and what you are. Of course you don't want to feel criticized for exploring your spiritual inspirations. Of course you don't want what feels fascinating, inspiring, and authentic to be marred by the negative judgments of others or to have what you experience as divine to be perceived as something evil.

Keeping our abilities a secret seems especially necessary when we feel like we haven't yet established a secure support system of people who understand or are at least open to learning about this side of us. Keep your secrets. Let your inner world blossom at its own pace. Within these pages there is no judgment, only support and encouragement for you to continue to grow.

The Challenge of Living Between Two Worlds

"How do I exist in one place when part of my heart feels like it's in another place too?" Pam asked me. When you're drawn to follow this calling of Spirit, at some point it's bound to leave you feeling as though you're living between two worlds. Part of this just takes getting used to. The more you learn to tune in, the more it will just feel like a natural sense. Say you're in the middle of a work meeting or are at the grocery store and the delicious smell of food cooking wafts its way to you. This sense of smell doesn't turn off your other forms of awareness. You can smell this wonderful scent and still keep your attention on the meeting at hand or on the surroundings of the grocery store, even if you're a bit distracted. So it is with the pull of intuition. Say you're in that meeting and you feel the tap of intuition.

You can tune in to that internal message while remaining aware of the space around you. It may feel odd at first, but with practice you'll get the hang of being equally in both worlds at once.

On the other hand, say you've just gone through a very intense experience in one of your meditations. It felt profound, and as you start to go back to your daily routine, you feel like part of you is still off on a spiritual exploration. Your mind is distracted as you contemplate the details of what you saw and heard. In this case, trying to get back into the motions of the physical world might end up feeling unnatural, as though you're split between two different realms.

Yet another form of this "living in two worlds" feeling is the potential juxtaposition of your past versus where you feel the call of Spirit is leading you in the present. This can bring up some emotional challenges. Commonly this includes grief over what you feel you need to let go of that's no longer a fit for you, fear over what might happen as a result of being true to yourself, and sadness over your sense of isolation from others who you don't think will understand the changes you're going through. As you feel yourself growing in a new direction, you might get the sense that you're living dual lives, playing the role of your old self to appease your family and community while internally there's a whole other side to you that no one even knows about.

I know this two-world's juxtaposition and can still viscerally feel what it was like when it was at its peak for me. I was in my second year of college and had been part of one of the religious organizations on campus up to that point. I'd found friends there that I really liked, but every time I left a devotional meeting, I felt heavy and unsettled. I tried my best to ignore those feelings. I didn't want to find out where they were coming from. I wanted to be good. I wanted to fit into the world that I'd always been told was right. *Why didn't this fit?*

In the past I'd pulled at the threads of tradition that didn't resonate with me while clinging to the bits that left me inspired. In this way I'd set up a kind of compromised patchwork to my spiritual life. But increasingly

I could feel it like a sweater that was too tight, and there were no more threads left to pull. I couldn't fight it anymore.

As I left one meeting in particular, grief that I'd suppressed all evening was especially heavy, like a weight in my chest. I made it into my car and cranked the music, trying to drown out the emotion. But it was no use. What I'd sensed growing inside of me for months, even years, finally made itself fully known. In the dark of the night as I drove my way home, waves of grief crashed over me, one after the other, and I cried as if someone I loved intensely had just died. This was the ugly, can't-breathe kind of cry. I felt like I was being ripped in two, the pain was so deep. When it was over, I felt exhausted but cleansed. Something had shifted and I knew change was about to follow.

I still had a lot of processing to do, and the adjustments that I ended up making as a result came gradually. But that was a defining moment where I knew without a doubt that I could not go back and try to pretend. I no longer fit in the world of my past, and it was time for me to find where I actually belonged in the present. I was meant to move in a new direction, and for me this meant shifting away from the religion I had been raised in and moving toward my own authentic form of spirituality that was wrapped in the use of my intuitive abilities.

Living in a State of Transformation

These types of shifts can lead you to a newfound place of true beauty that you might not have even been able to imagine for yourself before. Once you've made your way through the struggle of discovering your own potential and aligning your life with who you authentically are, looking back you'll be amazed by how far you've come. But even knowing up front that the end result might be magnificent doesn't mean that standing at the start (or right in the middle) of so much change won't be a painful or scary thing.

Just look to the metamorphosis of a caterpillar into a butterfly. It takes time inside the chrysalis for this transformation to manifest. Within that safe secret space, the caterpillar's tissue is digested and liquefied. *Just imagine that!* Knowing it's finally ready, the seeds of potential that have been held within it from the beginning are finally activated and a new state of being is slowly fed and rebuilt.

You might recognize that you're in a similar state. Maybe, like I did, you feel as though you're being torn completely apart. Or, as with the caterpillar, you might identify with the thought that life is eating you up and you're losing grasp of who you've been up to now. Within your own chrysalis state, you might have no idea what you'll find left of yourself once this transformation is complete. But neither, I imagine, does the butterfly. It follows the natural direction in which it's called anyway, and what a magnificent thing it becomes.

Breaking free of the safe space and leaving the old behind is also part of this struggle, but it's a necessary one. Before the butterfly lets go of the remnants of the past that brought it to that point, its transition isn't complete until it takes time to pause with the world upside down. During this time spent hanging in one spot, fluid from the butterfly's body moves into its wings. Eventually the wings are allowed to expand completely, dry, and harden. Only after this pause is the transformation complete.

You might be left feeling as though your life is being flipped upside down, but if you open up to the possibilities and allow your own transformation to naturally unfold, on the other side of that difficult transition you might emerge flying higher than ever before.

PRACTICE
Moving Through Transformation with Intention

If you find yourself in that upside-down place as you let go of your old self on the verge of spiritual transformation, take a moment here to pause. Even if you're at the very beginning of your transformation, we're going to envision the end point here and now.

Take a moment to settle comfortably into your space. You can practice this meditation sitting or lying down. If you fall asleep, that's okay. Transformation is hard work, and if extra rest is what you need, allow for it.

You can come back to complete the practice again another day when you feel more rested.

Take some deep breaths now and consciously relax.

Relax your feet, your calves, your upper legs. Moving up, now relax your hips. Take another deep breath and feel it filling your belly. Relax your abdomen. Relax your chest. Continue to move up, feeling the tension release from your neck. This relaxing sensation trickles down through your arms and into your hands. It spreads into your face now, and you feel your jaw, your lips, and the muscles around your eyes and in your forehead all relaxing. Take another deep breath now and feel your body melting even more into the surface that's gently supporting you.

Sit in this relaxed state for a moment.

When you're ready, in your mind's eye see yourself standing at the top of a set of stone stairs. With your bare feet, take a step down, then another, and another. The stones are rough underfoot and the air that was initially warm starts to feel damp and cool. You run your hand along the mossy stone walls as you continue making your way down. With each step, it's as if you're removing the weight of the day from your shoulders. Down wind the stairs, until the sunlight from above is almost entirely out of sight. Finally you reach the bottom, feeling light and free.

There you find a door, and looking at it you know there is something *fantastic* waiting for you on the other side. You wipe your hand across a film of dust that has settled over the front of the door and see that it reads "Set your intention for metamorphosis." You understand now that on the other side of this door are details about the transformation you're going through and where it's leading you. But before you can open the door, you have to offer it your intention.

Think about the reason you're here. Define what brought you to this point and why you picked up this particular book. Focus in on what you feel is calling you and clarify what your intention is for this journey. What is it that you desire to realize from this calling? If you feel at a loss for what your intention is, here are a few ideas:

- "I intend to realize my full potential and true self."
- "I intend to connect more deeply with Spirit."
- "I intend to realize the purpose of why I'm feeling pulled in new directions."

State your intention out loud. As soon as you do this, light shimmers around the edges of the door and it opens. You step through the doorway and see moments from your past all around you. As you walk among them, allow these memories to reveal themselves to you, rising up like bubbles in your mind, one by one. Take a moment to absorb what you find. Pay attention to what you see, what you hear, and what feelings come to you.

As you arrive at the edge of the space and move beyond those past memories, you see your future self standing before you. You look into each other's eyes for a moment, and the intense love that your future self holds for your present self washes over you. Your future self gives you a nod, letting you know they welcome your inquiry.

Take some time now to ask your future self any questions you have about the journey that they've completed and that is currently unfolding for you.

When you've run out of questions, it's your future self's turn. Listen now as they share any additional messages they have for you.

When they're done sharing their messages, your future self gives you a hug and steps back from you. From their cupped hands they present a butterfly that flutters over to you and lands on your shoulder. It rests there for a moment and you study its colors, the gentle flap of its wings, and the shimmer of light that reflects off its delicate structure. The butterfly flies off and your future self laughs. "A token of things to come," they say with a smile.

It's now time to go. You step away and move back through the doorway. Without looking back, you sense the door close behind you. You move up, up, up and back into the daylight ahead.

Take a moment now to get yourself back into the present moment. Feel your body. Wiggle your fingers and toes and take a good stretch. Drink a glass of water. If you'd like, jot down the details of the messages you received during your meditation. Also make a note of the intention that you set, so that you can refer back to it to use again or see how it changes as you progress through your transformation.

Notes of Caution

It's exciting to realize the potential you hold and to practice skills you might not have known you had before. As you move through the rest of the book, it's good to keep some notes of caution in mind so that your experience remains a positive one. First I'll address tips of ethical and safe practice, and from there I'll go into ways your practice might actually negatively impact you. As you open up to this subtle energy, there can be some unexpected and unwanted side effects. I don't want this to take you by surprise. Being aware of the potential for these issues will eliminate some of the confusion and can help you head off those problems right away if they come up.

Safe and Legal Practice of Subtle Abilities
These first couple of notes on safety and ethics won't really apply until you're sharing your abilities with others, but I include them here so they're not missed, and just in case you dive into sharing your abilities with others sooner rather than later.

In some places there are still laws against providing things like psychic readings or healing sessions, so be aware of what is and is not allowed in your location. For example, in New York fortune telling is a misdemeanor offense.[8] Laws like section 365 of Canada's criminal code (which was finally repealed in 2018) were said to have been passed specifically to protect people from those pretending to practice witchcraft. But even if you don't identify yourself as a witch, these types of laws may still apply to elements of what you're practicing.

----

8. "Penal Law: Article 165.35—Fortune Telling," New York State Law, accessed August 31, 2021, https://ypdcrime.com/penal.law/article165.php#p165.35.

These laws are usually framed as being anti-witchcraft or anti-fortune-telling. Their intention is usually said to be to protect people from being conned out of large sums of money and also to protect them from "super-natural threats" where the practitioner states there is the potential for harm and then claims that for a certain payment they can eliminate the threat.[9] However, even in instances where no threat was made, where large sums of money were not part of the exchange, and where the person providing the service showed evidence of special training and true belief in their practice, convictions have still been made. Only a few years before Canada's Witch-craft Provision was repealed, one assessment of it was that "the status quo appears that any representation of supernatural power outside of dominant religious contexts will trigger prosecution and conviction."[10]

While of course it's good to prevent true fraud, where these laws exist the line is often incredibly murky and subject to discrimination and abuse. Who determines what is legitimate and what is pretend or fraud? What one person views as legitimate practice another might consider to be criminal. What is prophecy, religion, or spiritualism to one person could very well be "pretend" to someone else. Many feel these types of laws are a form of modern-day witch-hunting and persecution. One study found that they disproportionately impact women and certain racial and religious groups, and they're noticeably a form of patriarchal suppression, "suppressing women's powerful positions in the community as healers, midwives, and holders of holistic herbal and agricultural knowledge."[11]

There are those who do take advantage, faking or making use of their abil-ities at the expense of others and for their own benefit. As with anything, one bad apple can ruin the bunch. Think of a physician greedily peddling a false cure. If you're left burnt by such an experience, you're likely to distrust future interactions with all other physicians. But that doesn't mean that all physicians

---

9. Natasha Bahkt and Jordan Palmer, "Modern Law, Modern Hammers: Canada's Witch-craft Provision as an Image of Persecution," *Windsor Review of Legal and Social Issues* 35 (December 2015): 133, https://papers.ssrn.com/sol3/papers.cfm?abstract_id=2606165.

10. Bahkt and Palmer, "Modern Law, Modern Hammers," 135–136.

11. Bahkt and Palmer, "Modern Law, Modern Hammers," 125.

are equal to the one who crossed you. In fact, all the rest you encounter may be very honest in their efforts to heal. The same is true in the world of intuitives. Some are noble, filled with a desire to share their skills for the benefit of others. Some are not. And in an effort to weed out those dishonest practitioners, laws have gone too far in some cases, painting with a broad brush that impacts even those who are honest in their practice.

In the United States these types of restrictions are found in individual community laws or codes. In many instances they're recognized as being very out-of-date and something that most people don't even know is on record. Once these laws are dredged up (often in instances of religious discrimination), it can be an opportunity for discussion, improved community awareness, and hopefully adjustment or removal of the law/code.[12]

This information isn't meant to scare you away from your practice. Instead, it's designed to make you even more aware of where your reservations may be coming from and, if and when you find yourself ready, to help you move forward with sharing your abilities safely. While such a law may never end up being an issue (or may be deemed so out-of-date that it's not even valid if it *does* come up), it's still good to know whether there are existing laws that could potentially be used against you.

PRACTICE
Preparing for Safe and Legal Practice

While the potential legal issues involved in practicing your psychic abilities can all feel really overwhelming, breaking those issues down into some smaller actionable steps for solution can help things feel more manageable.

Start Here

Start by reviewing your local laws/codes. Go to the city or county website and search for "codes" or "ordinances." Within those ordinances (usually

---

12. Heather Greene, "Virginia Priestess Raises Concerns Over Discriminatory Town Code," *The Wild Hunt*, May 11, 2014, https://wildhunt.org/2014/05/virginia-priestess-raises -concerns-over-discriminatory-town-code.html.

listed as "chapters"), if there's a search feature, you can search for terms like "witchcraft," "magic," "fortune telling," and "psychic." If you aren't able to find the information this way or you don't have internet access, you can call your city hall or county seat to request the information.

Obtain What's Needed for Safe and Legal Practice

Within your local laws, you might find that you're required to have a permit or license to practice. Or you may only be able to practice in certain locations, such as within a store but not at a fair or on the street. You might have to register, pay a fee, get a background check, have your fingerprints on record, or something else entirely![13] Review those details and assess what you need to do in order to practice legally in your area.

In my case, I was specifically interested in laws related to the combination of intuition and energy healing. If this is your interest as well, know that in some locations it's illegal to touch people in a professional context unless you have a license to practice, such as for a physician, massage therapist, or religious figure. If you don't have a formal license in one of those categories already, you can become a licensed minister. Even without an interest in energy healing, some intuitives also go this ministerial route, taking an oath and clarifying to their clients that they're offering life coaching or spiritual counsel. In the recommended resources section, I've included one such organization where you can become a minister with a small donation. You would then need to register this with your county office or potentially any other town that you're practicing in.

It's also good to consider having liability insurance. If you practice in person, this would apply if someone were to fall or be injured in some way. You could obtain this through the insurer that you already use for your home insurance. I've also included a couple of organizations in the recommended resources section that provide coverage for energy medicine and bodywork professionals.

---

13. Elizabeth Dias, "In the Crystal Ball: More Regulation for Psychics," *TIME*, September 2, 2010, http://content.time.com/time/nation/article/0,8599,2015676,00.html.

In addition, consider having your clients sign a liability form before they have a session with you. This could include a disclaimer clarifying that you're not a medical professional and that the reading is for entertainment purposes only. While the note of entertainment may not truly represent your beliefs, it's language that's often recommended as protection for the reader and as a disclaimer for the client. A sample release of liability form is included in appendix 1.

In some locations the acceptance of money, whether it's a charged fee or given as a donation, constitutes a contract between the two parties. I state this because some people recommend that you accept donations as a way to get around potential legal issues (again, check your local laws). To avoid client dissatisfaction or conflict, you might also guarantee your sessions, letting potential clients know that if they aren't satisfied, you'll reimburse their payment. Similarly, it can be a good idea to inform them of your cancellation policy, letting them know how far ahead of the session they would need to cancel in order to not be charged or to receive a refund.

And, of course, for legal reasons make sure you declare any income that you make from this work when doing your taxes.

Challenging a Law

If you become aware of an outdated law that's discriminatory of your rights and you want to challenge it, you can contact your city or district attorney. You should be able to find their contact information through your county website. If you find yourself in conflict and need support, you could also try reaching out to the American Civil Liberties Union (ACLU), Lady Liberty League (LLL), or Americans United for Separation of Church and State (Americans United or AU for short). See the recommended resources section for more on these organizations.

Ethics in the Practice of Subtle Abilities

In addition to all those legal details, it's good to keep in mind the ethics around the use of your subtle abilities and how you're putting them into practice.

This will also help to make sure you don't unintentionally cross the line into illegal practice.

- Share messages that you've received through your intuitive abilities only when asked or given permission.

- Be clear with potential clients about what they should expect from a session with you. Describe your process, letting them know what you do and *don't* do. For example, you won't diagnose or treat illness because you aren't a medical practitioner.

- Be careful with the words you use. Words have power! Be cautious especially on the topics of predicting death, medical events or illness, and infidelity. Kristy Robinett clarifies with this example: "Never tell someone their significant other is cheating, even if you see/sense it. Instead, word it as, 'I see fractures in your relationship. You may want to seek out couples therapy to better your communication and strengthen the relationship.'" Or, if you're receiving a message that someone is indeed near death, you could encourage the client to go visit that individual. Similarly, always take care that what you're saying isn't expressed in a way that's diagnosing or treating any known or suspected condition. Instead, you could share that you're sensing it would be a good idea for the client to see their physician. This caution is important not only for legal reasons if you're not a medical professional but also out of consideration for the other person. John Holland states, "It's important to keep in mind *impression* versus *expression* and the way you say things. If I'm with a friend and I psychically feel a spot on their chest, I am not going to turn to the person and say, 'Do you have a tumor?' I will say, 'Do you have a chest issue?' There's a big difference with the words that you use. You have to be careful how you express what you're intuitively getting, because you could scare people." We'll cover some of this more in chapter 4 when we talk about whether to do something with what you're picking up on or whether you should just let it be.

- Don't exaggerate or embellish the intuitive information that comes to you. Be honest about what you're getting.
- Let the client know that what you share is not black-and-white but is for their consideration and is open to interpretation. They should know that no matter what is said, they have free will and should decide what does or does not resonate with them.
- Don't allow a client to become dependent on you. Make sure they understand that you're a regular person and you don't have all the answers. If they seem to need more than an occasional session can offer, it might be good to encourage them to seek a professional therapist for counseling. Be aware of what else they might need that's beyond the boundaries of what you can offer them.
- Keep sessions confidential.
- Do not offer sessions when you're ill or under the influence of drugs or alcohol.

Negative Side Effects of Opening Up Energetically

There can be some negative side effects from opening yourself up to subtle energy connections. While I've been receiving spirit communication since around age fourteen, I ended up mostly shutting it down until my early twenties. Before I closed myself off, I taught myself how to channel through automatic writing. However, the messages were frustrating and often became looping nonsense, as though someone was just messing with me. At times I would also hear spirits as background noise, like static on a radio with moments of coherent breakthrough. This was especially prevalent while I was getting ready for school in the mornings. It was not a positive experience. The chattering was negative and intrusive. To try to drown it out, I would recite lines, sing, or read the shampoo bottle label in a hyper-focused way while I showered. Eventually I just gave up on the automatic writing for a while, and thankfully the chatter also eased off when it was clear that I wasn't giving it my attention.

My understanding now is that my energy was extra vulnerable because of my younger age and the fact that I hadn't yet established strong boundaries in the subtle realm, let alone in the physical one. Setting boundaries is something we can intentionally work on, but to some degree it's something we also grow into. We learn who we're okay with letting in and who we aren't through trial and error. In short, I needed to establish my footing more in this world before I delved so much into the other. The fact that I was extra vulnerable right after spending time in the dreamworld helps support this assumption.

If you're younger, it doesn't automatically mean you'll have the same experience I did. And if you're older, it also doesn't mean you're immune to these types of negative side effects. No matter who you are or whatever your age, if you begin exploring your energetic abilities and find that you have some negative experiences, first work on mastering practices that help keep you focused on *your own energy* instead of trying to reach out and connect with energy outside of yourself. Here are some exercises in this book that you might find helpful:

- Grounding Yourself Back into the Physical World (on page 35 at the end of this chapter)
- Tuning In (on page 42 in chapter 2)
- Clearing Your Subtle Energy and Setting Energetic Boundaries (on page 52 in chapter 2)

If you find that you're still having negative experiences, you may need to press pause on all of this and step away from spiritual and energetic exploration for a time. Focus your energy on being and growing within your physical space instead. Give it some time, and then when you feel like you're ready to try again months or maybe even years later, you can give it another go.

In my own experience, when I came back to actively engaging with my energetic abilities, I knew that if I was going to make any attempt at communication through automatic writing (something we'll get into more in chapter 3), it would be in order to receive a very purposeful and specific message. It would *not* be to sit and just see who and what came through. I intentionally make the window of practice very brief. Spirit knows this of me now. If they want me to "get" it, they know they need to impress upon me that they have a message to share and I'll then go get pen and paper and *bam,* they'd better be ready with something short and quick. Once it's briefly recorded, we're done.

Symptoms from Clearing Energy That You No Longer Need

While spiritual and intuitive development can be fun, it's not all play. Often we're creating energy shifts within ourselves, moving stuff around, and clearing out junk. When we open ourselves up to subtle abilities that have been shoved to the back corner for most of our lives, there can be some intensity as we open back up to this energy. This can lead to things like spontaneous remembrance of current-life trauma; visions of past life recall; emotional symptoms such as weepiness, irritability, or anger; and physical symptoms like headaches and fatigue. You may also experience intense emotional shifts and feelings of confusion about what's going on. This process can also be emotional for the fact that it may be the first time in a very long time that you're finally letting yourself be who you've always wanted to be.

All of this is an opportunity for healing but is a bit like detoxing your physical body. Before the benefits are realized and the junk is moved out to make room for healing, it can be uncomfortable. As you acclimate, practice self-care and be gentle with yourself in these moments. Get some extra sleep, take a bath, journal your thoughts, take a walk, get out into nature, or do whatever else you do to soothe yourself in healthy ways.

Becoming Obsessive

It's important to avoid becoming overly focused on the subtle and spiritual experience. While exploration into your secret psychic life is great, remember that *you still live in the physical world* and ensure that you aren't getting lost in Spirit. While subtle exploration can be an incredibly nurturing part of your life, it should not feel like it's your *everything* or that it's the most important thing. It is only one sliver of the pie making up your life on earth.

Sometimes it can be easy to become hyperfocused on your spiritual inner world as a form of escapism or running away from your life in this world. While it can be great to develop our understanding and abilities in the subtle world, we still need to participate in this concrete life as well. Intentionally working to maintain a balance between both sides is key.

If you find that you can't stop thinking about messages you're receiving, you're seeing absolutely every little thing as a potential sign, you're overly anxious about what it all means, or you're falling down rabbit holes of trying to psychically solve murders or other traumatic unsolved mysteries that are not a part of your life, then it's time to reel your energy back in. You only have so much to work with, and you might be giving too much of it away. Feelings of anxiety and worry, cyclical thoughts, tension, and an overall sense of "ick" are all signs you're using your skills in ways that aren't beneficial to you. It's time to refocus in order to avoid burnout. Practices around grounding and setting boundaries can be helpful in addressing this point.

PRACTICE
Grounding Yourself Back into the Physical World

Intentionally grounding into your physical body and the immediate space around you is an important mindful practice. This is especially true if you're "coming back" from an intense subtle spiritual experience and will come in handy as you work your way through the rest of the book and beyond. Whether you are doing a reading, have a spontaneous vision, are in deep meditative communion, or are participating in some other high-vibration activity, grounding is a very helpful close to such practices. If you're noticing looping or anxious thoughts, grounding can also come in handy to pull you out of your headspace or fight-or-flight mode and center yourself back in the present moment. Here are some potential grounding options to choose from:

- Go out into nature.
- Wash your hands and splash your face with cold water.

- Eat something.
- Take a shower or soak in a bath.
- Clap your hands and stomp your feet.
- Do an aerobics session or some other form of physical exercise.
- Play with your animal companion.
- Get your bare feet touching the earth.
- Bake something.
- Spend time in the garden.
- Smell an uplifting scent, such as a favorite perfume or essential oil. (Citrus is especially mood-enhancing.)
- Shift your focus by stating out loud five things you see and five things you hear in your immediate environment.
- Shift your focus by choosing a physical object to hold or touch and study all of its details very closely.

We've covered a lot in this chapter alone! I hope the initial practices have helped ease you into the deep work that can come about when connecting with the secret psychic side of yourself. Let's take it a step further now and dig into the foundational details of working with our intuition.

CHAPTER 2
Your Subtle Intuition

Now we're really getting into the heart of your practice. In this chapter we'll cover what subtle energy is all about, why it matters, how we actually go about accessing energetic information, and what the various forms of subtle intuition are. You'll learn what it means to "tune in" and how you can begin to intentionally do this to access your psychic skills. You'll begin to understand the framework of your own personal form of intuitive language and will have the opportunity to immediately begin practicing this language with newfound understanding.

Your Subtle Energy

The foundation of our subtle intuitive *senses* is our subtle *energy*, so before we dive into explanations of our various abilities, let's first review what our energy body is all about. Some of this information about our energy body and psychic senses can also be found in my previous book *Llewellyn's Little Book of Unicorns.*[14] If you've already read that book, you can consider this a quick refresher.

We all have a physical body that's easy to observe. Science has identified our organs, body systems, and basic functions. But on the energetic level, we also have a body that's difficult, but not impossible, to see. Many psychics and energy medicine practitioners are able to see the subtle body with their physical eyes or envisioned in their mind's eye to gather health insight and information.

---

14. Angela A. Wix, *Llewellyn's Little Book of Unicorns* (Woodbury, MN: Llewellyn, 2019), 41–42, 193–195, 214–221.

Our understanding of the subtle body carries ancient and sacred wisdom and has been handed down for thousands of years. Logically and scientifically, our understanding of these systems is still evolving. For example, in Traditional Chinese Medicine it's taught that we have different meridian lines through which vital life energy flows and moves around the body. This concept is utilized in a variety of healing methods, from reflexology and acupuncture to Chi Gong, yoga, and massage. Yet the physiological and anatomical existence of the meridian system has only really started to be understood scientifically in the twenty-first century.[15] As technology continues to improve, it's likely we will continue to receive scientific understanding and validation of many things that have long been intuited. Until then, ancient and intuitive wisdom continues to guide us. The pieces of your energy body that I want you to know about are the aura and the chakras.

The Aura

The aura is the electromagnetic bubble that expands out around your body. It spreads out about two to three feet around you, including above and below you. The aura can influence various states of wellness, from emotional and mental to physical and spiritual. It contains our own energy, but it can also collect the energy of others.

The Chakras

Chakras are wheels of energy that exist within our subtle energy body, overlaying the physical body. These energy centers run from the lower spine to the top of the head. Our original understanding of them comes from sacred Indian texts known as the Vedas. While there are a range of

---

15. Miroslav Stefanov et al., "The Primo Vascular System as a New Anatomical System," *Journal of Acupuncture and Meridian Studies* 6, no. 6 (December 2013): 331–38, https://doi.org/10.1016/j.jams.2013.10.001.

Liu Chenglin et al., "X-Ray Phase-Contrast CT Imaging of the Acupoints Based on Synchrotron Radiation," *Journal of Electron Spectroscopy and Related Phenomena* 196 (October 2014): 80–84, https://doi.org/10.1016/j.elspec.2013.12.005.

Bruno Chikly et al., "Primo Vascular System: A Unique Biological System Shifting a Medical Paradigm," *The Journal of the American Osteopathic Association* 116, no. 1 (January 2016): 12–21, https://www.cecity.com/aoa/jaoa_mag/2016/jan_16/12.pdf.

chakra and body energy systems found in different cultures, the following interpretation of the seven main chakras from Hindu tradition makes up the system that's most often described:

- **First chakra (root):** Color: red. Located at the hips/base of the spine. The root chakra is very focused on the physical body and has to do with stability and security in the material world.

- **Second chakra (sacral):** Color: orange. Located in the abdomen below the navel. The sacral chakra has to do with creativity, pleasure, emotional wellness, and the intuitive skill of clairempathy (psychic emotion).

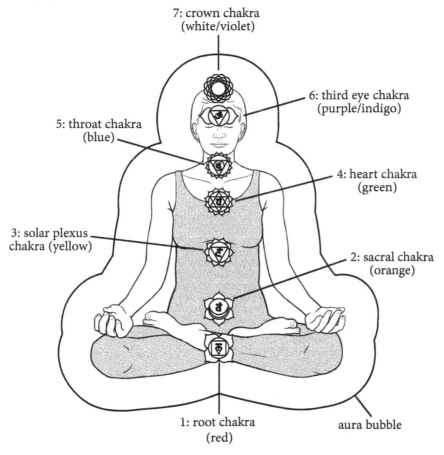

7: crown chakra
(white/violet)

6: third eye chakra
(purple/indigo)

5: throat chakra
(blue)

4: heart chakra
(green)

3: solar plexus
chakra (yellow)

2: sacral chakra
(orange)

1: root chakra
(red)

aura bubble

The Aura and the Chakras

- **Third chakra (solar plexus):** Color: yellow. Located in the abdomen above the navel. The solar plexus chakra has to do with personal power, self-confidence, mental well-being, the intuitive skill of clairsentience (psychic feeling), and the gut-level knowing of claircognizance (psychic knowing).
- **Fourth chakra (heart):** Color: green. Located at the heart. The heart chakra has to do with connection, compassion, love, and the intuitive skill of clairsentience, including clairempathy (psychic feeling and emotion).
- **Fifth chakra (throat):** Color: blue. Located at the throat/thyroid. The throat chakra has to do with communication and the intuitive skill of clairaudience (psychic hearing).
- **Sixth chakra (third eye):** Color: purple/indigo. Located behind the forehead. The third eye chakra has to do with visualization and the intuitive skill of clairvoyance (psychic sight).
- **Seventh chakra (crown):** Colors: white/violet. Located at the top of the head. The crown chakra has to do with enlightenment, connecting with higher guidance, and the intuitive skill of claircognizance (psychic knowing).

Tuning In to Connect with Your Subtle Energy

Learning how to become still and tune in to your energy in order to hear and learn from it is a foundation of working with your intuitive abilities. This doesn't necessarily mean you're required to sit and meditate every day or at regular intervals for a specific amount of time, although that kind of dedicated practice can be incredibly helpful. I still have not been able to manage that level of practice, and I used to feel bad about it, especially because it's so often recommended in spiritual and intuition development resources. It's true that the more you meditate and tune in, the more you can connect with the subtle energies, but even if you don't have a set, consistent practice of sitting down, clearing your thoughts, and tuning in, you might find that you're actually making the connection much more than you realize.

Taking time to tune in doesn't mean you have to sit in lotus position and try to empty your thoughts for an hour, although you can certainly go that route. It might be easiest for you to tune in when you go for a walk in nature. Part of why I don't have a traditional meditation practice is because I find I'm more devoted to regular tune-ins when I do it while taking walks, when I'm in nature, while in the bathtub, and as I'm lying in bed at night before I doze off. Eventually I realized that my tune-in sessions often occur when I just feel drawn to do it, instead of occurring on a set schedule.

That said, I'm a very (very, very, very) introverted person who loves to live in the realm of my inner exploration, so tuning in is part of my natural mode of operation. Even if that's also the case for you, once in a while it's still good to make an intentional practice of quieting your mind and tuning in to your energy. By putting more intention into it, you might get results faster, because you're actively remaining self-connected and in alignment with subtle experiences that you might otherwise have missed.

Your tune-ins might happen most when you're dancing or in that space of the runner's high, when physical movement is also moving your subtle energy. Another perfect opportunity for tuning in is after a yoga practice while in Savasana/Corpse Pose. Or your practice of tuning in might be while journaling. You might find that it takes writing out your daily thoughts and getting through the random jumble first, but eventually you can get into a flow where you're tuned in to receive higher wisdom.

Look for whatever makes sense to you. Whatever the case, your tuning-in moments should leave you feeling connected with yourself as well as a larger energy, putting you in a receptive state for whatever information needs to be processed.

PRACTICE
Tuning In

Take a moment now to practice finding stillness, clearing your mind, and tuning in to your energy. Once you get the hang of the process of tuning in to your inner guidance, you'll be able to find this stillness within yourself even in the middle of a busy external environment. Breathing is your first step. If you ever feel lost thinking of how to go about tuning in, look to your breath.

Step 1: Settle In and Find Stillness

Close your eyes now. Take a deep breath and then let it out. On your next breath, feel it go all the way down to your belly. Allow your breath to expand your belly before you let it out. Repeat this deep breathing until you feel your body and mind really settle into relaxation mode.

Once you feel that stillness, tune in to your energy. Pay attention to whether it feels as though it's reaching out externally. For example, while you're trying to relax, you might notice that you're also listening for your kids or anticipating someone needing your attention. Or maybe a part of you is trying to time your practice so that you can move on to your next task. If you find these types of reaching-out energies, notice them and see yourself bringing that energy back into yourself. Like an octopus with all its outstretched limbs, pull each arm back in one by one until all your energy is centered.

Sit in this stillness and continue deep breathing until you feel ready to move on to the next step.

Step 2 (Option A): Feel into Your Energy and See What Comes Up

As you tune in now, feel into your energy. Don't get lost in the random or racing thoughts that might arise. Just see what comes up. If you find that you're caught up in your mind, pause, breathe, and bring yourself back to your center. Focus on the feeling of that energy. Then begin to observe once again. You might see certain colors, feel a specific mood, have words pop into your mind, or notice other forms of intuitive messaging. Just settle in, observe, and enjoy the ride.

For example, you might see the color red and then feel rising anger. Focus on that emotion and try to follow it back to its source. Maybe you see the image of a coworker and then you think of an important work project. Suddenly you intuitively know that the anger isn't yours, but is that of your coworker due to their frustration around this project. Just by making this connection, you're left feeling lighter, knowing that energy isn't yours to carry.

Step 2 (Option B): Yes or No

Option A offers a more open-ended experience for tuning in, while option B has a focused direction. If you find with option A that you don't really get anything or are unsure about what you're getting, you can try this option instead.

I think of this option as something akin to muscle testing. If you've never tried it, muscle testing is something that's used to determine things like allergies or sensitivities. (Disclaimer here: This and any other practice in the book should not be used as a substitute for medical advice, diagnosis, or treatment.) For example, a practitioner might first have you state something true, like "My name is _____ (your name)." With your arm outstretched, the practitioner presses against it while you hold your arm strong to keep it in place. With a true statement, you'll notice that you're stronger, while with a false statement, when resistance is applied, it's much easier for your arm to be moved. The same is true for things that are beneficial or not beneficial for you. If you hold an apple and muscle testing is done, you might see that you hold strong. But if you hold an orange, something you're physically sensitive to, you'll probably find it much harder to keep your arm up when resistance is applied.

There are versions of this practice that you can do without a practitioner. In one version I found, I would lean forward if something was yes/beneficial and I would feel a sense of being pushed backward if something was no/not beneficial. You can also try a version where you link closed circles of your fingers (pointer finger touching thumb on both hands, with those two circles looped together like chain links). If something is yes/beneficial, the link holds when you pull to try to break them apart, but it breaks easily when something is no/not beneficial. In this way, you could be perusing the grocery aisles and test items in real time while you're out in the world.

I personally found self-muscle testing to be frustrating, partly because I felt odd practicing it in public spaces when I most needed to utilize it. I eventually discovered that it was actually easier for me to do this practice internally, which also makes it much more discreet.

In my version (in the case of assessing food items or supplements), I'll hold the item, take a deep breath, let it out, and settle my energy. This means that my energy is focused internally and I'm not reaching out to listen to the music or observe other shoppers or noticing whatever else is going on around me. I'm tuned in to my inner world. Once settled, I silently ask, "Is this item beneficial for me?" In my mind I see a lotus flower. If the item is beneficial, I see a closed lotus flower that opens its petals wide. If it's *not* a beneficial item for me, I see an open lotus that closes its petals tightly back up. Open means yes and closed means no.

You'll need to play around to see what your best form of imagery is. In your version you might just see the word *yes* or *no* like a sign that is being held up for you, or maybe you won't see anything but instead you'll hear the words.

Try it now. Close your eyes and take a couple of deep breaths. Settle in and find stillness. Now ask, "What is my intuitive sign for *yes*?" Once you understand that, ask, "What is my intuitive sign for *no*?" Now to confirm them, say, "My name is _____" and say your correct name. Tune in and see which sign pops up. Repeat again, but this time use a name that isn't actually your name. See what sign pops up. Once you have those signs, jot them down to help cement them in your mind.

Once your signs are confirmed, you can try testing this out in other areas. This technique applies beyond just sensing for what is beneficial or not for your body. It can be used as a way to learn to clear your mind and tune in, to connect with your energy and listen for the message of your inner guidance in many different situations. Maybe you want to see a clear yes or no response on whether you should make plans with your friend on a certain day, which job to consider, whether a certain relationship is something to continue putting your energy into, and more. The possibilities are endless.

PRACTICE
Sensing Subtle Energy

Now that you've learned how to tune in to subtle energy, let's take it another step further and try feeling it. You can try this on a houseplant, your animal companion, or even yourself. If you have someone else you know who is open to these explorations, they could certainly be your subject as well.

As you did in the previous practice, close your eyes and take some deep breaths. Settle and center your energy. Now extend your hands and hover them a few inches above your subject. Take a moment and see what you feel. Some examples of what you might sense are warmth, a fuzzy feeling in your palms, or a sensation as though you're trying to push two magnets together between your subject and your hands. If you do feel something, this is the energetic charge. You're sensing the aura of the subject.

Now feel into your own energy at the center of your palms. Notice what happens when you attempt this next step: *extend your energy to your subject.*

Did you sense anything? You might have sensed a pulsing sensation or pressure in your palms. It could also feel like something is flowing or being pulled from your hand toward your subject, like a very subtle string being pulled through the center of your hand. Or again, you may have felt the same heat or reversed magnetic sensation as before. If so, way to go! You've just sensed subtle energy. If not, it may just take more time. Keep trying with other subjects. As you progress through the rest of the book, at some point you might suddenly realize that you've grown more sensitive and can now easily sense this energy.

How Subtle Energy Translates into Information

The subtle energy that you've been sensing in the previous exercise is part of what translates into information through our energetic senses, or what we think of as our intuitive/psychic abilities. Here I'll share a breakdown of some of these psychic skills, including clairvoyance, clairaudience, claircognizance, clairsentience, clairempathy, clairolfaction, clairgustance, and clairtangency.

We traditionally consider that we have five basic senses: sight, hearing, touch, taste, and smell. But we actually have more senses than that, including a sense of spacial awareness, pain, balance, temperature, and acceleration, as well as perceptions like time or the feeling that something is familiar. Some people even perceive senses in entirely different ways. For example, they might see sounds in the form of color or experience something they're seeing as a smell.

In addition to these traditional and nontraditional senses are our energetic senses. These are known as the *clairs*, because the terms all begin with *clair*, which means "clear." These senses connect us to our intuitive guidance. Even though you may not have been aware of them previously, you've certainly been using them.

Clairvoyance (Sight)

Clairvoyance is the ability to visually perceive energetic messages through your psychic vision. This usually appears within your inner vision in the mind's eye, and not with your physical eyes. However, some people do perceive psychic imagery that way as well.

To get an idea of how clairvoyance works, picture your bedroom. Now see your bed and envision the pattern on your blanket or bedspread. The way you've internally seen the images and details of the space is the same way that we see with clairvoyance. This ability becomes very useful during meditation and energy work.

Clairaudience (Sound)

Clairaudience is the ability to perceive energetic messages through the inner ear. By "inner ear" I don't mean the internal structure of the physical ear. Instead, this is the ear's version of our inner vision/mind's eye. When you get a song stuck in your head, you're using the inner ear that I'm referring to. For some people, though, clairaudience can come across as sounding the same as our normal physical hearing. Most often we'll psychically hear in a way that's internal, and on rare occasion it will come across as external noise or communication, like a loud noise or your name being called.

Usually clairaudience ends up sounding a lot like your own internal thoughts. Because of this, it can take time before you're able to clearly perceive the difference between clairaudient communication and your own thoughts. With practice it becomes much more obvious. Like a fingerprint, we all have a distinct voice and energy. When communication is coming from a source other than you, it feels different, but this can be a subtlety that takes time to distinguish.

Claircognizance (Knowing)

Claircognizance is an energetic sense of knowing. It's when you know something down to your core, even when you aren't sure why. There is just no logical reason for how you know the information.

This used to happen with me and my older sister Amy all the time. It seemed that whenever either of us called the other, the receiver always knew who was calling. This never happened for me with anyone else and our calls were very random, so there was no pattern or reason to support our knowing. It was simply a connection and energetic communication that left us certain of who was on the other end.

Clairsentience (Feeling)

Clairsentience is the ability to perceive energetic messages of sensation or feeling. This is the gut instinct that we often hear about. You might feel pushed in a certain direction but can't quite define why. Or perhaps you've just met someone and you get the sense that there's danger or mischief about them. Without words, you're reading spaces, people, events, and situations to feel out information that's helpful for you to know.

If you perform psychic readings or energy therapies, this ability allows you to feel specific messages and energy that you're working with. If you're giving someone a massage, you might feel a stabbing pain in your head if they get frequent migraines that need attending to on an energetic level. In a psychic reading, the psychic might feel tightness in their chest while connecting with someone who passed away from a heart attack.

Clairsentience is closely related to clairempathy, the difference being that with clairsentience you are feeling within the physical body, and with clairempathy you are feeling within your sense of emotion.

Clairempathy (Emotion)

Clairempathy is the ability to energetically feel another's emotional experience. It's a form of clairsentience but is specific to emotion. People who are strongly aligned with this ability are known as empaths. It's very common for these individuals to confuse these energetic connections and messages as their own. Because of this, they might go through the day taking on a teacher's anger, a friend's distress, a cashier's depression, and more. While positives can be felt as well, negativity is something that empaths unknowingly tend to soak up like a sponge and struggle with, which can cause this to be an exhausting ability.

Unconsciously, we as empaths want to heal and help resolve pain, but we need to tend to ourselves first. If you feel down, anxious, burnt-out, or overwhelmed, make it a regular practice to ask yourself, "Where is this feeling coming from? Is it mine? Is it someone else's?" Listen to the internal answers that come to you. If the feeling is yours, try to trace it back to its origin so that you can work through it. If it *isn't* yours, ask Spirit to help you release the energy for the other person to heal and resolve. Afterward, ground yourself with a physical activity. Go for a run, dance around the house, or stomp your feet. This will pull your own energy back into your body. Clairempathy is a wonderful ability, but it's one that demands a lot of self-care and awareness.

Clairolfaction (Smell) and Clairgustance (Taste)

Clairolfaction (also known as clairalience) is the ability to perceive energetic messages through your psychic sense of smell. The smell is perceived without the assistance of your physical nose, since the scent isn't actually coming from anything in your physical environment. Clairgustance is the ability to perceive energetic messages through your psychic sense of taste when you're not actually eating anything.

These two often come together, since our physical experience of these senses often happens in union. Perhaps your grandfather always chewed spearmint gum, and this taste and smell come to you when he wants you to know he's near.

Clairtangency (Touch)

Clairtangency is also known as psychometry. This is the ability to receive energetic information through touch. Some mediums (psychics who connect with those who have passed on) use this ability during readings by holding an object that belonged to the person they're trying to communicate with. In doing so, they're able to gather information about the history of the object and the person connected with it.

After having each of these abilities individually defined, you might have a better sense of those you've already been using, even if you didn't realize it until now. A common assumption that people make when they hear about someone seeing a vision or hearing a spirit is that the person saw or heard in the same way that you normally would see or hear something in the physical world, but now you know it's more common that you will "see" or "hear" internally, similar to how you see or hear your own thoughts. This point can be a huge revelation, and you might now begin to realize that you have in fact seen or heard (or sensed in other ways) spirit communication before, especially when you were younger, but you just didn't have a frame of context to understand what you were experiencing.

We don't have to be skilled in all of these abilities. Like left- or right-handedness, we're usually stronger in one or a certain collection of abilities rather than all of them. Clairaudience, clairvoyance, clairsentience, clair-cognizance, and clairempathy are usually the most prominent senses. Being aware of what each of these abilities is all about can help you better understand your experience moving forward.

How We Access Energetic Information

The energy body is where information is stored and interpreted with the use of our psychic senses. In my experience, the various ways in which we gather energy information in order to read it include reaching out to it, accepting drop-ins/downloads, and immersing ourselves in it.

Reaching Out

Some psychics say that as they're connecting with their client for a reading, they're reading the information that's in their client's aura. With this kind of reading, I see it as a "reaching out" action. You're two distinct and separate energies. You extend your own energy outward in order to access the energy of someone else, gather that data, and interpret it.

You've probably done this before without fully knowing that's what you were doing. You might do it when you enter a room and try to read the people in the space to get your bearings. If you grew up in a house with turmoil, you probably did this to gather data from your caregivers and determine the current energy in the home. While the action in these types of instances would be more instinctual and automatic, reaching out during an intuitive reading for someone else is usually very intentionally done.

This type of "reaching out" reading connects especially with the lower chakras (root, sacral, and solar plexus chakras).

Downloading Intuitive Drop-Ins

Another way that some people describe how we access energetic data is when information "drops in" like a mental download. In this instance it's as though someone tipped opened your head like a mailbox and dropped in their messages for you.

This version might just spontaneously happen without you consciously being aware that you're trying to access a message. Without any effort on your part, you just suddenly have access to data that's there within your energy for you to interpret, like someone plugging in a flash drive. Or without the sense of reaching out, you might tune inward and ask a question to receive a message, and it comes to you with this drop-in sensation. Instead of there being an outward-reaching action on your part, the seeking comes from, and is received, within.

In instances of downloading intuitive drop-ins, the energy can feel very much like it's being received through the headspace, connecting with the crown and third eye chakras.

Immersing Yourself

In this form of accessing information, your energy merges with the other person's energy and you exchange information. If a deceased loved one or guide also gets involved, they become another merged part of the same bubble of energy. This is why boundaries become so important when you're working with your subtle abilities. When you connect with others in this way, you need to know how to separate your energy from theirs, clear your energy, and close yourself off again when you're done. This is important so that your energy is once again defined as *your own* and you don't have any lingering attachments to others, whether on the physical plane or in Spirit.

Because I usually only actively give intuitive readings during energy healing sessions, this immersive version is how I would describe my experience. During energy work, I'm already immersed in the other person's energy. I'm open to universal energy that moves through me from the crown of my head and into my client. At the same time, any energy they no longer need moves out of them, through me, and out into the greater body of energy (sometimes through my crown, usually through my feet). I'm also tuned in and reading their subtle energy body in order to see where I need to move and what might need my attention. Since there's already an exchange of energy taking place, the next step of allowing information to consciously present itself becomes very natural.

Receiving energetic information this way can happen even if you aren't someone who does energy work. If you're a highly empathic person or know you need to consciously set healthy boundaries with others in order to maintain your well-being, this immersive experience is probably something you've already experienced, even if you weren't really aware that that's what was going on. If you're really close to someone, like a friend, parent, or significant other, to the point where you finish each other's sentences and seem to read each other's minds, you're in this type of immersive energy.

Immersive readings especially connect with the solar plexus, heart, third eye, and crown chakras.

PRACTICE
Clearing Your Subtle Energy and Setting Energetic Boundaries

Anytime you begin to feel overwhelmed by others around you or burdened by your connections to even those you love, practice this meditation. Making it a regular habit will strengthen your energetic boundary and mentally set you up to advocate for your own energetic space and wellness. Once you get the hang of it, in moments when you can feel your boundaries waning, you'll be able to just envision this practice briefly in your mind and it will act as a quick reset button.

See yourself encircled by a clear bubble. Now, one by one, see all of your connections to other people (such as your best friend, your parents, your significant other, the person you watched on the news, all the people you read about on social media today, etc.) as bubbles that merge into yours. You're all crammed into a murky bubble that's hard to see through. Inside that bubble, see your energy tangled up with the energy of every other person there. The threads from their energy wind all around you, tying up your wrists, tripping you at the ankles, and winding around your chest. Frankly, it's hard to even breathe in this space.

Take a deep breath now and see a radiant light shine down from the top of your bubble into the top of your head. Like a ray of sunshine reaching you for the first time in spring, feel that warmth and let it spread deeper and deeper, filling you up from the inside. Soon you begin to feel the ties around you loosening. Like ice thawing, the threads drop away one by one. As they do so, the individuals attached to each thread are suddenly encapsulated within their own bubbles and they move outside of yours. One by one, see them drift away. As each one escapes, the space around you brightens and feels increasingly lighter. And now, finally, they're all outside of your vibrant, clear bubble, and you're glowing from the light that fills you from head to toe.

Sit in this space and soak up this good energy for as long as you need to. Remember to ground back into the present moment when you're done.

°⋘⃝⋙°

The Importance of Your Personal Symbolic Language

No matter how or when you find that intuitive information comes to you, know that it's frequently revealed through symbols, and these symbols make up the foundation of our intuitive communication.

While you can find popular meanings of common symbols in dream dictionaries and other interpretation resources, practicing intuitives will be quick to clarify that the meaning of any one item may differ for you personally, varying from what you might find others saying it means. Initially, this can make things *extra* complicated. But just like anything we learn, all we need to do is take it one step at a time.

Think of the process it took for you to learn how to read. You didn't just pick up a book one day and start cruising through all those letters and words with clear comprehension of the story they were telling. Instead, it took dedicated attention, repetition, and practice in order to arrive at full understanding. First you probably learned about each individual letter in the alphabet. You were shown what it looked like. You spoke it out loud. You learned how to write it down. And you learned to associate it with different things that you already understood in order to better commit it to memory. *A* is for apple. *Z* is for zebra.

Once you knew the alphabet, only then did you learn how to put those letters together and figure out how they influence one another. Finally, you started to learn how to put together and read whole words. And what a thrill that moment was when you finally understood! This quickly led to reading whole sentences, and from there you could fly. It was as though a whole new world had finally been opened to you.

So it is with psychic signs and symbols. We grow up being told that it's good for us to learn another language, and most of us were required to learn one at some point during our education. Well, this is another language for you! Because symbols usually come to me visually (instead of hearing the symbol or just knowing it), I've always thought of this process as learning to read sign language or as a complex game of charades, because both of those are visual forms of communication. In fact, when my sister chimes in from the other side, she often appears in my mind's eye doing sign language, as a cue that she has a message for me and that I should more fully tune in to access it. If you speak sign language or are fantastic at charades, it makes me wonder if you'll find that this new intuitive language comes very easily to you. But perhaps not! Maybe you'll still find learning these symbols to be a clunky process.

Your analogy for the process of learning to read psychic signs and symbols may differ, but whatever the case, it will force you to shift your normal way of processing language and think about communication in a whole new way. To throw a wrench in it, here the language isn't standardized. *A* might not mean apple. Instead, it might mean zebra! A rose to me means hello, as a greeting of love from a deceased loved one on the other side. For a friend of mine, it means romantic grief and trauma. And for one well-known professional psychic medium, it means the literal flower or the name Rose. For someone else, it might mean a funeral, wedding, or something else entirely.

Part of this understanding comes through experience and learning as you go. You don't have to overwhelm yourself with thinking you have to study all possible meanings of all potential signs and symbols. Instead, you can dip your toes into learning more about symbols that you know are likely to come up, and tune in to find out what your own personal meanings are for those items. Once you have a bit of a foundation built, Spirit also knows this and will use those symbols that you've already established. As new symbols come to you over time, you'll be able to tune in to those to figure out your meanings for them and add them to your log.

You don't always have to reach out to interpretations found in external resources. Maybe the symbols of squirrel, turtle, and crow stood out to you while you were on a drive, and this felt like it was the string of a meaningful message. Instead of looking up those symbols in a book, you could first tune in and ask what each symbol represents for you personally. The understanding might come to you as a gentle download. Suddenly you just know that this combination of symbols represents lots of options that you have right now for where to expend your energy. But instead of going around and trying to gather every single nut, you should take a second to slow down and be discerning about what you actually decide to do. Like a crow picking out the perfect shiny thing, go for the one or two things that stand out the most for you.

If you already have a symbolic language in hand, Spirit is likely to make use of that as well. For example, if you know a lot about flowers and their symbolic meanings or essential oils and their uses, those types of things might pop up for you as symbols associated with meanings that you already have some understanding of. Or if you get a message and are unsure of the meaning, you can actively bring your existing symbolic language into your practice by directly asking Spirit to clarify by adding in an associated plant (or whatever your previously understood category might be) to pair with the original message.

Even as you gain an understanding of your symbols, confirm their messages when they come up to ensure their meanings are still consistent with what you've known them to mean in the past. For example, maybe you're practicing with a friend and see a forget-me-not flower, which is usually a sign to you of a recent loss, but you aren't quite sure because it feels like there's something more to it. You tune in to double-check if the meaning is consistent with your norm, and find that you also see a feather, which for you means a message from a deceased loved one, so it feels consistent. However, you still feel like there's more to it. You also see another symbol of a small garden shovel, which is new to you. Once again you see some forget-me-not flowers, and along with them you have a motherly feeling. You share this with your friend, and they confirm that their grandmother recently passed away. She'd had a thriving flower garden that was one of her favorite places and she would often share bouquets that she picked from it with her. Now, you know that feather and forget-me-not are consistent with your past symbolic interpretations, but here the flower has a dual meaning (message from deceased loved one + garden lover) and was clarified by the new symbol of the garden shovel, which indicated someone who loved to garden. Moving forward, you'll have that new symbol in your back pocket to work with.

In another example, you see a peace lily, which is a leafy green plant, and this is representative to you of a healthy and thriving home space. But in one instance when you're tuning in for a friend, you see a peace lily alongside a stop sign. When you tune in and ask to confirm whether the peace lily still means a healthy home, you see the plant wilting and turning brown. You then see a dog next to it. Putting the three symbols together, you let your friend know that they should probably check their plants to make sure their animal companion isn't getting into them. Your friend looks startled and shares that their dog has been mysteriously sick lately and they haven't been able to figure out why.

In one instance, my friend Pam saw three symbols in rapid sequence: rose, mustard, muffin. She asked Spirit to show the message to her in another way, because even though she knew that the symbols went together, she was baffled by what it meant. The symbols repeated, so she thought about each one individually. To her, rose equaled love or a relationship that's been lost, and, as unusual as it may sound, muffin represented emotional trauma. (You'll learn why later in chapter 4 when we talk more about recalling past energetic trauma.) The bottle of mustard meant nothing to her, but when she shared the symbol with the person she was reading for, they immediately knew its meaning as an inside joke from a former romantic relationship. She tuned in further, asking Spirit to show her the message in another way, and saw a figure covering her heart with her hands and making a very weepy and pained face. She asked if there was a message, and the figure showed the same heart-holding pose but then changed her expression and lifted her hands to reveal that there was now a flower blooming over her heart. Pam intuited the message "Hold on, the bloom is coming." She's very into flowers and essential oils and noticed that the blooming flower was Cistus, which in essential oil terms is used for emotional trauma and opening the third eye. When she shared these things with the person she was reading for, it all resonated for them.

Later, Pam checked in with me, asking, "Could this be kind of how it works, with tying things together and reading the message?"

Yes! Exactly! I was so excited that it was all starting to really make sense to her. "This is totally how it happens for me as well," I said.

She was left a bit shocked by her own ability. "I think it still doesn't feel real," she said. "It's... *confusing*... but I also love it."

When you start trusting what you've previously dismissed as "just your imagination," it can be amazing to realize that there's validity to this subtle style of communication. You're learning and creating a language based on images, feelings, and emotions. It takes time to get used to that! It can feel so much like guesswork and imagination, but when you speak it out loud and find that it hits for someone else, the confirmation can leave you reeling and thinking, "Oh my gosh, this *is* real." If you aren't yet sharing with others, you might find that messages are confirmed for you as the details play out in your life after the fact or as additional synchronistic messages that affirm your original interpretation.

Symbols are fluid, just like intuition itself. In the example of the peace lily, what was once a symbol of health was turned on its head to show an example of illness. There are no locked-in rules when it comes to symbols, but with these basics we have a starting point of understanding. From there, we can then follow up by tuning in to our internal guidance to confirm the full meaning of the message.

PRACTICE
Tune In to Your Personal Meaning of Common Symbols

I asked various practicing psychics, mediums, and subtle energy intuitives what they thought the top symbols that one would come across might be. The following list is a compilation of those that they mentioned, in addition to some that I've always found useful. You can find sample interpretations of these items in appendix 2, but before you jump to look at those meanings, in this practice you're going to tune in to each of the symbols and write down the meaning that comes to you. Have your journal and pen ready to record those insights.

While it's always good to keep in mind that symbols may sometimes be representative of the literal thing they're showing, here we'll be focusing on the spiritual and symbolic meanings. These are listed as categories (such as "animals"), for which there are endless options that might come up. I've just provided a sampling of what some of those might be (bunny, deer, etc.). If any other specific items come to mind when you see the category, make sure to add them to your list, along with the meanings that come to you.

Take a moment now to settle your energy. Look to each word and tune in to discover what each symbol means to you.

- Animals (bear, bunny, cat, deer, dog, fox, horse, snake)
- Birds (blue jay, cardinal, crow, eagle, hummingbird, parrot, robin, swallow)
- Colors (blue, green, orange, pink, purple, red, white, yellow)
- Flowers (baby's breath, carnation, dahlia, forget-me-not, iris, lily, rose, sunflower)
- Geometric shapes (circle, diamond, oval, pentagon, rectangle, square, star, triangle)
- Insects (ant, bee, butterfly, cricket, fly, grasshopper, mosquito, moth)
- Numbers (0, 1, 2, 3, 4, 7, 666, 1111)

- Other common symbols (aura, birth/labor, cheerleader, coins, cross, door, feather, fire, fork in the road—could also be shown as just a fork or just a road, mirror, moon, radio, rainbow, ring, stop sign, sun, telephone, water, window)
- Plants (aloe vera, cactus, *Echeveria imbricata* 'Blue Rose' succulent, fern, jade, peace lily, shamrock/clover, spider plant)
- Trees (balsam fir, banyan, birch, eucalyptus, maple, oak, palm, weeping willow)

If you have trouble intuiting your own meanings for these symbols right now, you can start out by relying more on interpretations gathered from other resources. After you feel more established in your abilities, you can come back to this practice and see what comes to you.

Whether your understanding of a symbol comes from your own interpretation or from an external resource that resonates with you, you can add those new meanings to your list as you go along. Psychic Melanie Barnum recommends logging this list in your computer so you can more easily add entries and keep things organized alphabetically, which I agree is a great idea![16] You might jot things down as you go about your day, and set those random, sporadic notes in a designated place. Then once a week or once a month, you can pull out your notes and type them into a single document that you've set up to hold your personal symbol meanings.

Gathering Symbol Interpretation Resources

In your symbol interpretation journal or document, also have a section where you record your favorite external resources. There is an abundance of books and websites that you might find useful. Dream and symbol dictionaries can be a vital source of assistance. When you're initially gathering your favorite resources, one way to go about it is to do an internet search for

16. Melanie Barnum, *Intuition at Work: Trust Your Gut to Get Ahead in Business and in Life* (Woodbury, MN: Llewellyn, 2020), 48.

"dream interpretation" and you'll find different sites that list various symbols alphabetically for easy search.

Some books on psychic development also cover symbol interpretation, but it can be harder to search for what those might be. You can look to the recommended resources section in this book for a collection of titles that get into this topic to start you out.

When you're looking at these types of interpretation guides, remember that the meanings you find may not match your own. As you look to someone else's interpretation of a symbol, pay attention to whether or not it resonates with you. If it doesn't, you shouldn't force that meaning into your own repertoire. Stick with things that feel authentic to you. As author and lucid dream expert Clare Johnson states, "How can a dream cow mean the same thing for a butcher as it does for a Hindu, for whom cows are sacred animals? A dream moth will have a very different meaning for an insect enthusiast than for someone who is moth-phobic."[17] She adds that dream dictionaries can be helpful in gathering insight on how symbolism works, especially when it comes to archetypal imagery, but trusting your gut and how a symbol fits into the context of your experience is key. I agree!

PRACTICE
Interpret Symbols in Dreams

As you continue to learn about a range of potential symbols, you might look to your dreams to start understanding your personal intuitive language. To make this part of your practice, keep paper and pen by your bed so that you can immediately record your dreams and any prominent symbols that stand out to you. Taking an active role this way signals to your mind that these are details it should pay attention to and remember. The more you record, the easier it becomes to recall your dreams.

---

17. Clare Johnson, *The Art of Transforming Nightmares: Harness the Creative and Healing Power of Bad Dreams, Sleep Paralysis, and Recurring Nightmares* (Woodbury, MN: Llewellyn, 2020), 43.

The next time you're able to recall a dream, choose some symbols that stand out and work with them as you did in the previous practice, where you tuned in to determine your personal meaning for each one. You can also look up the symbol in your favorite resource and see how your meaning compares to someone else's interpretation and to see if anything else stands out as extra insight. From there, you can record the new symbol and its meaning in the list that you've started keeping.

Dream interpretation is an area that can be an easy way to start sharing with others, if you have that desire. Since everyone dreams, it's an approachable topic. Try to think of someone you might share your dream with and ask them what they think it might mean. You might discover it's really helpful to talk it out and play off someone else's interpretation of the details. Hearing their dreams and offering them your interpretation is yet another way to flex this interpretation muscle.

PRACTICE
Interpret an Intuitive Message

In this practice you'll be receiving an intuitive message that you'll then interpret.

Option 1: Interpret a Message for Yourself

Take a moment to settle your energy. Practice breathing and centering yourself until you feel really calm. Once you're in that place, ask Spirit to clear and protect your energy so that only messages for your highest good can come through.

Tune in now. Ask Spirit to reveal the message they have for you. Sit in this space until you feel you've received the full message.

Once you feel you have all the details, come back to the present and write down what you received. Note colors and things you saw, heard, felt, etc. Highlight the details that you've never received before that could be added to your symbol log. Focus on each of those details and tune in to determine what each symbol means in this instance. Now look at all of the details as a whole. Try to string the individual items together, as if putting words together to make a sentence, and see if it makes sense. If you don't feel you're getting the message, tune in again and ask for Spirit to reveal it in a different way. If the same details are shown and you still don't get it, ask if there's anything that can be added to it to help nudge you in the right direction.

Once you have the meaning of the message, write it down and ask Spirit to send you confirmation in the form of additional follow-up signs or messages. If you still don't feel like you understand the meaning, ask Spirit to help it be communicated to you in the following days. Pay attention to follow-up details, synchronicities, and things that make you go "aha!" As Spirit works in the background, the meaning of all those details might suddenly click when you aren't even actively thinking about it.

Option 2: Interpret a Message for Someone Else

I anticipate that many readers of this book won't have a trusted person they can work with, and that's fine. Independent practice is equally valuable. That's certainly where I started out, and it's still the main way I practice. However, having even occasional access to someone you can practice with or bounce ideas off can be really helpful as a form of external confirmation that you're hitting on the correct interpretation of messages. If you *do* have a trusted person you can work with, consider it a bonus.

To make this practice even more unique than the independent version, you'll be practicing by immersing yourself in the energy of the person you're reading for. If you're not there in person with them, ask them to sit or lie down as the practice unfolds, and just envision that you're making direct contact with them.

Sit facing the person you're reading for. Take their hands in yours and ask them to close their eyes. Close your eyes as well and take a moment to settle your energy. Practice breathing and centering yourself until you feel really calm. Once you're in that place, ask Spirit to clear and protect your energy and the energy of the person you're reading so that only messages for your and their highest good can come through.

Now reach out to the person energetically. See your energies as one combined bubble. Imagine a radiant light coming through the crown of your head and down into your body. It lights you up and flows out of your hands into the person you're reading for. Soon it has spread throughout their body, clearing out energy they no longer need. Take a moment to see if you feel any of their energy moving back out through you and into the larger body of energy. (You might feel the energy move down to your feet and into the earth, or up to your head and out your crown chakra.) This is energy that was ready to be released.

With a clear connection, you're both now open to receive an intuitive message. Tune in now. Ask Spirit to reveal the message they have for the person you're reading. Sit in this space until you feel you've received the full message.

Once you feel you have all the details, come back to the present and write down what you received. Share the symbols or words that come to you as is. If you have a sense of their meaning, you can share that, but first just share the basics as they come and ask if they have any immediate meaning for the recipient. Let the person sit with it for a second.

If you don't feel you're getting the message, you can tune in again and ask for Spirit to reveal it in a different way. If the same details are shown and you still don't get it, ask if there's anything that can be added to it to help nudge you in the right direction. Once you think you have the meaning, share your interpretation with the person.

If the message still doesn't seem to be making sense for either of you, ask Spirit to help it be communicated in the following days. Let the person know that they should also pay attention to follow-up details, synchronicities, and things that leave them feeling as though the pieces are clicking into place.

How to Know Whether You've Interpreted a Message Correctly

There aren't any hard-and-fast rules when it comes to the interpretation of messages. Sometimes I feel that the symbol is just that, and I'm able to apply the symbolic meaning that I'm familiar with, as in "I'm seeing this symbol, which to me means _____." In other instances, if I'm not sure, I might say, "I don't know if this is literal for you or symbolic, but I'm seeing _____. Does that mean anything to you? To me it feels like it might mean _____." In this type of instance, intuiting the meaning becomes a mixture of both your own interpretation and the external assessment and confirmation of the other person you're sharing with. If you aren't yet sharing with anyone, it could be confirmation from other external resources like symbol interpretation books. If you're new to sharing, this type of instance might feel like you're being nudged to have a conversation with someone as an opportunity to finally share with others.

While the interpretation of symbols and messages can be very subjective, there are some indicators you can watch for to help confirm that you've understood correctly. These might include the following:

- **Physical and emotional sensations:** Chills, smiling, laughing, mouth open with a sense of surprise, etc.
- **The "aha!" moment:** A dramatic moment of clarity that comes with a sense of excitement and recognition, where the meaning is clear and you just know *that's it.*
- **Repetition:** The same message might keep coming up for you. This cue can be a bit tricky, because the repetition could be confirmation itself but could also be the message still trying to be heard. When you're experiencing repetition and it leaves you with the warm fuzzies and a sense of happiness about the message you've received, that's a cue that it's confirmation. On the other hand, like a continued tap on the shoulder, repetition could be asking you to pay even more attention in order to fully get what's being spelled

out for you. If you aren't quite getting the meaning or there's more to be understood about the message, the repetition might continue until things click, so long as you're open to receiving it. If you get tired of it, you can close off and ask for it to stop. Two practices in this book that can be especially helpful if that's the case are Clearing Your Subtle Energy and Setting Energetic Boundaries (on page 52 earlier in this chapter) and Setting Boundaries with Spirit (on page 128 in chapter 4).

- **Synchronicity:** You notice things that occur independently of one another but feel meaningfully connected as significant coincidences. If such synchronicities happen in relation to your message, it might be confirmation.

- **External confirmation:** This form of confirmation might come from the person you're sharing your intuitive insight with or from another resource that you check, such as a dream or symbol dictionary, or it could be some other form of confirmation from the world around you. External confirmation could be part of the synchronicity as well.

- **Write or vocalize the message:** I often find that when I'm not totally sure about a message's meaning, it usually takes writing it down or speaking it out loud for it to fully tell its story. Try writing about it. Note the details, how the message came to you, what they were, what you thought and felt about them, etc. Often the message will feed you additional information once you open up to writing it down in this way, and new realizations will click in. You can also try speaking the message out loud. Since you're connected to the energy of the message, this helps to keep it moving and allows for more insight to drop in for you. These are both forms of channeling the energy and downloading more of the message.

- **Tune in:** Remember the yes or no part of the Tuning In practice (on page 42 earlier in this chapter)? Use this to confirm whether or not your interpretation is correct.

Here is one example of receiving a message and confirming it through synchronicity, repetition, and emotion. After decades of illness, I asked for Spirit to confirm if I was going in the right direction, as I was about to have two surgeries to try to improve my condition. I was conflicted over whether this direction would provide benefit or lead to an even worse state. I'd tried so many things over the years, including other surgical procedures that hadn't helped at all and had even made things worse. I was cynical and unsure.

While I did experience some reassuring synchronistic messages before the surgeries, I still was not totally convinced of things even after the first surgery, and I still had another one to go. During the slow recovery after the first surgery, I was gifted an oracle deck that I had owned before but had let go of at some point. I found it interesting that it had made its way back to me. The cards themselves shared angel imagery and were a symbol of a time in my life when I'd been much more trusting. An interest in angels had been the beginning of my spiritual journey, and they'd been the ones I had cried out to for years when solutions to so many health issues seemed out of reach. Eventually I'd felt jilted by both Spirit and the medical system and was left wary of placing my trust there again.

Three times on three different days, I tuned in to Spirit to ask about these health situations, and each time I pulled the New Beginnings card from this angel oracle deck. I got chills every time. The first time, I felt wishful but still unsure. I would stare at the card with an angel staring back at me and feel afraid to let myself open back up to hope. *Could this really be my new beginning?* After so long, it almost felt unfathomable.

When I pulled the same card the fourth time, I cautiously accepted the message. I allowed myself to hope again. As an act of claiming my new beginning, I kept that single card and let go of the rest of the deck, holding the message close and letting go of what I didn't really need. Eventually, as things unfolded, I knew directly from my lived experience that this was indeed a new beginning for me in very significant ways.

As another example, one time I was driving and was lost in thought over a dilemma that I'd previously asked for insight into when I found myself pulled from my thoughts by the surprising appearance of a bird. I wondered if it was a sign, but didn't dwell on it. I continued driving, once again lost in thought over my dilemma, only to be shocked out of my thoughts a second time by the appearance of a bird that nearly hit my car. I started laughing in amazement, because I instantly had a knowing of what these signs meant. In these moments, it was as though time stretched on, moving in slow motion and magnifying the presence of the animal symbol, its synchronistic occurrences, and the meaning the symbol had for me that was attached to the thoughts I'd been contemplating when the birds appeared.

When in Doubt, Ask for More Information

Keep this note in mind from here on out: *If in doubt, ask Spirit.* If you're unsure whether a symbol you get is meant to be interpreted or is just a literal representation of that image, ask Spirit. If you're reading for someone and aren't sure whether a symbol is something you're supposed to ask the person about, ask Spirit. If you're unsure whether a symbol has the same meaning that it has had in the past or it has a new one in this instance, ask Spirit. If you don't get the meaning of a message or understand what to do with it (keep it to yourself or share it), ask Spirit.

This isn't a multiple choice quiz. You're allowed to ask for help. You're allowed to receive more information in the moment. Just check in with your spirit guides and make a request for clarification. Then tune in and see what they respond with. Keep asking questions in the moment and feel out what other associations your intuition is leading you toward. Once you think you've got the message, ask if you've got it right and tune in to see whether the response is yes or no.

The Potential for Delay in Understanding a Message

On the surface, the process seems straightforward: we open ourselves up to receive a message, we receive it, and we understand it. But the truth is it doesn't always feel so smooth and linear. I know for me, personal messages often come slowly and need to be processed over time before I fully understand them. We can ponder and struggle over the meaning of a message, but in the end we may need to just set the pieces aside until, one day, *click*.

Suddenly we get it. Maybe we needed a bit more information. Maybe our brain was working on the problem in the background. Or perhaps Spirit was tinkering with things to ensure the message was eventually received at just the right time. Sometimes the pieces that make up the message may not be for you to understand. Instead, the message is meant to be shared with and interpreted by someone else.

Even if you've been successfully interpreting intuitive messages for a long time with symbols that have become familiar to you, these delays in understanding can still occur. There will probably *always* be times when you find yourself in the midst of learning what a new symbol is going to mean for you moving forward. One time I was visiting with someone who asked if I could feel anything about his retirement. He was contemplating whether the timing was right, and while I didn't receive much detail on the circumstances, I saw a heart and shamrock in my mind. I had no idea what this meant or how it was related, and somewhat uncomfortably I said, "I don't know what this would mean, but I'm seeing a heart and shamrock."

He smiled and said, "I've been thinking of retiring around February or March."

New to all of this, I was floored, because at the time I didn't know these were symbols of holidays, but he recognized the meaning right away. From that day forward, I had a new understanding of symbols for myself. I now know that if I see a pumpkin, a turkey, an evergreen tree, a heart, a shamrock, etc., it's probably an indicator of time as holidays on the calendar year.

Another time I was working with someone who was pregnant, but I didn't know it at the time. I was being thrown all kinds of baby symbols and feelings, but I couldn't piece it all together. The meaning remained foggy, just out of reach for me. Instead of interpreting the symbols, I shared exactly what I was seeing and sensing: fuzzy blankets, a feeling of being really cozy, warmth, and a sense of preparation for something new. It was energy I wanted to snuggle into. To me, these were random details that weren't yet interpreted, but to the person I shared them with, it was a literal message of me picking up on a pregnancy that she wasn't yet sharing.

Sometimes the message isn't for you to know; it's for you to share and let the other person connect the dots.

One of the clearest examples of a delay (and message persistence) that I've ever experienced came after the death of a grandparent. In all the time I'd known him, Ed was someone who always seemed ready with a smile and conversation, but everyone knew not to disturb him during football! After he passed away, I unexpectedly had a vision one day of him on a throne that was bedecked with flowers. Ed had never struck me as someone who'd want extravagant attention lavished on him, so seeing him on a *throne* of all things seemed odd. I wasn't part of the scene, but instead was viewing it from an outside perspective. There were people celebrating all around, and I saw my sister Amy trying to get up to him to say hi. She was so excited to see him again, and the first thing she exclaimed once she finally reached him was, "Wasn't that the *weirdest thing you've ever done*?" (as in being human). The vision was such a surprise and the message so humorous that all I could do was laugh.

The message reappeared some days later with another random pop-in. I was fully immersed in some landscaping when suddenly Amy chimed in, but she wasn't talking to me. Instead, she was talking to Ed, as though she was giving him a tour and I was just overhearing things. Unfazed by my eavesdropping but fully acknowledging my presence, she continued on, saying, "Oh, and see, sometimes she can hear me." She continued with her tour, letting him know that his transition was different from what hers had been like, because he needed less healing and recovery time. Because of this, his "space" was different from what hers had been. Throughout her orientation it felt like he was humoring her, kind of like, "Okay, I got this," but because of her enthusiasm, he was letting her give intros anyway. I was thoroughly entertained by these exchanges and was happy to sense that he felt good-humored and at ease.

For a week, these kinds of pop-ins kept happening randomly. The image of him on a throne kept showing up in my mind, as though someone was trying to get me to look at it more. When I finally focused in, I saw that the flowers that people were bringing and that were all over the throne were carnations. There were so many, it was like they were drowning him in them! I thought that was weird, because I find them unappealing and I think of them as a cheap flower. *Couldn't they be a little more elaborate up there?* I wondered. Then I started feeling like it wasn't so much a throne that I was seeing but instead was actually something more like a parade float. *Okay, they're celebrating for him at the level of a parade,* I thought. *Cool. Message received.* But the throne and carnation images still kept coming up.

Finally, I wrote about it one night in my journal and happened to write that I was seeing things *from the sidelines,* and then the word *homecoming* slipped out. *Click!* I sat there looking at those words on the page, and it was like I was being slapped in the face with the meaning. What a neat way for him to put it. *Homecoming.* In true Ed fashion, his message from the after-life was a football metaphor. It was so consistent with who I'd known him to be that I was blown away once I finally got it. And as the pieces fell into place, the energy from those in Spirit seemed to exclaim, "Finally!" Once again, I had to laugh.

Confirmation of certain messages may not come to you for days, weeks, or even years! In one case, a year after Amy passed away, my friend Pam received her first auditory message while in the shower, telling her to send me blue flowers as a remembrance gift for the anniversary of Amy's passing. I confirmed for her that blue had been Amy's favorite color and had been a special part of her memorial service. Pam had multiple visits from Amy following that, which, at the time, was an entirely new experience for her. During a meditation in which she envisioned her favorite spot on a beach, Pam saw Amy beckoning her to come into the water. Once in the water, Amy mimed having an underwater tea party with her. Many years later, Amy popped in for her once again with a vision, waving her back into the water. Soon they were zipping all over the place, laughing and relishing in the fun. When Pam looked down, she realized they were both mermaids.

These events were very powerful for Pam. They held a lot of symbolic meaning, imparting feelings of lightness, play, and encouragement to take the leap and trust enough to jump into the deep end of her abilities. But it wasn't until years later, when she shared all the details with me, that I was able to add external validation to what she was getting. Amy and I used to play tea party under the water all the time growing up, and *The Little Mermaid* is one of my top nostalgic things in connection with her. It's the first movie I remember seeing in the theater, and we used to play as mermaids in the pool all the time. I'd recently gone to see a live orchestra performance of the music set to a showing of the movie, and it was all I could do not to burst into tears as I thought of Amy throughout the entire thing. In addition, the first time Amy communicated with me after she passed, I was in the shower, and the parallels between Pam's experience and mine seemed significant and intentional. All of these things added up to confirm that Pam was on track with accurately assessing her intuitive messages.

The connections between symbols and their meanings may be made later on, as those in Spirit continue to work at it to get things to click for you. I find that their persistence through repetition and the building up of their message with additional details without my even trying to connect with them is one way that helps me to know the message is authentic, because I know I haven't logically been trying to work out a problem. The message and messengers were the ones doing all the work. I just eventually accepted and understood what they were pushing through to me during their occasional pop-in moments.

When we don't understand a message right away, or if we haven't completely interpreted it, as long as we express to Spirit that we're interested and open to it, the messenger will keep feeding us information. If the message is meant for us, it will find a way, but it may take time for the pieces to align and fully reveal themselves.

CHAPTER 3
Recognize the Natural Occurrence of Spirit Communication

While some people perceive communication with those in Spirit as miraculous or a rare occurrence, it is a natural and common phenomenon. I believe we're all born mediums with a direct line to Spirit. While some may have an easier time receiving messages than others, it's still an ability that we all possess to some degree. In this chapter I'll clarify who it is that's communicating with you from Spirit and the different ways they go about reaching out to you. From these examples, you might be surprised to realize that you've already had these types of experiences but were dismissive of them or weren't ready to believe it at the time. We'll also review different reasons why you might be resisting this type of communication and what you can do if that's the case.

Spirit Guides, Guardians, and Other Honored Spiritual Figures

If you're feeling a tap from someone specific in Spirit, it may be one of your spirit guides or guardians. These are beings who have your back and really know the map of your life. Some are with you through the long haul of this lifetime, while others dip in and out, bringing their specialized assistance in specific instances. Some might feel like close relations, while others have more of a professional feel about them. One of my long-haul spirit guides, Sarah, feels very "big sister" to me. Another, Nejú, doesn't have such a personal connection and comes mostly in times when I'm processing new training around energy medicine.

As you become familiar with these guides and guardians, you might identify some as iconic spiritual beings or specific figures from traditions you're most familiar with. For example, from Christian tradition you might identify a high-frequency spiritual figure as Jesus or Mary, while from Buddhism you might sense Buddha, or from the Hindu tradition maybe you recognize Ganesh. Even if you don't identify with a specific religion, you might still find high-frequency spiritual figures from these traditions that come to you. A common one for me is the archangel Michael, who is referred to in Christianity. He first showed up to me in a dream and pops in every now and then, always with a very encouraging, protective presence, like a loving big brother.

For our purposes, moving forward in the rest of the book I'll refer to these various categories of spiritual beings and figures as "spirit guides."

Family and Friends

There's a special connection you have with those you've known in your life, as well as those from your lineage that you may not even know much about. Aside from spirit guides and guardians, family by birth and family by choice (aka your friends) are most commonly who you'll be hearing from.

It was never a surprise to me that my sister Amy became a key voice for me from the other side after she passed away. Another that's been a steady connection is my maternal grandpa. He's someone I occasionally call on, and he also pops in unexpectedly now and then.

This is all unsurprising once you become aware of the high prevalence of what are referred to as "continuing bonds" and "extraordinary experiences" or "post-death contact." Kenneth J. Doka, PhD, a world-renowned expert on death, dying, and bereavement and a senior consultant for the Hospice Foundation of America, explains continuing bonds, saying, "We retain an ongoing relationship with the deceased. This can occur in a variety of forms, including in our rituals, beliefs about the afterlife, and memories—

to name but a few."[18] This type of bond could manifest as an astonishing or seemingly unusual experience, like seeing an apparition, or it could be as simple as the warm connection felt through memories of the one who has died.[19] A continuing bond could include everything from sensing a presence or having a sensory experience (sight, sound, touch, taste, smell) related to the deceased loved one to encounters within your dreams, symbolic experiences, or messages delivered to you by a third party.[20] If you find yourself having conversations with your passed loved one or feel as though they're watching over you, these are all forms of this connection. And it's actually very common. It only feels like it's not, because so many people don't feel comfortable sharing about it.

In a paper assessing available data on sensing the presence of those who are deceased, it was found that "while the incidence of sense of presence experiences tends to be given as approximately 50% of the bereaved population (Datson & Marwit, 1997; Grimby, 1998; Kalish & Reynolds, 1973; Klugman, 2006; Olson et al., 1985; Rees, 1971, 2001; Shuchter & Zisook, 1993), the true incidence is thought to be much higher, as there is still a great reluctance among the bereaved to disclose its occurrence (Datson & Marwit, 1997; Olson et al., 1985; Parker, 2005), particularly vis-à-vis doctors, therapists (Sormanti & August, 1997) and clergy (Rees, 2001) for fear of ridicule (Rees, 2001), having it 'explained away' (Parker, 2005) or being thought of as 'mad or stupid' (Hay & Heald, 1987)."[21] They found that once individuals were reassured that the experience was very normal, they were then willing to speak about it.

All that is to say continued connection with those who are deceased is recognized as something that *does* happen. Even if no one around you has

---

18. Kenneth J. Doka, *When We Die: Extraordinary Experiences at Life's End* (Woodbury, MN: Llewellyn, 2020), 148.

19. Doka, *When We Die*, 178.

20. Doka, *When We Die*, 106–120.

21. Edith Maria Steffen and Adrian Coyle, "Can 'Sense of Presence' Experiences in Bereavement Be Conceptualised as Spiritual Phenomena?" *Mental Health, Religion & Culture* 13, no. 3 (April 2010): 273–91, https://www.researchgate.net/publication/233272815_Can_sense_of _presence_experiences_in_bereavement_be_conceptualised_as_spiritual_phenomena.

mentioned their own experience with continued bonds before, it's likely that others you know have experienced these types of occurrences as well. Some people may have been encouraged to try to emotionally disconnect from the deceased loved one in order to move on, which is part of why these occurrences often aren't talked about. But a new understanding of the widespread and often lifelong experience of these continuing bonds is shifting things, allowing people to accept and be more open about it.

PRACTICE
Meet Your Spirit Guide or Family Member/Friend

Take a moment to allow someone in Spirit to make themselves known to you. Go into this practice without anticipation of who specifically you're going to connect with. Allow the individual(s) to reveal themselves. This way, you have the opportunity to meet whoever is most important for you to be aware of at this time.

Take a moment to settle in. Get comfortable and take some deep breaths. As you did in the Moving Through Transformation with Intention practice on page 23 in chapter 1, progressively relax all areas of your body and deepen your breathing. When you're ready, once again see yourself at the top of those stone stairs.

With bare feet, take a step down, then another, and another. Feel the cool stone underfoot as you go. The air that was initially warm starts to feel damp and cool, and the sunlight dims with each step. Notice the details as you move downward. Finally you reach the bottom, where you find a beautiful door. Light coming from the other side seeps out around its edges. Rest your hand on the handle and open the door, letting the light spill completely around you.

Stepping across the threshold, you find yourself in a favorite meditation space. See what this looks like. Maybe you're on a tropical beach, in a clearing on the edge of the woods, or at the top of a mountain with a fantastic view. Walk deeper into this space and find a place to sit down. Settle in and take in the details of the space. Notice what you see, hear, feel, smell, or taste. Touch the surface you're sitting on with your fingers and notice the details there. Enjoy the scenery for a bit before moving on.

As you're scanning the space around you, you notice another door nearby. On the other side is someone in Spirit who wants to connect with you. Go to that door now and open it. Your guide/relative/friend steps over the threshold toward you. Notice the details of their appearance and the feeling you get from them.

Take time now to receive the message they have for you. Pay attention to how this message comes to you, whether it's spoken by them, shown through pictures or other visuals, felt through emotion or other impressions.

After you receive their message, ask any questions you might have for them.

When you feel your meeting has come to a close, say your farewell and see them leave through their door. Move back to the door you came through and follow the path back up the steps.

Gently come back to your physical space by wiggling your fingers and toes, stretching, and opening your eyes. Take a drink of water and do anything else that you like to do to ground back into your physical space. Jot down any details that were significant to you.

In this practice you got to meet with someone special to you in Spirit, but you also were able to see what psychic skills come most naturally to you. Note which subtle senses you most naturally leaned on to receive your message. As you move through this chapter, you'll see more examples of different ways we use our range of subtle skills for spirit communication.

°⋖⟠⟡⟢°

Sight: Visions

When seeing those in Spirit comes across in the same way that you see using your physical sight, instead of seeing a full-bodied figure, it's more likely that you'll see lights and shadows, especially out of the corner of your eye.

It's like a flicker of "hello" to get your attention and to cue you to tune in further.

But most often you're seeing within your mind, the same way you would envision a memory. Seeing visions is one way that those in Spirit can connect with you. These visions can play out like mental snapshots or mini movie clips within your mind. They can come suddenly and flash by quickly, leaving you wondering if it was a true event or just an anomaly.

The day my sister died, I experienced just such a vision. My phone snapped me from sleep on a damp January morning and I glanced at the clock as I reached for my cell phone: 3:00 a.m. This couldn't be good. I grabbed my phone without hesitation, knowing we'd unexpectedly turned an ugly corner. Only five hours earlier, I'd texted my younger siblings saying, "Amy's at the hospital again. Acute liver failure, but her test numbers look like they're improving a little again, so she could bounce back from this like last time." I ended it on a positive note. No need to over-worry them, right?

A little over a year prior to that point, we'd all discovered that Amy had been dealing with liver disease, although she'd managed to keep it a secret for some time. It had been a dramatic moment after so much wondering to realize point-blank that she was struggling with alcoholism. She was also battling an eating disorder, and the combination had sped up the progression of damage to her body. She could die in days, or weeks, or months, or years. Maybe a decade? That would only get her to age forty. How could this be happening? The doctors were frustratingly unclear, but any option that didn't end with us growing old and gray together was unbearable. As a family that tended to avoid openly expressing our emotions, this finally had us breaking down in each other's arms.

Amy had come back around, though. Her skin maintained an orangey jaundiced tinge and the whites of her eyes were shaded yellow most of the time, so the reality never let us fully sink into a comfortable "things are back to normal" denial. Still, she was alive, and that was more than we'd been given to hope for at first. I'd been planning to pack up my things and visit her that weekend. Her numbers were improving again after all.

She'd make it out okay, right? There had been so many false emergencies. It could be another year, another decade, they had said…

Now, as my phone jangled me awake and flashed away the dark morning in my clammy palm, I knew that either I would be running out the door far ahead of the weekend on my way for last moments with my big sister or I would already be too late.

"Ang?" Dad said, low and broken. *Too late*, I thought to myself.

"Yeah… Is everything okay?" I asked, already knowing that everything was the very opposite of okay.

"No, Ang," he paused. "Amy just passed away." Wailing grief swelled in my chest, but I had to at least gather the basics. I walled off the tears to the back of my heart for later; I wouldn't break down on the phone.

"Okay," I said. Okay? This was so *not* okay, but what other words were there to say? Why hadn't someone warned me or told me to rush down there instead of wasting those final hours with sleep that I now resented?

"They weren't expecting it," Dad responded to my silent thoughts. "The doctors were even surprised, but there was a nurse with her. She wasn't alone."

"Good." I imagined a loving hand holding hers, a soothing voice easing any final fear. *Go, find your peace*, her nurse would have said. *This pain is no longer yours.*

"We're meeting to tell the younger siblings."

"Yes, I'm coming," I croaked out.

"They shouldn't be alone," he added.

"No," I agreed. With panicked realization, I thought, *I'm the oldest sister now.* "Call me when you leave," I croaked. "Okay?"

"I will." He paused. "I love you, Angi." The air pitched in my chest, trying to force its way out in sobs. I bolstered the wall I had set against the tears.

"You too," I squeaked before hanging up. My husband, Luke, was sitting up and rubbing my back with a knowing reassurance. I sat forward, ready to let the grief explode from my body, to seep past my eyes and wash out some of my pain. The second before it all let loose, I decided this was not the time. I stamped it down somewhere below my hollow stomach, and with dry eyes I turned to Luke. "I'm going. I need to get ready." I was shaking and my teeth chattered through my words.

"I'm coming too," he said resolutely. "We can pack and head out right away." I nodded.

"I think I need to take a shower first," I said as a violent round of chills shook my body.

"Okay," he said as we moved from the bed into action mode. He could sense my need for time alone probably more than I did. Before we parted to our separate chores, he took me in his arms. "I'll handle packing. Take your time."

I turned on the shower as hot as I could stand it. Clouds of steam bellowed out and filled the bathroom in a thick white cloud. Good. I wanted to be hidden. I stepped my ice-cube toes into the hot water that pooled around the drain, and the breath I'd been holding escaped in a sigh. The heat moved to the tension in my shoulders and then rained down on my scalp. Now that I was warming, alone, I tried to open the gate I'd slammed down against my grief. I couldn't find the way, though, and the tears wouldn't come. I stood silent, waiting for it. Still it wouldn't come, so I let the streaming water fall in place of my tears.

Even among the rolling clouds that told of heat filling the cold around me, shivers continued to rumble through my body, revealing that their source was not only a chill in the air. I'd never experienced this kind of shock or grief before. I wasn't alarmed by my reaction, but observed the peculiar-ness of it. Instead of tears wracking my body, moving my shoulders in waves of sorrow, grief stole my warmth all the way down to my bones and shook me with little earthquakes.

Little earthquakes. Tori Amos's "Happy Phantom" sang through my head. Her album *Little Earthquakes* was the soundtrack of my middle and high school years with Amy. It had rung out from her bedroom, belted out on drives to school and back, and played out in a sister-thief battle wherein I would sneak the CD for as long as she didn't notice, until she came stomping into my room, demanding it back. Maybe she was the happy phantom now?

A flash of her holding our family dog displayed in my mind like the snap of a photo that was quickly removed. Was Amy with her? Another quick flash of Amy walking in snow, all white around her, with a trail of animal companions we'd had in life following after her.

What was that about? I wondered, moving my head from side to side to shake away the involuntary images.

I squirted some peppermint shampoo onto my hand and smooshed it between my palms, lathering it up. The smell wafted to my nose and the potency cleared my nostrils. I closed my eyes and took a deep breath, trying to allow the aromatherapy to calm me. *Flash*—a hummingbird fluttered in the front of my mind. An impression of being light, carefree, and uninhibited came to me and a feeling of pure joy washed over me. I opened my eyes, my attention fully present. My voice caught in my throat and I could only let out a whisper.

"Amy?"

Following this moment, I eventually received confirmation that I had in fact received visions from my deceased sister. I was left wondering why in the world she would leave this muck and go somewhere with snow. Of all things, why would that be what she decided to show me? Amy hadn't especially cherished winter. In fact, we'd often talked and schemed about ways to run away on tropical vacations when we were stuck in the middle of yet another Midwestern freeze. The significance of the winter symbolism was lost on me. The mystery lingered through even further confirmation when I found out that a family friend, to whom I hadn't divulged my vision, had gone for a reading with a trusted psychic. That psychic also saw Amy in snow. I was absolutely amazed at the repeated message, even though I still wasn't sure what it all meant.

Hearing: Sounds and Words

As with sight, hearing is another way that spirits connect with us through our energy and psychic abilities. The very first communication I remember receiving from Spirit came completely unbidden in the form of hearing.

I was no more than five, admiring a toy in a jar. Inside was a cute little bee hanging on a string. Because the bee was magnetized, when you moved the bottle into different positions, it would look like the bee was actually flying around. I was hypnotized by it. This little yellow shape captured my full attention as I watched it shifting and darting from one side to the other.

Bzzzzzzzzzz! Suddenly I was startled out of my focused attention when someone made a buzzing noise right in my ear. I jumped and looked all around me, but was equally surprised to see that no one else was there. It hadn't been the noise of an actual bug but had clearly been the sound of a bug being made by a person. I wasn't scared by it, just totally confused. Even though I didn't see anyone, I felt like someone was laughing.

At the time I had no idea what had just happened. I didn't have a context for hearing someone who didn't seem to actually be there. But I never forgot it. As I started learning about subtle abilities and the potential for spirit communication, it eventually made more sense. I still wonder who exactly it was. When I tune in to try to figure it out, I don't get a specific family member or guide that I'm familiar with, but I do sense that it's someone I have a connection with, and they weren't trying to scare me but were just having a moment of playfulness.

It's also worth noting that this was one of the very few times that I've psychically heard something in a way that was actually perceived by my regular physical hearing. At other times this has happened only when I was drifting off to sleep, in between the states of awake and asleep, and heard my name being called.

Usually, though, we "hear" in a way that's perceived internally, much like hearing our own thoughts. But when it's clearly a message, you can sense the difference between your own thought and the communication from someone else.

One good example of this came the day after my dog died suddenly and unexpectedly. Emotionally broken the day after his death, I distracted myself from the grief by burying myself in work. I was locked in, listening to music and typing up notes. There was no room for my mind to wander, but suddenly I psychically (and internally) heard, "Oh, *that's* what you do all day!" Startled, I focused in on the source of the voice and saw my dog Jasper in my mind's eye, smiling and wagging his tail. I sat there shocked for a moment and let the message linger in my mind. I'd never had an animal connect with me like that before, and it took me completely by surprise. And of all the things he could have communicated, he had broken through to express his shock at finally having the answer to his longtime question of what the heck it was I did all day without him. Now he was getting a kick out of being able to go wherever he wanted to answer all of those mysteries. I could see that he was following me and my husband into our vehicles, to work, on errands, and anywhere else we might be venturing, and he loved it. I had to laugh, and his connection was so comforting. I hoped he would come through to me again somehow.[22]

While this is an example of a clear message through hearing, sometimes it is much more subtle and is experienced as your own thought, with those in Spirit trying to get your attention with random thoughts that make you think of them. When you find yourself randomly thinking of your deceased loved one, it might actually be because they're around you at that moment, trying to cue you in to that fact. Of course, it could then be easy to claim that they're around in *any* moment. To get confirmation, you can tune in to see if it's actually them or ask them to provide additional confirmation in some other way.

Influencing Physical Objects

Spirits can be sneaky, making a connection with us through lost, found, moved, and otherwise influenced objects. This category of spirit communication also includes an influence on electrical objects, such as your TV randomly turning on. In these instances, the influence of items feels significant and will leave you with the strong sense that this was an intentional connection from Spirit.

I knew Amy had been interested in this sort of phenomenon, so it was unsurprising when she appeared to be taking action in this way after she

---

22. A version of this story first appeared in *Gone Dogs: Tales of Dogs We've Loved*, edited by Jim Mitchem and Laurie Smithwick (Charlotte, NC: Thomas Woodland, 2019), 27–30.

passed away. In one instance, her boyfriend shared just such an experience with me. "I just had to tell you this thing that happened," he started. "I knew you'd want to hear it. You remember that lighter you gave me when we were cleaning out Amy's apartment?" My mind jumped back to the image of a sunflower set against a blue sky. I'd picked it out of the candles and clutter of other things on her dresser, and her boyfriend was the one person I thought would put it to use. When I'd handed it to him, asking if he wanted it, he'd paused. I'd thought maybe he didn't really want it but in the end had taken it because I'd offered and he didn't want to be rude. The slow-motion exchange had left me with an awkward feeling because I didn't understand it.

"Sure, I remember," I said.

"It struck me because you purposefully handed it to me and it was *so Amy* to have a lighter like that. I set it on a dresser at home and kept meaning to put it somewhere safe where it wouldn't get wrecked. Every time I walked past it and saw the sunflower, I would think, *I should put that in a safe place.* But I'd move on to let the dogs out or whatever and forget again. Then today when I finally went to move it, it was flipped over!"

"Really?"

"Yeah! I mean, Amy used to always talk about this kind of stuff. She'd go on and on about finding pennies from her grandpa and that sort of thing. At first I just blew it off, but damned if I didn't start finding them everywhere too!"

"I know, it's uncanny. You start feeling like you're going a little nutty sometimes," I said with a laugh.

"She always said if she ever died, she'd come back and let me know she was around. I kept telling her, 'Amy, you know me. If you're going to give me something, you've got to dumb it down.'"

"I think she's been getting pretty specific!" I said.

I had also experienced the penny phenomenon with Amy, which was extra meaningful because, as her boyfriend noted, it had been something she'd felt a connection with during her life. After her death, it seemed that in significant moments I was sure to find a rogue penny, and it would be dated from the year of either her birth or mine, as if to emphasize the point.

The morning of Amy's funeral, our family also experienced rogue electronics behavior that had no real explanation, such as an alarm clock that blared us awake randomly, even though we'd never had an issue with it before and haven't ever since. When Amy was alive, she had also shared an experience she'd had on the first anniversary of our grandpa's death. She was suddenly woken when the VCR in her room came on, spit out a tape, and turned itself off around the same early morning time when he had passed away.

If you notice these kinds of influences, it's usually just a way for those in Spirit to say hi and let you know they're around. Make sure to give them a wave and say hi back!

Knowing: Feelings and Impressions

When it comes to spirit communication, some of the ways that knowing/feeling can come across are as an impression, a nudge, a subtle physical feeling, or an emotional feeling.

An impression is when you have a sense of something and you just *know* it. You might just suddenly get the impression that your loved one is with you. It's something that's almost impossible to explain, but in the moment you just feel them and know they're present with you.

A nudge is a pulling in a certain direction that leads you to do or find something that you may not have otherwise or is especially meaningful in that moment. Maybe you were all set to settle down and read a book, but then for some unknown reason it feels important that you wash the dishes. A bit perplexed about this feeling, you set down your book, get back up, and head into the kitchen. You don't know why, but you just feel like you need to do this. Then, as though someone was intentionally leading you to it, you immediately find the lost ring you've been looking all over for sitting underneath a plate on the counter. Or, as I once experienced, instead of heading to bed as I intended, I suddenly felt the urge to turn back around and dive into an overwhelming pile of a loved one's many papers. There I unexpectedly came across a message that was so synchronistic to the events of that day that it felt overwhelmingly like she was sitting right there, handing the note directly to me.

Feeling could include the sense of a physical feeling. It could be knowing that a spirit is messing with your hair or pressing your nose the way so many of us lovingly "boop" the nose of our animal companion as a silly sign of affection. While physically there isn't an indication of your hair actually moving or your nose being pressed down, there's still a subtle feeling that you just *know* is there and being imparted to you by Spirit. For mediums, knowing/feeling in this way comes across when, for example, they feel as though they're having trouble breathing when a deceased loved one who passed away from lung cancer is sharing that information to help confirm their identity.

Feeling in terms of emotion might be something that is being shared with you, or it might be emotion that you naturally feel as a result of the occurrence of spirit connection. After a signing event for the launch of my first book, I experienced both of these types of emotion. I was driving home, thrilled that the book was finally out and that I'd gotten to celebrate it with others, including many of my family members. The day had felt like a kind of baby shower, a reunion of my loved ones all celebrating a momentous milestone in my life. I was equally happy about the coming of my favorite season, and as I drove home, I watched for the trees that were just starting to turn their autumn colors. Lost in song, scenery, and a sense of accomplishment, I suddenly started to feel like I was going to cry.

This caught me off guard and confused me, because up to then I hadn't been sad. Logically, I tried to think about where this sadness was coming from. I thought about how happy I was in that moment, so I initially assumed that maybe I was crying from happiness. But that didn't seem right. When I tried to feel into where the emotion was coming from, it felt like the kind of crying and heartache that comes from grief. I followed that grief and it led me to thoughts of my deceased sister. Suddenly I realized she was trying to get my attention, and while I hadn't consciously realized it until that moment, energetically feeling her had triggered latent grief around her not being in the physical world. It wasn't that her present visit was sad; it was just that I held an energetic memory of her that was associated with grief, and feeling her had triggered that emotion.

I tuned in to her then and noticed that there were many other family members with her. I could feel a swelling of joy from them as they were all congratulating me on the release of my book. I was floored. It felt like I'd just walked into a surprise party. The euphoria juxtaposed with the grief was so intense that it left me crying the ugly cry! The message had been so unexpected and caught me totally off guard, but I was grateful for it.

During the phone call that I'd had with Amy's boyfriend, he'd shared an experience that offers another example of psychically hearing, along with knowing/feeling in the form of impressions, nudges, and subtle physical feeling. He prefaced his story by saying, "I never told anyone this before, because I didn't want anyone to think bad of Amy, but I know you'll understand. She used to say how you 'got' all this stuff."

"We did talk about some unusual things sometimes," I said with a laugh.

"She used to talk about this one guy she'd hear. It sort of freaked me out, but she swore it. We used to walk through this cemetery path and she'd say someone was there. She told me what he said his name was and she'd tell me, 'He's pulling my hair,' or he's saying this or doing that."

"I remember her telling me something about that once," I recalled, smiling at the thought of the playful spirit. I definitely remembered her talking about someone who would mess with her hair.

"Yeah, I mean, I'd just smile and nod. It worried me a little, but I just left it alone. I never really believed, but then one night she started weaving through the headstones, saying he was telling her that he was buried there. She walked around like she knew where she was going." I imagined Amy disregarding any sense of creep factor as she played a sort of graveyard hide-and-seek, following the internal nudge. "And wouldn't you know, Angi, she stopped right at his headstone."

PRACTICE
Feeling into Your Emotions

In this practice you'll work on tuning in to the emotions that you're feeling in order to determine their origin. This practice assumes that the emotion you're feeling is truly your own and is not the effect of empathic connection where you're actually feeling someone else's emotion. We'll cover practice around empathic connection later in chapter 4.

Becoming self-aware and assessing where an emotion is coming from can sometimes lead you to understand that the emotion is actually being triggered by spirit communication. Practicing with your own emotion will make it easier in the future for you to determine whether Spirit is making you feel something that is an example of *their* emotional experience or if what you're feeling is your own emotion as a result of connecting with them in the moment.

The next time you feel a wave of emotion, tune in to it. Really let your barriers down and allow yourself to feel the emotion completely. Ask, "Where is this emotion coming from?" As you sit in the emotion, allow your mind to wander and see what drifts to the surface, like memories popping into your mind. If you're open to the experience, you'll find that the bread-crumb trail leads you to an explanation of the emotion's origin.

Sometimes it's immediately obvious where your emotion is coming from. Someone made a joke, you laughed, you're happy. The origin is the joke and possibly your connection with the person who told it. The best form of practice here are those instances when the feeling is like a nagging tick that's bothering you, where it's not obvious why you're feeling that way. While this experience can seem irritating, think of these moments as an opportunity to dive into this practice and flex the muscle of your emotional intelligence.

Disturbances

You might notice spirit communication in the form of disturbances around you. I separate this experience out from the previous category of lost/found/moved/influenced objects because in this case it's specifically something that causes you momentary trouble or unsettled feelings.

I know someone who had two dogs, and one of them passed away. After about a month, the surviving dog started acting strangely in a way that was noticeable. It was the same way the dog had acted when this person had been pregnant, as though the dog was again aware of the presence of someone else who was unseen. Coinciding with this were issues with the TV, where it would randomly turn off. While this person believed it was her dog that had passed away saying hi, her spouse wasn't convinced. This went on for so long that they decided to replace the TV, only to find that the new one turned *on* a couple of times at random. With the combination of circumstances, the skeptical spouse was finally also convinced that it was the dog, and the TV issues stopped.

When this person shared this with me, I told her about how after our cat died, Luke and I noticed that our surviving dog acted very strangely for a couple of months. While we could have attributed it to his own process of going through loss, his oddness coincided with noises, and we would say it was our cat from the beyond messing with him, as she'd very much *loved* to do that in life. Then, after our dog died, we started hearing odd noises again. We would just look at each other as if to say, "You heard that, right?" It was creepy, hilarious, and awesome all at once. When we again found no physical source for the disturbances, we attributed it to our deceased dog letting us know he was still around. The disturbances stopped after a couple of months.

Maybe *you* aren't directly feeling or seeing anything, but you keep noticing your young child or animal companion consistently staring at a certain spot in the house. In one such instance, a relative of mine noticed that their cat would sit and stare down the basement step or would be in the basement staring at a specific spot. Random clunking noises were also occurring, and they were feeling creeped out by it all. When she shared this with me, I finally let her know that when I had been over helping with the house and had gone into the basement to check the fuse box, I had sensed something and was left with a very creepy vibe. I hadn't mentioned anything at the time because I didn't know if I was just imagining things.

I went to her house to do an energy clearing and noticed stuck energy in one room upstairs, but mostly the issues resided at the bottom of the basement steps. When I tuned in, upstairs I saw a girl and boy running around playing. In the basement the energy was much more depressing, and I saw an older woman and a man lingering there. It was the woman who was sticking to the spot at the bottom of the steps, and her energy was the strongest. She was the anchor. I knew that if she moved on, the rest of the energetic disturbances would be resolved as well.

To try to get some kind of external confirmation that I wasn't just making this up, I brought a camera and took photo after photo all around the space. Only in the spot at the bottom of the steps where I'd felt a presence did an orb appear in a photo. I went through the entire house listening to what this lingering energy had to say. At the same time, I did energy healing. As I talked with the spirits, eventually I felt them letting go of the space. Once I'd cleared everything, I took photos all over again, and no orbs showed up. Afterward, the disturbances stopped and the cat completely ignored the spot that he'd previously been very drawn to.

In another instance, I found I was having spirit-induced insomnia, where someone was visiting me while I was trying to sleep. I suspected they were an earthbound spirit. Tuning in, I asked them why they were there. I let them tell me their story as I sent them energy to heal any trauma. When these visits kept on, I eventually went into a meditation where I connected with this person and asked for someone in Spirit who was connected to them to join us and offer extra support to help this soul find their way to the other side. All the while I wondered if I was just making it all up, but after this practice the nightly disturbances finally stopped.

Some would call the type of energy or spirits that I encountered ghosts. Others would just refer to what I encountered as an imprint of energy, a kind of replay or residue of energy that's been left behind. Whatever the case, the feeling is different from when you interact with the spirit of someone who has passed on and clearly transitioned over. In this kind of instance, it feels more like a holograph than a real being, like looking at old photos instead of full-color images. There's a dull hollowness to the energy, with less substance or "spark."

It's important to keep a grounded mind when assessing this type of thing. Many times orbs in photos are just dust and not actually evidence of spirits. Moving curtains could just be the leaking of air from outside into the space. Electrical flashes or malfunctioning devices could just be broken equipment or power issues. Odd noises could be pipes or uninvited mice moving around the house. Insomnia could be due to that extra cup of coffee you had. At the same time, you don't want to totally disregard the possibility of these types of things being part of spirit communication. It's a fine line.

If you notice something, ask for more evidence. Let Spirit know it has to prove itself to you. In the case of the house clearing that I did, the orb I found was in the *exact same spot* where I had first sensed a presence, which I had felt even before it was ever brought up by the homeowner. When they finally told me about it, without my even asking they confirmed that was also the spot where their cat had sat and stared. After I cleared things, the disturbances ended and the cat stopped acting weird. All of this compounded as confirmation.

PRACTICE
Clearing Energetic Disturbances

You've noticed some unwanted energetic disturbances that you want to resolve. Now what?

First, before you tune in to the source of the disturbance, look around for any sign of a physical source that might be causing the issue. If nothing is found, your next step is to energetically protect yourself. Envision you and anyone else living in the space surrounded by a beautiful shining light. Only beneficial energy is allowed within this light.

Once you feel your boundary established, settle your energy. Think of the details you've noticed with these disturbances, like creepy feelings, odd noises, or electrical issues. Now ask that the source of these details make itself known. Pay attention to what you psychically see, hear, and feel. If someone presents themselves to you that you know is friendly, ask them if they have a message they've been trying to share with you. Once they share that, let them know you got it and you'd like the disturbances to stop now.

If it's someone you aren't familiar with, sit with them for a moment and see what you sense. Ask them why they're there and why they're disturbing you. If you get a weighty or negative feeling and suspect they're a being or energy that needs to move on, you can first ask them to share their story and then follow that by sending them light. See this light coming down through your head, into your body, and out your hands to them. It fills them, lightening what has been weighing them down.

If they still feel stuck, ask for someone from Spirit who is connected to them (whether a loved one, guide, or some other being of support) to please come and assist them in moving on. You can watch this interaction unfold and continue sending light to support the process.

Once you feel things have resolved, send light to the space where these disturbances were felt. You can also play music you love, spray a favorite scent, bake something with an aroma that wafts through the whole house, dance around in the rooms singing, etc. The goal is to reclaim the space and raise the energy of the rooms that have been affected. When the space feels "clean," see the flow of the energy that's been moving through you stop. Your energy bubble is disconnected from them now. Wave your hands as if you're wiping cobwebs out of the air around you. Blow air out of your nose like you're blowing out an unwelcome smell. Stomp your feet and wash your hands. All of these things will help to clear you and disconnect your energy.

°⋖⌀⊘⋗°

Dreams

Dreams are a commonly accepted way that Spirit gets in touch with us. Communication through dreams is usually something that even those who aren't necessarily open to the idea of psychic connection accept. When dreams are used by Spirit, they stand out from ordinary dreams. The details are vivid, emotion is heightened, and memory of the event is easy to access. You might awaken feeling amazed that the dream wasn't reality because *it just felt so real.*

A little over a week after my dog Jasper passed away, I had a dream that I was at a house that wasn't mine, but I had a strong sense that in this place I was coming home. I was touring the space as though it was an open house, but it was as if I had already claimed it as my own. In the next instant, I was hugging and petting Jasper. The pleasant and loving emotion lingered with me after I woke.

Soon after, my sister-in-law who'd had a special bond with Jasper shared her own experience. When she was pregnant and before she had announced it to anyone, Jasper knew and was obsessive about getting at her belly. He remained focused on her belly throughout the pregnancy, but once my niece was born, his obsession promptly shifted to this little girl. Even though I hadn't shared my dream about Jasper with anyone, the night after my dream my sister-in-law also appeared to have had a visitation dream from Jasper.

"I walked into a house that wasn't your house and Jasper came running to greet me as usual," she said. "He jumped up and hugged me around the neck and gave me a quick lick on my chin. Then he got down and started frantically licking my stomach. I was happy to see his face and give him a smooch. He was such a good pup."

I couldn't believe the similarities in our dreams. "I think he wants us to see that he's happy in his new home," I told her, a bit dumbfounded.[23]

23. A version of this story first appeared in *Gone Dogs: Tales of Dogs We've Loved*, edited by Jim Mitchem and Laurie Smithwick (Charlotte, NC: Thomas Woodland, 2019), 27–30.

Most visitation dreams that I've experienced have been from deceased loved ones trying to show me they're okay, to reveal details about what they've been up to, and to express their continued love for me. A visitation might also come about from someone in Spirit wanting to communicate something specific about a life situation. I had this happen when a grandparent came through to let me know he was supporting me through the challenges of a project.

Before major surgery for endometriosis, I called on my grandpa and asked that he watch over me through it all. As I was going through the motions of surgical prep, he was brought to mind when I smelled coffee that someone was brewing and when the nurse offered me spearmint essential oil to help soothe my nerves. These are the two scents that I have always strongly associated with him, because he always chewed spearmint gum and whenever he came over we always made sure to brew coffee. I felt comforted at the thought of his presence.

Years later, in a dream I realized he was *still* watching over me specifically in relation to endometriosis. At the time I was stressed out trying to finish up a survival guide for those with endometriosis that I'd been working on for nearly two years. Throughout the process I'd been faced with so many hurdles that I'd been left wondering if life was trying to tell me the book just wasn't meant to be. While I'd put in so much effort, it felt a bit like things were falling apart, and I was having a hard time tying up loose ends to wrap it up. That's when my grandpa visited me in a dream.

In the dream I found myself in a hospital that was in total chaos. As in life, I had been mistreated in the dream and decided I wanted to make sure no one else ever faced a similar fate. Throughout the dream, my grandpa was calmly there at my side. When I would get overwhelmed and lost in the drama, he would pull me back to a steady state so that I could assess what was going on and determine what I needed to do to take control of the situation. Calm in the midst of the storm and without words, he made sure I knew he was there to guide and support me in reaching my goal of helping others. With his reassurance, I woke up knowing that I should continue the project and that I would meet my goal in the end.

Messages from the External World

In the last chapter we looked at some common symbols and their potential meanings. These included animals, insects, trees, flowers, and other plants. Your interpretations of these symbols can also come in handy when you encounter them as signs in the physical world as you're going about your day.

Messages from Nature

The fact that you're reading this book tells me you've probably always had a deeper connection with animals and occurrences of nature bringing spiritual messages to you. This may have even been such a natural part of your life that it came as a surprise when you realized it isn't something that everyone pays attention to. If you *haven't* noticed these types of messages much up to this point, I've probably just shattered the glass and now you're going to notice them all the time! Animal messages are signs that especially tend to get my attention.

When a friend of mine was going through a somewhat intense phase of her spiritual transformation, water and fire had become constant symbolic messages that were being thrown at her in dreams and throughout her daily life. At the same time, she noticed that animals were coming to her in ways that felt very purposeful. Raccoons were one animal that started showing up for her, and one day one even pooped on her porch, the same day her daughter brought home raccoon artwork that the class had made. Finally driven to know more, she looked up the meaning of this animal, and one of the first things that jumped out was a note in a book that said "raccoons are fascinated by water."[24] It was one of those moments when the messages align so perfectly that you kind of freeze from surprise at the pieces clicking into place. She was stunned. The book also mentioned that raccoons like to wash their hands and their food. With thoughts of cleansing and immersion, I told her she must be in a mode of "baptism by fire," an experience of intensity where you're thrown into an experience and just have to learn as you go.

---

24. Ted Andrews, *Animal Speak: The Spiritual & Magical Powers of Creatures Great & Small* (Woodbury, MN: Llewellyn, 1993), 305.

Eagles were another animal sign that showed up for her over and over again. This bird is also symbolically associated with water and sun. When my friend wondered if maybe she was reading too much into it, as if to add an exclamation point to it all, she found an eagle flying low right over her vehicle in the middle of the city, where it coasted along with her for a bit. Soon after and in an entirely different location, she saw not one, not two, but *five* more eagles, two of which hovered along right in front of her car. She concluded that the emerging animal symbols in combination with the water and fire messages all seemed to be about perspective, transformation, disguise, and camouflage. She felt the overall message was that it was okay for her spiritual transformation to be taking place in secret and for her to be the one to make the call about when and with whom she shared it all.

Instead of animals, maybe it's a plant that has come to share a message with you. In the midst of overwhelming stress, another of my friends went to let her dog out. He sat smiling at her until she noticed a single blooming dandelion—the first of the season—resting sweetly at his paws. "You might think, *a dandelion, what's so special about that?*" she said. "But to me it's my grandpa checking in. It was everything." Anyone who grew up around him knew how fastidious he had been about removing dandelions as soon as they showed up, so much so that it became a humorous and recognized sign for the family. In that moment she felt his presence and the love and reassurance he was imparting to her.

As intuitive Jurema Silva says, "Nature tends to give answers to our challenges and is in constant communication with our energies." Here is some additional insight from Jurema on some signs from nature that you might encounter:

- Birds that get close to you or visit you frequently may indicate that your spirit guide, guardian, or loved one in Spirit is trying to deliver a message.
- Suddenly seeing a wild animal near you may be an important sign. Wild animals are closer to the Source, and they can deliver insight into a situation that needs an answer.

- Houseplants are very sensitive to our energy and how we feel. Pay attention to the signs they emit. A happy houseplant is picking up a good vibe from you. An unhealthy houseplant (besides maybe not having enough nourishment) may be sensing some form of negativity in the house or an unpleasant outcome.
- Outdoor plants and trees that appear unhealthy may also be a sign to pay attention to.

As with the symbols that you covered in the previous chapter, when you receive a sign from nature, you can tune in to perceive the meaning and also check the meanings in appendix 2 to see what they have to say.

Other Messages from the External World

You might also come across messages meant for you from things in the external world. These are things that show up at *just the right time* and leave you feeling blown away. Maybe it's a song on the radio. Maybe it's a billboard that you've never noticed before but that seems to be shouting its words to you now.

One particularly astonishing sign from the external world came to my dad the day after my sister's funeral. My family and I had spent the day going through her things to clear out her apartment. It was either that or everything would soon be thrown out. Her place was a small upstairs apartment in a two-level house. When we walked in the first time the day she died, all I could think about was how her home resembled what I'd seen on the show *Hoarders*. It was full of clutter, dirty dishes and clothes, spoiled food, and stacks upon stacks of stuff. It was chaos. After trying at first to walk carefully, I gave up since there wasn't a clear spot to be found. Over the years I've learned that my outer world matches my inner world. When I'm stressed, I explode. It never happens gradually. My house could be pristine and then all of a sudden in a single afternoon it could look like a tornado swirled through it. All it takes is an internal storm that I just can't deal with. Amy's mess hadn't been sudden. Hers was a building storm expressed through years of stashed notes, old magazines, and childhood mementos that showed the past colliding with the present in turmoil.

As we stood in the middle of each room, frozen by the immense task at hand, we could all see that her ending had been completely overwhelming. When we set to work, we simply had to disassociate from the meaning of it all. We organized piles of clothes and good-condition items for donation, and each of us started our own pile for things we wanted to hold on to. I settled down to flip through a stack of books to make sure there wasn't anything hiding inside. Most often there was some form of bookmark, photograph, or note. As I fanned through the pages of one book, a plastic card fell to the floor. It was the driver's license from Amy's high school years. I picked it up, studying her well-fed frame, healthy skin, and glowing smile. She looked so happy, with a life ahead that was so much more promising than what she'd been given.

I didn't really want to keep the card. It had a bitter note to it, seeing the contrast of what should have been hers but now wasn't. I didn't want to throw it away, either. Unsure of where to place it, I jammed it in my back pocket and forgot about it as I kept on cleaning. By the end of the day, we'd made a good dent but still had a lot to do. Exhausted, we headed back to my dad's place. We'd originally planned to go out with extended family that evening, but by the time my behind found a cozy living room chair, there was no getting back up. My dad decided to head out on his own, but a few minutes later he called my phone.

"Hey, what's up?" I asked.

He hesitated for a second and then asked, "Do you believe in coincidences?"

"Uh, no." I said. "I always feel like they're more than just a coincidence, like a sign. Why?"

"I was praying all evening for a sign that Amy was okay, you know? I pulled my truck out of the driveway and the neighbors were having a get-together, it looked like."

"Uh-huh," I encouraged.

"My lights hit on this car's license plate. In all the time we've lived here, there's never been a car in front of our mailbox, but that's where it is right now. *Right in front of our mailbox.*" I wondered where he was going with this.

"I drove for half a block and then drove back, wondering what had caught my eye. I shone my lights on it and holy cow! The plate says 'Amy Joy.'" He gave a dramatic pause for the message to sink in. "Amy Joy!" he exclaimed again. "It didn't hit me right away. I drove away thinking how odd it was to see a license plate that said that. I got down the road and thought, *Amy Joy, huh…* And then it really sunk in. *Amy Joy!*"

"That's so cool," I said.

"You know, you wonder if she's okay and you hope and you suspect, but I needed something to confirm it. In church today I even asked if God could give me any sign that Amy is happy… but 'happy' didn't feel like the right word. I thought on it and changed my prayer. I asked, 'Please let me know Amy is *joyful*.' Dang, I can't believe it!" I could just see him shaking his head back and forth, and smiled. It really was amazing.

I was glad for him, but even in the midst of his awe-inspiring occurrence, a bit of jealousy fluttered inside of me. It was like going to buy a lottery ticket with a friend and watching them hit the jackpot instead of you. I'd been waiting for my own hit-me-over-the-head sign from Amy, and a little piece of me was envious. "Would you go out and take a picture of it for me?" he asked.

"Sure thing, Dad."

I grabbed my coat and a camera, and sure enough, there was *Amy Joy*. I took a picture from a distance and another dozen up close, just to make sure I captured the moment for him. When I went back in, I showed it to my younger sister and walked back to my chair. I stopped short, staring at Amy's smiling face that shone from the driver's license on my chair. "Did you put this here?" I asked my sister. She shook her head.

The presence of those two objects in that same moment, the license plate and the driver's license, shocked me. I realized that I'd forgotten all about that morning's occurrence. It seemed like eons ago. Yet here it was again, turning what had been a bitter note earlier in the day into something that was far more comforting. To see my sister's youthful beauty, so full of life and happiness, impressed me now not with the life she'd missed out on, but the joyful piece of herself that it seemed she'd finally gotten back.

Channeling and Divination

Channeling and divination are ways of connecting to energy and receiving messages from Spirit. These could include tarot and oracle cards, spirit boards, pendulums, automatic writing, and more. Some people have reservations about these tools and practices, but when it comes down to it, we all have different preferences for what works for us and what doesn't. It's all a personal decision, seeing what you're naturally drawn to and finding what's actually effective for you.

I see these tools as nothing to be feared, but simply as forms of spiritual connection that should be used with a balance of caution and grounded critical thinking. I occasionally use cards for extra insight and like to see where my intuition leads me with the message that is imparted by the imagery. I find this tool extra helpful when I feel like I need an objective outside perspective. If I'm having a hard time tuning in on my own to receive a message, I'll use the cards as a secondary tool to help me figure things out, and this is how I really love to use them. Instead of perceiving a message directly myself, adding in cards puts some distance between me and the message I receive. It can allow me to perceive the meaning in a way I might not have otherwise.

With automatic writing, just like with tuning in, you're making a direct connection with Spirit that may pose more boundary challenges than some of the other tools. Because I've encountered challenge with automatic writing, I now put a time limit on this type of connection, because the longer I go with it, the more I find that the messages become looping and nonsensical. If I'm going to get a true message, it will come immediately and directly or not at all. Before I realized this, I felt as though someone was messing with me whenever I tried to practice it. I was so frustrated by automatic writing that I gave up on it for years. I now mostly use it in the same way as cards, as a secondary tool to confirm the message I'm already directly connecting to myself.

In the end, remember that you are your strongest tool. Any other items are just providing secondary confirmation.

PRACTICE
Using Secondary Tools to Enhance Spirit Communication

If you need a little more confirmation that the message you've received internally was accurate and not just your own thoughts, try adding in automatic writing. Set your hand out as though you're about to write something down. You can have a piece of paper and pen, but that's not even necessary. With the movement of your hand and arm alone, you should be able to tell what's being written. The message flows through your mind at the same time it flows through your arm/hand, and feeling the physical movement enhances the energetic movement, making it even easier to "hear" and sense the message that's being communicated.

Hold your hand as though you're about to write, firmly enough that you could hold a pen but loosely enough that someone could easily move it. Ask the question you've been trying to intuit a response to and see what happens.

You may find that you don't even need to follow the full movement of writing out the complete words, but that all it takes is just getting the start of a word here and there in order to really make the message appear more prominently for you. You can also extend this method to your voice, saying the words out loud and creating even more energy movement, which amplifies the connection.

Acknowledge Any Resistance to Receiving Messages

You might notice that you are resistant to receiving messages, especially if you've recently experienced the loss of a loved one. If you do receive a message, you might find that you believe it, but at the same time you don't. The logical mind takes hold and you find it hard to trust what you're getting intuitively. Even as we desperately crave connection, we might also fight it. Time can make it easier to allow your barriers to fall, but even if it's been years since your loss, it can still be hard to accept the communication that's coming to you. This is okay. If you feel like it's too much to open yourself up to the communication, Spirit will understand. But know that even with that understanding, it doesn't mean they won't still keep trying to get their messages through to you.

The Connection Might Be Too Painful

We might resist connection as a form of self-protection. This was especially true for me following Amy's death. It was impossible not to sense her all around me, but since I knew I intensely wanted her back, I fought against that subtle awareness. Instead, I tried to convince myself I was making it all up. It was my imagination. It was wishful thinking. It was a chance happening. The already broken part of me didn't want to allow even a microscopic space for any kind of deception.

Even though the continuation of life after death and our ability to communicate with those in Spirit were topics that had long been validated for me, I knew that if I found I was only fooling myself with fairytale hopes in this instance, I wouldn't have been able to handle the fallout. So up went the concrete wall. But if I took a moment to tune in to my heart, underneath all the fear I knew I wasn't spinning fantasies for self-comfort. The stories shared and goose bumps felt by others around me with similar perceptions confirmed that I wasn't orchestrating anything. Amid the ugliness of tragic loss and grief, we were all in a magical dance of confirmation, and Amy was making sure we knew she was the wielder of the wand. Still, when I needed to, I allowed myself to keep that connection at arm's length.

Even a decade later, I still feel that the connection to my sister is too painful sometimes. Even though it's often wonderful to hear from her, I don't always have the energy to deal with the grief that arises with her presence that will forever be a part of my life without her physically in this world. While she respects that resistance on my end, that doesn't mean she fully holds back from sporadically making herself known to me.

Make It Good

If you find that you're in a state of resistance, give yourself permission to not fully acknowledge or connect with the messages that seem to be coming your way. Let Spirit know you're not ready right now. If things *do* break through, you might ask that Spirit make sure this happens only for really necessary messages. And if that's the case, also request that the message be *really* convincing in order to get your attention and to help you be less doubtful about it. Otherwise you aren't going to pay much attention to it at this time. Let them know that if they really want to reach you, *they'd better make it good*. Here is one such example.

Just before I headed out for the long drive home a couple days after Amy's funeral, I went to lie down on the couch to rest. I curled up on my side, with my back facing the room and my face toward the back of the couch. I shut my eyes and took a moment of stillness before more activity started up. After a moment I felt Amy's presence at my back. I tuned in, in a way I hadn't done much since she'd passed. I'd felt enough without trying to connect with her so closely, and I hadn't been ready for any more than that. But now I was simply too tired to resist. I could tell she wanted me to acknowledge her. I allowed myself to be open and accepted what came without fighting it.

In my mind's eye, I could see her there in white clothes and a scarf that wrapped across her forehead. As if responding to my acknowledgment, she rested her hand on my shoulder in reassurance. "I'll sit with you, if that's okay?" she asked. I knew she stated it in the form of a question as a way of respecting the boundary I'd put up against her so far. I nodded slightly in acceptance of her offer. She slid down to the floor, sitting cross-legged in front of the couch, and rested her back on mine. It almost felt like she was guarding my space. I didn't have much time before I was called to get packing and move on, but in that moment Amy was simply with me, resting in my grief.

As if knowing I'd cracked the door open to Amy's world, a family member caught me just as I was ready to head out, asking about visions.

"I don't know if I'm crazy or if this is how it works, but I've been getting these flashes. Do you think they could really be Amy?" This person had always been very open to my spiritual experiences, which I'd otherwise been cautious about sharing, but she'd never divulged an experience of her own like this before. I was intrigued.

"Really? What are you getting?"

"Yeah, I mean, it's just quick flashes, like photo snapshots. Is that the way it happens for you? Or am I making it up?"

"That's what happened for me the morning Amy died," I said. "I saw images like flashes, real quick and then they were gone." I could tell she was encouraged by this. "What have you seen?"

"Well, at the funeral service I felt like Amy gave me a hug and wrapped her arms around me to hold my heart with love. Another time I saw her with a white scarf or band around her head over her forehead." She moved her hands to her own forehead, demonstrating where the scarf had been.

"I've seen her with a wrap on her forehead too!" I exclaimed. The confirmation between our two separate experiences felt incredible.

"And yesterday," she went on in a more confident tone of excitement, "I saw her in snow." My jaw dropped. This was one of three visions from three different people where we had all seen Amy in snow. While I still didn't know what the forehead cover or the snow meant, the repeated messages most definitely got my attention.

But I'm Not Resisting!

On the other hand, maybe you don't think that you're resisting making a connection, and yet you still aren't making one. What's the deal? You might be trying with all your might to connect, hoping that a clear message will come to you, but sometimes the connection just isn't meant to be had. This seems especially true when we're deep in the throes of grief. We might just need to give it time for our emotions and energy to level back out, which can make it easier to be receptive to messages. In addition, the one you might be trying to connect with might be going through a phase that also inhibits clear connection at the moment. It's easy to imagine that those who have passed away are now in a perfect state and have complete understanding of everything, but that isn't necessarily the case. They might need time to heal as well.

Eventually the Resistance Will Resolve

Given time to process and heal, you'll likely find that the resistance you've been dealing with will resolve on its own, at least to some degree. When you feel that moment arise, make sure to communicate to Spirit that you're ready to make a connection. This can be as simple as silently stating, "I'm ready now to connect with and receive messages from Spirit." Or it could be more involved, like taking time to go into a state of meditation and envision yourself meeting with the person you want to make contact with.

When I finally felt ready to open up more to Amy, I connected with her in a meditation. To get myself into a deeper state, in my mind's eye I saw myself walking down a steep set of stairs. Once at the bottom, I saw a door and set the intention that it would open to wherever Amy was. I opened the door and saw a dreamy paradise. I stepped forward and my bare feet sunk into grains of sun-soaked sand and a warm breeze whipped at my loose hair. I looked around at the lapping turquoise water, white beach, and waving palm trees and found Amy sitting on the shoreline. She was in comfortable white clothes and still had the white scarf wrap around her forehead, tied with the threads hanging down her back and winding into her long hair.

I walked over to her and sat in the soft sand. I was surprised that I didn't see her as fully healthy and glowing. She was still skinny, with an off-color orange tinge to her skin. It seemed strange. Energetically she was almost unrecognizable. Even though her outward appearance was much the same as when I'd last seen her in life, energetically she reminded me more of a young Amy, around age seven, when she was my play partner and life was simple and fun. Instead of being frazzled, angry, and distracted, she was calm, light, and focused. Although I tried to stifle my questions, without her defensive shield or sarcasm to deflect me, the questions couldn't be stopped. *Why did you have to go? How can you be gone? Where are you? What have you been doing? Are you happy? Are you better now? Why don't you look better?* On and on it went. My stream of questions passed by unanswered until I hit on, *Why do you have that wrap on?* She drew her hand to the center of her forehead, touching the space delicately.

"It's to heal my third eye," she responded. Instead of speaking with her voice, she communicated telepathically and I heard her transferred thought in my mind; I sensed she was working to conserve her energy. She went on to explain that early-life trauma had deeply affected this energy center, which is connected to psychic vision, mental thought, imagination, and insight. "This is part of why I had such racing thoughts and chronic insomnia. My third eye was always open, watching for the next danger to come. It was wide open in fear, and the wrap is to hold it closed and help it heal."

I recalled learning in a healing class that you can place a hand over your forehead with the intention to shut down the third eye in order to help remedy racing thoughts and insomnia. While I always forget to use this healing technique on myself, I found it intriguing that she was practicing it in the afterlife. I'd assumed that she'd find instant release from what had bound her in life, but apparently that wasn't the case.

"I'm not using my third eye at all right now, but instead I'm developing a sort of secondary eye at my heart chakra." She pointed to her heart in demonstration. "Instead of seeing with my mind, I'm seeing with my heart." She sat up, as if puffing up in pride. I found peace in hearing her express such sincerity and seeing her with a calmness that was all her own.

"Why do you feel so young to me?" I asked, still wondering why she still appeared the same age but her energy felt so different.

"That was when my trauma hadn't rooted so deep yet and I was still more myself. You're sensing what's really me instead of the false protection I projected during most of my later life, more and more as time went on."

"But if you're more yourself, why aren't you all better? Why do you look the same to me? Is that just my perception? Or are you really not all better?" I was so confused. My beliefs about what transpires after this life were being flipped and turned.

"I'm so much better, but I still have a long way to go for healing."

"Oh," I said, still confused. She laughed, seeing my assumptions crumbling right before her.

"Think of it as phantom pain. If someone loses an arm, a lot of times they still feel pain in a phantom limb. Even if the physical arm isn't there, the pain is still very real. It's the same for me. No physical body, but a phantom body and a real experience of all the pain that existed there. Just because I lost my body doesn't mean I don't still need to recover from it all." This all made so much sense. I wondered why I'd never heard it before. "It's not punishment and I'm not resentful about it. It's just the natural way of things and I'm glad to finally have the tools I need to get through it all."

"I'm glad for you," I said with a note of sadness. I wished so much that she'd had the tools she needed to get through it in life instead.

"Everything still needs to be dealt with. There's no running away. Plus, I don't *want* to run away," she said with a smile. "I need resolution as much as all of you do. We'll get there." She rested her hand on mine reassuringly. With my questions run dry, we sat quietly side by side, watching the waves wash in and out. After many nights of insomnia following her death, I was now easily lulled to sleep.

When I woke up in the morning, another answer to a question was waiting at the very edge of consciousness. Spontaneously I realized what we'd all been seeing in our visions. Perhaps Amy saw my confusion and impressed me with the answer while I slept, waiting until morning to be sure I would remember. As swiftly as the visions had come and gone, I suddenly knew that we hadn't seen snow. We'd seen *light*. With our earthly eyes and assumptions, we'd interpreted our visions of elevated energy as the glare off sparkling snow, not recognizing that it was actually the intense glow of a higher realm. When I tuned in to the vision's message again, I could now see that what I'd originally been shown was actually a field over-flowing and alive with flowers. As I took in this new understanding, a message sprang into my mind: *She opened her eyes and saw wonders she hadn't known were hers to see.*[25]

---

25. This moment is something I reflected on in the painting *She Saw: Flowers Everywhere*, part of my *Sister She* series. A detail of this painting is featured on the cover of this book.

CHAPTER 4

When Intuitive Senses Seep into Everyday Life

As you become more aware of subtle energy and intuitive messages, you'll also notice when your psychic senses start picking up on things unbidden in your everyday life. In this chapter we'll cover what that might look like, including hearing others' thoughts, feeling others' feelings, seeing spontaneous visions, sensing unexpected energy, receiving breakthrough messages, and experiencing spontaneous recall of past energetic trauma. We'll cover when these types of occurrences are acceptable or not and what you can do about it if they become disruptive. Addressing energetic entanglement, setting boundaries, and regularly downloading your intuitive messages are just some of the practices we'll cover to make sure you're left feeling empowered by (and not the victim of) your abilities.

Hearing Others' Thoughts

Telepathy is the direct communication of thought from one individual's mind to the mind of another through extrasensory ability. We all use this form of communication, but most of the time we have no idea we're doing it. This is because telepathy so often comes through as though it's your own thought. As you become more aware of intuitive occurrences, you'll start to suspect when thoughts just might be coming from someone else, whether in the physical world or in Spirit.

I first noticed this phenomenon with my husband. As our years together ticked on, we both started noticing with ever-increasing regularity that sometimes we would simultaneously share the same thoughts. We called it "marriage brain." It was a bizarre realization and we started to wonder if it was both of us or if it was just one of us hearing the other. When one of us said something that the other had also been thinking, we got into the habit of calling it out: "I was just thinking that too!" or "I heard you before you said that!" When we started getting even better at it, we'd call things out before either of us even spoke it out loud. Usually this would happen while watching movies that we'd already seen together many times. "Did you see _____ just now? Did you ever notice that before, or was this the first time?"

Eventually we concluded it's usually me hearing him. For example, when I find myself noticing something new from a film that I've watched repeatedly, almost 100 percent of the time I know it's actually Luke picking up on that detail and I've just caught onto it through him. The thought actually does feel different, as though I'm being nudged to pay attention to that detail instead of just naturally noticing it on my own. Even though this recognized telepathy between us has been going on for years, it still surprises us. Along with a laugh, a common declaration from Luke when I unintentionally speak his thoughts is, "Get out of my head!"

As I became more aware of this occurrence with Luke, I started to notice that I was also hearing others. Usually this occurs with people I'm emotionally close to, but not always. Even just going through a checkout line, I was once shocked to hear a full sentence from the cashier in my mind before she said it out loud. Soon after, while I was out for tea with a friend, I found the same thing happened while I was with her. I think what shocks me the most is that it's as if a gong has gone off and I'm the only one who noticed. *How did no one else notice?*

These kinds of instances reveal just how connected we all are. It's also a way for your intuition to blatantly get your attention and reveal that, *yes*, you do in fact have psychic ability. It might be a reminder of a need to work on boundaries, especially if the thoughts you're catching feel intrusive or leave you feeling anxious. It can also be an indication that you need to give your intuition opportunities to unload at better times. The practices in this chapter will help you do these kinds of things.

One of my favorite examples of the use of telepathy comes from the memoir *Life, Love, and Elephants*, in which Dame Daphne Sheldrick shares her extraordinary experience as a conservationist living among African animals that she devoted her life to raising and saving. In working with the elephants and other animals, she and her husband, David, became convinced that the animals communicated telepathically, in addition to other subtle ways, such as through infrasound, body language, and chemistry.[26] They noticed that the animals seemed to automatically know what others were going to do, and they frequently witnessed instances where animals would appear promptly upon their caretaker's return, somehow able to gauge the exact time of their arrival. At other times they would notice an animal standing for a long period in a very focused way until (sometimes hours later) a relative of theirs would appear, as though they'd been called.[27] Daphne states that her experience "proved to me that… many animals are able to pick up thought process and that telepathy is a real means of communication, especially among family members with strong emotional bonds."[28]

Elephants are very emotionally intelligent animals, and this has caused their subtle nature to be more noticeable to us humans. In yet another example, after conservationist and "elephant whisperer" Lawrence Anthony passed away, two herds appeared at the house. His son is quoted as saying, "They had not visited the house for a year and a half and it must have taken them about twelve hours to make the journey."[29] They remained there for two days as though in memorial to their deceased friend. This could be an instance of telepathy, where the elephants were alerted by thought about the death of someone they cared about, but it may also be an example of psychic feeling.

------

26. Dame Daphne Sheldrick, *Life, Love, and Elephants: An African Love Story* (New York: Farrar, Straus and Giroux, 2012), 138.

27. Dame Daphne Sheldrick, *Life, Love, and Elephants*, 198, 215.

28. Dame Daphne Sheldrick, *Life, Love, and Elephants*, 213.

29. Tanya Waterworth, "Elephants Say Goodbye to the Whisperer," Independent Online, March 10, 2012, https://www.iol.co.za/news/south-africa/kwazulu-natal/elephants-say -goodbye-to-the-whisperer-1253463.

Feeling Others' Feelings

Our interconnection with others is very immediately grasped through psychic feeling. In the instance of the elephants mysteriously knowing about the death of their friend, Rabbi Leila Gal Berner, PhD, says, "If there ever were a time, when we can truly sense the wondrous 'interconnectedness of all beings,' it is when we reflect on the elephants of Thula Thula. A man's [heart] stops, and hundreds of elephants' hearts are grieving. This man's oh-so-abundantly loving heart offered healing to these elephants, and now, they came to pay loving homage to their friend." [30]

Our emotional connection to others is subtly nuanced and incredibly powerful. This is where clairempathy, or psychic emotion, is at play. The level at which it's involved in your interactions with others can be shocking once you start to become aware of the extent of your entanglement. Trying to consciously separate out what feelings are yours versus what you're feeling from others can be a challenge! Those who identify as empaths (highly sensitive individuals who recognize they're very susceptible to taking on and feeling others' feelings) need to be extra mindful of this ability for the sake of their own well-being.

Assuming psychic feeling was at play in this story of the elephants, they understood that the source of that information was external, and they didn't confuse it as their own sensation or emotion. This may not be the case for you. Without realizing it, you've certainly interpreted other people's emotions as your own. This is very common. I've felt this in a positive way at weddings when the bride enters the space and starts walking down the aisle. The swell of emotion from everyone else in the room gets me *every time* and it's all I can do to keep from crying. I've felt this in a negative way when a friend handed me her baby and he started crying for his mom. The emotion was something I immediately took in and I almost started crying right along with him.

---

30. "Elephants Journey to Pay Respect … But How Did They Know?" All-Creatures.org, February 2013, https://www.all-creatures.org/stories/a-elephants-journey-respect.html.

When I first learned about clairempathy, it immediately put into context a distinct memory that I'd always been confused about. I'd been riding in the car with a few other friends, something we'd done countless times before. A familiar song came on the radio and someone said, "This is my *favorite* song!" Someone else responded, "Hey, me too!" Immediately I was awash in anger and jealousy, but I was utterly confused by what I was feeling. Logically I didn't think I had anything to be jealous about in that moment. What did I care if they both loved the same song? I didn't! So what was this feeling about? Years later I learned that the fourth person in the car had been jealous about the connection that the other two people shared. In hindsight, I now clearly understand that what I'd felt was actually that person's jealousy and not my own.

In another instance, I had a lengthy dream, one of those that seems to last all night and makes for fitful sleep. In the dream I was with a friend and she was deeply distressed. I watched situation after situation unfold that left her feeling helpless and as though things were out of her control. When I awoke, I assumed the dream was just that—a regular dream—because I was in the midst of my own stress. But it spurred me to get in touch with her to make a date so we could get together and catch up. "Thank you for reaching out," she said. "It's exactly what I need. My life is insane right now."

When we chatted more the next day, I realized just how overworked and stressed she'd been the night that I'd had the dream. I shared the details of it with her. "You feel me, girl," she said. "I was freaking out that night."

When we're aware of what's going on, these kinds of moments can feel truly amazing. That we can feel someone else's emotions or sensations in such an immediate way is baffling. With our separate physical bodies, it's crazy when those solid boundaries become blurred. Yet we do it constantly and in ways that we're usually not entirely aware of. As a result, we can end up mistaking what are actually other people's emotions for our own. It can take a lot of awareness and reflection on our part to sort out what's what.

I've always felt very responsible for other people's moods, and as a result I'm constantly assessing where others are at on the "happy-wellness meter" that I've created in my mind. Without even consciously trying,

I'm automatically assessing my space and the energy of others in it. For this reason, family gatherings can be exhausting. No matter how much I'm looking forward to it, if I'm not mindful I can be left feeling depleted for days afterward. Trying to be energetically responsible for everyone else when I'm with them is something I have to make myself aware of and continue to monitor in order to stop. Even if I pull myself back, I might still find later that I'm again energetically reaching out and checking on everyone. Once again I have to consciously pull the extensions of my energy back into myself, like octopus tentacles.

In other instances, if I've been really upbeat all day and find that I'm suddenly irritable and grouchy, I'll often realize that the change occurred when someone else came into my space. This doesn't necessarily mean I'm irritated or angry about them being there. Usually one or all of the following reasons are at play:

1. They are irritated and angry and I'm taking on their mood.
2. I sense that they're not feeling all that happy, which makes me grouchy because my built-in assumption tells me I'm responsible for raising their energy to build them back up, but I just don't have the energy for it.
3. I sense that they aren't feeling all that happy, and because of my built-in assumption that I'm responsible for raising their energy, this means I'm a failure, which leaves me feeling low about myself.
4. I sense that they aren't happy and become resentful at the thought of things I've done to try to build them up (now or in the past) and become frustrated, depressed, and angry that nothing I do is ever good enough.

If you start noticing these kinds of thoughts around how you're feeling, take a moment to check in and confirm whether or not you're catching someone else's emotions. If this is the case, work with the next practice to address that energetic entanglement.

In addition, you might take on other people's physical sensations. Maybe a friend got in a car accident and you're thinking about them a lot, wishing that you could help them in some way. You notice that the area around your neck and shoulder on one side starts to feel uncomfortable and tight. The next day you go to visit your friend to make sure they're doing okay and find out they have an injury on the right side of their neck and shoulder as a result of the accident. Coincidence? Many would think so, but we know better! It is commonly known by people who practice energy work that in an effort to heal others, you might unintentionally end up taking on the person's issues. Working on clearing energy and setting boundaries can help to avoid this.

PRACTICE
Addressing Energetic Entanglement

All of us experience tangled energy with others at some point. While it looks like we're living in clearly separate, independent bodies, we're actually moving through energy that connects us intimately with one another. Some we're bound to much more than others. There's a reason why I hear my husband's thoughts more than those of anyone else. He's the person I live with, see almost every day of my life, and love above all others. I also most easily recognize when our connection is empathically having a negative impact on me (where I am taking on his energy), while the same kind of impact with someone I'm less connected with might slip under my radar and be interpreted as my own issues.

I've also found myself very entangled in Amy's energy, and I felt it viscerally with the sudden divide after her death. I kept thinking of the 1982 movie *E.T. the Extra-Terrestrial*. In this story an alien with paranormal ability is accidentally left behind on earth and a boy named Elliot finds him and takes him in. The longer they're together, the more they become energetically entangled, with Elliot empathically connecting to E.T.'s feelings. It evolves to the point that when E.T. becomes sick and is dying, Elliot experiences the same thing. After Amy died, I realized how real that empathic connection is. My energy needed to figure out that we were actually separate entities and that I could still live even though I was no longer bound to her within this world.

You might be able to easily identify someone with whom your energy is most merged, where connection comes easily because your lives are so integrated. Perhaps it's a partner, best friend, or relative. But empathic connection can also happen with, say, a cashier you've never met before, a relative you haven't spoken with for a while but have been meaning to call, or a long-lost friend you haven't been in touch with for years.

Whether it's a super close connection or someone you don't really know, these energetic bonds sometimes need to be brought more into your conscious awareness, to be tuned up or even disconnected so that you aren't expending energy in ways that aren't beneficial to you. This exercise will help for those purposes. Part of this practice (the listing of emotions) comes courtesy of my friend Pam Paulick and is a great insight.

Earlier in chapter 3, you practiced tuning in to your own emotions in order to determine where they were coming from. In that exercise, you assumed the emotion was actually your own. You were becoming more emotionally intelligent by recognizing your emotion and following it to its source. This time, we're considering emotions you're feeling that are *not actually your emotions* but instead originate from someone else. In this case, you're energetically tapping into someone else's emotions and feeling them as if they're your own. Because of this, the first step in addressing energetic entanglement is figuring out if the emotion you're feeling is yours or someone else's.

Step 1: Is This My Emotion or Someone Else's?
Have paper and pen ready before you start. When you're ready, get comfortable. Close your eyes, take some deep breaths, and relax your body. Once you're settled, feel the emotion or sensation that you want to resolve. Whether you perceive the feeling to be positive or negative, acknowledge it as an energetic message and thank your intuition for this opportunity to understand that message better.

Take some time to write down all of the emotions and sensations you're feeling in this moment. Once your list is complete, go back through each individual item and intuitively ask whether it's yours or someone else's. Think back to the Tuning In practice on page 42 in chapter 2, and use your form of receiving yes or no answers. As you get confirmation one way or the other, make a note of it next to each item.

Rewrite these emotions and sensations into separate lists, one for what is yours and one for what is coming from others. For the list that is your own, you can go back later to the Feeling into Your Emotions practice on page 88 in chapter 3. For now, you'll focus on the list of items from others.

Go back through each individual item and intuitively ask where this energy entanglement originated. You might see or hear a name, get flashes of places where you were when you picked up that energy, or sense it in some other way. If you have trouble, you can ask your guides to help you out. As you get confirmation of the source, make a note of it next to each item. If you aren't sure of the source in some instances, that's okay. Move on to step 2.

Step 2: Disentangling Your Energy

Ask your guides to show you where the energy of others is entangled with your own and to help in removing this energy from your space. Like a deep clean, you'll practice this in several ways to make sure you wipe away all the layers of this unwelcome energy.

See your energy as octopus tentacles reaching out in all directions. Notice where those attachments show up on your own body, and see if this seems to make sense with any physical sensations you've had lately. Focus on each individual tentacle and see what it feels like. See the color of each tentacle. Notice if there are identifying words attached to any of them clarifying the emotion, sensation, or origin point. If you can, see where each tentacle is reaching out to. If you're ready to let any or all of these tentacles go, feel the tension in them relax and watch as they shorten and curl back into you.

Assess your energy again and see if it feels like there are any lingering connections. If there are, see them as heavy coats that you're wearing.

Maybe you have on one coat, or you find that you're actually layered in many of them. These aren't coats you recognize and you realize they aren't yours! See yourself taking them off, one by one, and handing them back to their owners. Feel the weight of each connection lifting and the relief of no longer being confined by it. Once you've handed out all of these coats, see yourself walking away from those former connections.

Tune in one final time and see if you sense any remaining or unwanted energy. Focus on those areas. Envision these sensations rising like steam, up and away from your body. Gather the energy all together like you're collecting bits of stray yarn. Scoop it up and roll it into a ball in your hands. Now extend your open palm and allow your spirit guide to carry that unwanted energy away.

Step 3: Reestablish Your Boundaries

To close, envision your aura as a clear bubble encircling your body, cleansed and radiating light. As a final form of clearing and to get yourself back into your body, shake like a dog, stomp your feet, and/or vocalize. I like to do a form of Lion Pose where I open my mouth wide, stick out my tongue, and forcefully exhale, making the sound "ha."

Step 4: Energetic Maintenance

Whenever you're aware that you've made a connection, you can perform maintenance for any energetic entanglement that might have occurred. If you're doing some kind of healing work with someone else, always intentionally reestablish your boundaries and clear yourself at the end of the session. This could even apply to things like prayer, where you're really emotionally and energetically reaching out to impact someone else.

When you've finished with these types of activities, close down both your energy and the other person's energy. You can visualize the separation, seeing your energy bubble as separate and distinct from their energy bubble. Tune in to see if you notice any of their lingering energy that's stuck or bound to you, and see yourself passing it back to them. Invite your guides and say something like, "Please clear my mind, clear my body, clear my spirit, clear me energetically." Repeat this a few times. Breathe deeply. Wipe down your energy like you're wiping cobwebs off of yourself. Wash your hands. Stomp your feet.

Spirit Counseling for Entanglement Issues

After completing all of these steps, if you find you're still having trouble, visualize yourself with the person you're having energy entanglement issues with. Ask your guides for insight into anything you need to know about whatever caused a negative energy shift between the two of you. Similar to how you've followed step-by-step guided visualizations that I've provided in other practices, start here by meditating and then ask your guides to walk you through a unique practice specific to your situation that will help you resolve the connection.

If you find that this connection is one that you know is very damaging for you, ask Spirit to tie it off until you're ready to open back up. See the bond as a tube that they flood with radiant light. The more light it receives, the smaller it gets, until it's pinched shut and no longer moving energy to or from you. If you prefer, you can continue on and see the bond dissolve entirely. When you're done, close down your energy at the end, as described in step 4.

Additional Practices to Avoid Energetic Entanglement

Some previous practices on clearing energy and setting boundaries can help you avoid energetic entanglement. These types of practices keep you focused on *your own energy* instead of trying to reach out and connect with energy outside of yourself.

- Grounding Yourself Back into the Physical World (on page 35 in chapter 1)
- Tuning In (on page 42 in chapter 2)
- Clearing Your Subtle Energy and Setting Energetic Boundaries (on page 52 in chapter 2)

Spontaneous Visions

Spontaneous visions can appear as flashes of pictures or mini video clips that show snippets of a story within your mind. They're likely to occur when your mind is otherwise distracted or in daydream mode. For example, you might be mindlessly doing chores, driving your car on autopilot, caught in a groove at work, mowing the lawn, or taking a shower. Earlier I shared some instances of spontaneous visions that occurred for me. This included the visions I and another relative received independently of each other of my sister in "snow" shortly after her death, as well as the visions I had that showed a recently deceased relative now apparently alive and well on a parade float!

Spontaneous visions like these might be a one-time deal, or, like the one with the parade float, the details might repeat, possibly with more specifics each time, until you make sense of what's being shown to you. If you aren't sure whether what you saw was actually a vision, tune in and ask your intuition and Spirit for confirmation one way or the other.

Sensing Unexpected Energy

In the previous chapter I mentioned the occurrence of disturbances, which can certainly be considered unexpected energy, but unexpected energy isn't always necessarily a disturbance. It might just be energy that you notice or that feels a bit off but that isn't necessarily bothering you. You might just feel surprised by it. In one such instance, Pam was busy dancing away in an aerobics class when all of a sudden she noticed what seemed like a slippery spot on the floor and felt an energy connected to it. She sensed it had been there long before the studio existed. She was more curious about it than anything and wanted to know more. When she inquired about it with others who worked in the space, she was told that it had been there as long as anyone could remember, and no matter how much the floor was cleaned, even to the point of refinishing, that spot always remained that way. She found that when she danced in that particular room, she would spontaneously download information about the energy that was connected there and it just seemed to want to share its story.

Unexpected energy could also be coming from an object you've obtained where the energy of the previous owner is stuck to it. Or it could even occur with an object that's familiar to you but for some reason now feels different. In one example, someone I know shared that their necklace felt like it had negative energy in it, because they'd noticed they went into a funk whenever they wore it. The unexpected part was that they'd worn it for years without issue, but now the energy had changed and was so disruptive that they'd stopped wearing it altogether. It turns out, they'd been wearing it when they went through a traumatic experience, and that energy had stuck with the item.

The source of unexpected energy isn't always easy to pin down. When you can't quite place where the energy is coming from or aren't able to shield yourself from it, it can feel extra creepy. Pam calls this conscious awareness of unwanted unexpected energy the "creepy spidey sense." In these instances, she feels like she's getting a tap from intuition and then gets a sense of something icky, dark, suspicious, and hair-raising that puts her on high alert. I break down this type of occurrence into two different instances:

- An intuitive hit from sensing unexpected energy that's telling you you're not safe
- Intuition that's tapping into harmless unexpected energy but that's unintentionally also activating your fight-or-flight mode as a secondary reaction

Sometimes our sensing of unexpected energy can activate our survival instinct, putting us in fight-or-flight mode, which cycles back to feeling like we need to be extra vigilant of our surroundings. It may or may not be that our intuition is actually telling us directly that there's danger. Instead, it could just be a secondary effect of our subtle energy awareness. If you feel this creeped-out sensation, tune in and ask about it. If you get a message letting you know that things are okay, like "harmless" or "safe," it may just be that your psychic sensing of this unexpected energy tripped the switch for the primal safety alerts to go off.

You might wonder what to do when this type of unexpected energy comes up. First, if you get the creepy sensation and aren't sure whether or not it's your intuition warning you of danger, it's a good idea to err on the side of caution and take the safety measures you need in order to feel protected. Any other version of this type of occurrence outside of a true safety warning may be a cue that you need to work more on setting boundaries and clearing energy.

Beyond that, sensing whether action is called for or if unexpected energy should just be left alone is a judgment call. In the case of the slippery floor, Pam was left wondering these exact things, but she sensed that she wasn't supposed to do anything specific. She resolved that it was simply there and was to be left alone. In the case of the unexpected energy in my relative's basement, which I mentioned in the previous chapter, I left it alone. When it was brought up to me as a disturbance from someone who was living in the space after the fact, this was a clear indication that it needed to be resolved in some way and was worth giving more attention.

You might be inclined to just let the unexpected energy be, but at the same time part of you might be chiming in to say you shouldn't leave it without help. Even if you decide to assist in some way, maybe you're still worried that if you do, you might just be interfering in something that's not your business. So many conflicting thoughts! We'll look a bit more at the question of whether or not you should engage with an energetic experience later in this chapter, but for now I'll make it easy for you: *When in doubt, give it light.* This will relieve the pressure of answering the question "Should I or shouldn't I?"

PRACTICE
Give It Light

This is a practice you can use to extend light to unexpected energy that you encounter. The light you give in this exercise is not your own energy. This is an important detail, because you don't want to go around depleting your own energy. Instead, with this energy work, you open up to receive and share universal energy. To start, tune in to the unexpected energy. Ask to receive a clear yes or no as to whether it's okay for you to engage with it. Don't force your assistance if it's clearly unwanted. If you have the green light or are left unsure, you can move ahead with this practice.

Begin by envisioning your aura filled with light and encircling you with a strong boundary. Ask your guide to be with you and assist you. Before you actually offer energy, state, "If the light I offer is not welcome for this situation, then let it go out to wherever else it might be needed." This emphasizes your intention to not force your assistance.

Option 1: Clean the Energy

If the energy you've sensed feels negative or heavy, envision a sponge soaking it up. If the unwanted energy is in an object, see yourself sponging that object off. Hand this sponge to your spirit guide for them to take care of in whatever way is best. Now see a spray bottle in your hands that's filled with light. Spray this all over the area (or object or person) until you feel a shift, and envision it sparkling. This may seem silly, but remember, we're working with a symbolic language. Just as Spirit speaks to us through symbols, so can we speak back in the same way. Trust that the message will be translated.

Option 2: Channel the Energy Directly

If you don't like the cleaning version, you can also go the way of simply standing in or envisioning the space where you experienced the unexpected energy. If the energy was in an object, you can hold it or envision it. If you sensed a being, you can stand near them or envision them in your mind.

Once you're ready, see a powerful universal energy enter through the top of your head and fill you up. Act as a conduit and allow this light to spill out of your hands and fill up the unexpected energy, leaving no room for anything that's unwanted. Once you feel that the energy has shifted, you can bring yourself back to the present again.

Option 3: Add in Extra Positive Vibration

Another way to go about clearing and shifting the energy would be to pick a very meaningful song, something that already has a very positive association for you. It should make you think of *very* happy times, like a wedding song or a favorite holiday tune. Fill the space with this music, or in the case of a small object such as a necklace, you could hold the object directly. While in the space or holding the object, also envision shining light all around. Sing along with the song yourself and feel that positive emotion that you associate it with. Think back to the euphoric memories that it brings up for you and savor the details. Don't force the emotion; allow it to arise naturally.

Add in anything else that will enhance the ritual and mental associations, such as favorite scents, essential oils, or crystals. In the example of the necklace, I would recommend wearing it only at special times for a while, to ease it back into remembering that it's a positive token. This will all help to reprogram it.

In addition to giving unexpected energy light, you might also find support in this instance by looking back to the Clearing Energetic Disturbances practice on page 91 in chapter 3.

°⋘❀⋙°

Breakthrough Psychic Slip-Ups and Pop-Ins

Sometimes communication from Spirit slips in without us intentionally trying to receive it. I break this type of communication into two groups: slip-ups and pop-ins.

Slip-Ups

Psychic slip-ups occur through other people but may go entirely unnoticed by them, even when it's extraordinary for you. In these instances, Spirit uses others around you to communicate with you. It might be something that's very obviously meant for you. Or it might be a bit more subtle and seem a part of natural discussion and just be something that Spirit nudged the other person to say as a way of trying to inspire or influence you.

I had the extraordinary version of a psychic slip-up happen once when I was in the process of trying to buy a house. Just before Christmas the same year Amy passed away, Luke and I found ourselves climbing an ice-covered driveway and wondering just what we'd find at the top of the hill. We'd somewhat reluctantly sold our own house a couple of months prior. It was a home we'd really loved, but because of job moves it hadn't made sense to stay there. We had purchased it as a foreclosure, and after all the work we'd put into it to make it home, it had been very hard to let it go. We were now putting our hopes in the potential of finding something that we could love just as much.

In the interim, we'd moved into a small apartment, determining there was no rush. We would give ourselves time to find the right place. As it turned out, only a couple months later, in the dark of winter, we got to the top of that unplowed hill and found home. Or at least we thought we did. Others were viewing the house at the same time and also appeared excited, so we knew there was competition. Points in our favor were the fact that it was a foreclosure (our forte), the home had *just* gone onto the market that day, and there was only one terrible grainy photo of the outside from a distance in the listing. Still, we were nervous. *We wanted this house.*

After checking out the house and neighborhood in the daylight the next day, we went to put in an offer. With knots in our stomachs, we gave a figure that was well below the asking price but the max of what we could manage. As we sat with a real estate agent we'd never met before, she pointed out lines on pages from her stack of papers and read hypnotically, "Lucas sign here, Angela sign here. Lucas sign here, Angela sign here. Lucas sign here, Amanda sign here. Lucas sign here, Angela sign here…" Amy's legal name, Amanda, rang in my head like an alarm bell. Luke and I were looking at each other, mouths gaping and eyes wide. The real estate agent, completely oblivious to her slip, kept on with her instruction, so we were forced to put our amazement on pause. But it was like I could feel my sister right at my shoulder, laughing. *Chill out, girl, you got this,* she was saying. I took a deep breath and felt the knots in my gut loosen.

When Luke and I stepped out of the office, we were grinning at each other from ear to ear. "You heard that, right?" "Yes! Oh my gosh!" "And she didn't even notice!" We took it as a good sign and, as it turned out, our offer was accepted the next day.

Pop-Ins

Pop-ins are psychic breakthroughs that happen directly through you. Some intuitives will say that if you're experiencing breakthrough moments of psychic information or spirit messages without trying to actively tune in, that means you're not developed enough in knowing how to handle your abilities and you especially need to work on your boundaries. I think that can be true in some instances, especially when you're not okay with the pop-ins that you're getting. If they feel intrusive, then boundary work is definitely called for.

On the other hand, you can think of these breakthrough events as an overfilled voicemail box that you never check. If you don't regularly take action to tune in to Spirit to download your messages, then these spill-over moments end up being a way they can force you to check at least some of the messages they have for you.

Like I shared in the first chapter, I used to find myself in the first group. I would hear random spirit chatter that felt very intrusive and negative. At different points in time I also experienced spirit-induced insomnia, where I was kept awake because of the intrusion of spirits that lingered around me, trying to communicate things when my barriers were down as I attempted to sleep. These are examples of unacceptable pop-ins. Now that my boundaries are better, I don't really experience those negative instances of pop-ins anymore. I do, however, still experience the full voicemail version! And I'm okay with that, because they're usually wonderful messages from my departed loved ones that leave me filled with gratitude and affection.

For me, pop-ins happen most when I'm distracted, such as when I'm driving or landscaping, when I'm focused on music or lost in a task. For a friend of mine, it happens when she's dancing. My deceased loved ones are my invited inner circle, but it's usually my sister who chimes in, as she's become a primary contact for me to the other side. Select spirit guides also make the list, but in one instance I'm not really quite sure who it was that decided to speak up in an attempt to keep me safe.

I was with my mom, siblings, and some friends. We were on a day trip and heading to a children's museum. We all piled into a van that sat seven people, and we were full to the max. We'd just piled back in after getting a bite to eat. A few of us were settled in the back row, but since we weren't going far, we hadn't buckled up. The van was full of chatter and tunes chiming from the radio when suddenly the thought ran through my mind that we should buckle up. I dismissed it, but the thought felt pressed upon me, so much so that I turned to one friend next to me and said, "We should really be buckled up." We laughed, but didn't act on it. Still, as we continued on, the message nagged at my gut and grew even stronger, to the point that, once again, I said out loud to no one in particular this time, "We should buckle up." In hindsight, I now know I was speaking words that a spirit guardian was feeding me. But we'd waited too long, and before we could do anything, we heard the screeching of tires. My friend and I looked at each other again, our eyes widening, and *bam!* We were hit from behind. I rose into the air, hit my head on the roof, hit it again on the seat in front of me, and found myself on my hands and knees on the floor.

This was a moment that, obviously, has never left me. While it could be dismissed as a coincidence, the strength of the message has remained with me. As with hearing a playful spirit buzzing in my ear, this event occurred before I had any real understanding of subtle abilities. Once I started learning more, I knew that message wasn't only my own intuition; it was most definitely a pop-in message from Spirit. And, of course, being a warning about an emergency, this is an example of a very acceptable pop-in. Someone had my back and was trying to keep me safe. With chronic neck pain that I experienced for decades after, it was a literal hard knock on the head that helped the message sink in: *Listen to that intuition. Pay attention to those messages.*

PRACTICE
Setting Boundaries with Spirit

If you're experiencing instances of pop-ins that you don't want, this practice can help build up your boundaries.

Settle into a quiet meditative space. Take some deep breaths and feel your body relaxing. Now imagine you're in a space (a room, an outdoor garden, or whatever feels right to you) that's packed with many spirits, all awaiting their chance to get to talk with you. They're talking over one another and shouting out their messages, all trying to get your attention. Envision a line drawn across the space. Now see all of these spirits on one side of the line, while you walk to the other side. They continue shouting out to you, but instead of reacting to them, you turn around so your back is facing them. In your mind, you call on someone specific to join you on your side of the line. This could be a deceased loved one, a spirit guide, or an honored spiritual figure. They move through the crowd and step across to your side of the line. They walk to your back and come around to face you. Taking both of your hands in theirs, they smile and ask, "What do you need?"

"Please help me to secure a boundary around myself against all uninvited energy, including messages from those in Spirit." They nod and you immediately see an orb encircling you. It pulses outward, pushing away those who aren't invited. The chatter of the spirits outside of your bubble is now silenced, even though they're still bustling about. Some recognize that reaching you is now a lost cause and they take their leave. They know they will only be able to connect with you now at your request. Others may persist and linger, but as long as you continue to hold this boundary and don't give them the attention they're hoping for, they too will eventually get bored and leave.

"What else do you need?" your invited spirit asks.

"Please help me to continue holding this boundary. I consciously invite you and [name those you're okay with, such as a deceased loved one, spirit guide, or other spiritual figure] to enter this space. Also please adjust the energy so that others who are beneficial for me to be in touch with can enter this space."

Here you can also specify whether or not you're okay with your welcomed contacts reaching out to you through sporadic pop-in messages that they might want to share with you when you're not consciously asking to connect with them. If you're *not* okay with that, specify that as well. If you don't like pop-ins at all, you could clarify to your invited circle that unless it's an emergency, you *only* want to receive their messages during download sessions, which we'll cover in the next practice.

The orb around you shimmers as it adjusts to your specifications, and others you've invited into the space walk from the outer boundary into the orb, encircling you. The rest who have been lingering outside depart now, knowing they will not be invited. Take a moment to sense whatever comes to you. For example, perhaps you feel warmth from the loving presence and positive energy of those you've allowed into your space. See if anyone has a message to share with you. If so, they step forward from the circle to stand in front of you. They take your hands in theirs and share their message. Each spirit inside of your boundary who has a message takes a turn.

As the messages wind down, thank everyone for helping you to create and sustain this boundary. When you feel ready, gently come back to your present space.

When you don't give unwanted spirits attention for their negative actions, they figure out what it is that you *want* them to be doing, so they can earn the attention from you that they so desire. By stating clearly how you want them to proceed, what was once chaos is now a functioning system of communication.

PRACTICE
Meditation to Download Your Intuitive Voicemails

This practice is based on a discussion I had with psychic Sherrie Dillard many years ago when I was experiencing unwanted psychic breakthroughs randomly throughout my days. Ideally it would be good to have a daily meditation session, because taking the time to regularly settle and tune in can help to curb the overflow of intuitive energy showing up as pop-ins and other sporadic occurrences. I know this, but that doesn't mean I always master actually putting daily meditation into practice. I tend to swing back and forth, where at times I'm very devoted to practice and other times it's not a world that I'm so active in. I know I'm not alone here.

If you find yourself in the same boat, consider doing this meditative practice. It is simple and fun and can be done at any time. If you're anything like me, it's easiest to remember to do this as part of your bedtime routine. Put on your jammies, brush your teeth, and take down your intuitive messages that intuition has on hold for you. Just five or ten minutes before you head off to dreamland is all you really need.

If you have trouble committing or just don't want to do this practice daily, set an alarm or mark it on your calendar with the goal of practicing it once or twice a week for whatever amount of time you want. Five minutes? Great! Twenty minutes? A perfect sweet spot! An hour? Look at you go! But really, the time can be fluid, guided by however long it takes for you to feel like you've received all the messages that were waiting for you. There's no need to force it to be any longer than it naturally plays out. I want you to feel committed enough that you'll do this meditation regularly but not so committed that if you miss it here and there you end up feeling like a failure and just give up. Once you get into it, you might find that you crave practicing it more frequently and don't find it to be a chore at all. It just becomes a part of your routine.

Now that we have that settled, let's begin.

Have paper and pen available. Get comfortable and take some deep breaths. As you did in past practices, progressively relax all areas of your body and deepen your breathing. When you feel settled in, with your energy centered, tune in and ask your intuition to reveal any messages it's holding for you. Don't force it or try to engage. Just allow the details to naturally rise into your awareness. As you would when taking a phone message, jot down the key details that are shared with you.

After you receive your messages, you can end the meditation. Or, if you want, you can ask any questions you might have about the details you just received and end when you feel the responses winding down.

To end the practice, write down this statement: "I will only intuitively receive information that is in my highest good." Include this as a closing every time you do this practice. Writing it down cements it in your mind.

As Sherrie Dillard explains, "What this does is train your intuition to surface when you are listening. It prevents psychic awareness from surfacing throughout the day in random situations that seem to be of little importance and consequence."[31] With intentional effort on your part, you'll be able to handle these confusing intuitive eruptions by funneling messages into a purposeful outlet that you manage yourself.

°◁⟨∂.℘⟩▷°

Recall of Past Energetic Trauma

You might also experience spontaneous energetic breakthroughs that aren't messages from anyone in particular but instead are actually experiences from this life or even from a past life that have spilled over into the present moment. They potentially could also be breakthroughs from what's called the *collective consciousness* of stored memory from our united experience. Energetic breakthroughs can also come from DNA, from energetic memory that's been passed down the familial line. These types of energetic recalls are usually based in trauma and might come up as an explanation

----

31. Sherrie Dillard, email message to author, January 6, 2016.

for questions you've had or as an opportunity to heal an energetic imprint that's ready to be resolved.

I experienced a spontaneous energetic breakthrough once while I was in the middle of an expo. One of my energy healing teachers was there, and I took the opportunity to get a mini energy session with her. In the middle of the session, I spontaneously experienced a past life recall. This was the first time I'd ever experienced such a thing, so I was extremely surprised and didn't know what to do with it.

Suddenly I saw myself much older than I actually was in my current life. I was a woman in my mid-fifties or early sixties, with white hair that was partly tied back. I lived alone and mostly kept to myself, but I was quite happy and comfortable with the life I'd built for myself. I was in a small house in a much simpler time. There was no electricity or plumbing, as those types of things hadn't yet come about. I worked with herbs and developed my own remedies, which I shared with others. While I wasn't a doctor, I was someone people came to with various health issues. As in my present life, in this past one I had found a natural ability in energy-based healing. This wasn't something I advertised, but there were select individuals who knew what I did and people often came to me through word of mouth. Most of the time, though, I provided energy healing without people consciously knowing it was something I was doing.

In this vision during my session, I saw that I was in my house, cornered by a man I knew from the town I lived in. While he didn't physically harm me, he hovered over me, yelling, with an ax held threateningly in his hand. I cowered as he cursed, calling me a witch and demanding that I never come near his son or family again. His son had been very ill, and I'd recently attended to him. The mother had known I was providing an herbal remedy to her son, but I had also unobtrusively done some energy work on him. While it wouldn't have been obvious to anyone else, the boy had felt the energy and talked about it afterward to his parents. Based on his response, the father obviously didn't want him or his family associated with me or my work, because it was considered by some to be based in evil sources.

Back in the present time, when my healing session was over, I just looked at my teacher, waiting for her to say something about what had just happened. I mean, she had to have seen what I had just witnessed, right? But she hadn't noticed it. The vision had been a pop-in for me alone.

The story from this vision helped me understand the passion I had for the healing arts in this life and also why I was so afraid to own those abilities and interests. That traumatic moment in the past had impacted how I lived out the rest of that life. I was afraid in this current life of the same kind of repercussions that I'd known then.

My friend Pam experienced energetic trauma breaking through from a past life remembrance during a meditation. While she knew going in that the guided meditation was about traveling to the past, the intensity and high level of emotion that came with her experience left her feeling blindsided and, as she put it, in "pure emotional hell." You might recall that I mentioned in chapter 2 how Pam had interpreted the symbol of a muffin to mean emotional trauma. That was a result of this experience, where Pam saw herself in a past life at around seven years old being attacked while she was walking in the woods. She was carrying muffins in a tin at the time the assault occurred. In the midst of reexperiencing the horror of the attack, she wondered how this was possible, why she was being shown this horrible event, and whether she even believed it was real or if she was just imagining it. While it was a challenging experience, she found that in the end there was a feeling of resolution and she was left with a dramatic new understanding. As with my experience, she also felt like the revealed energetic trauma explained a lot about her intuitive abilities and the way she exists in the world in her current life. In short, she says, "It was mind-blowing."

Should You Engage with This Energy Experience or Leave It Be?

Determining whether a breakthrough moment is really important for you to engage with or not can be a challenge. In this instance I'm referring to a breakthrough of past energetic trauma, but it's also something to consider if you've heard someone's thoughts, felt someone's feelings, received a pop-in message from Spirit, or experienced some other type of intuitive breakthrough.

The breakthrough experience that I just shared about being a healer in a past life came up as the result of an energy healing session. It was a moment from my past that was being healed and just happened to come into my consciousness as it was being resolved. There wasn't anything more that I needed to do with it. I had a better understanding and felt a sense of intrigue, but I did not feel further traumatized by it. Energetically it felt neutral. If you experience something that lingers or brings a sense of panic, anxiety, depression, irritation, fear, etc., then this is something that needs extra work around it in order to be resolved.

In the end, each instance of energetic breakthrough is unique and requires tuning in so that you can make a call on how to act (or not act) on it. If you feel ready to resolve these energetic issues, that's great. If it feels like too much or you don't feel ready to work on resolving the energy imprint and just want the breakthrough experiences to stop, that's also okay. Either way, there are some things you can do to support yourself. Here are some helpful practices:

- Grounding Yourself Back into the Physical World (on page 35 in chapter 1) can be used to help bring you back to the present moment and ground you outside of the uninvited energy.

- Tuning In (on page 42 in chapter 2) can help you tune in to see if you get more specific information on what, if anything, should be done. The yes or no part of the practice can be especially help-ful in determining whether the situation is something you need to engage with or just let go of.

- Clearing Your Subtle Energy and Setting Energetic Boundar-ies (on page 52 in chapter 2) and Setting Boundaries with Spirit (on page 128 earlier in this chapter) can both be used with some adjustments. For your purpose here, your goal would be to clear and set boundaries with the breakthrough experience instead of with spirits who might be trying to communicate with you.

- Give It Light (on page 122 earlier in this chapter) can be used to try to resolve the energetic imprint.
- Healing Past Energetic Trauma (later in this chapter) can also be used to resolve energetic ties that are specific to past life recall.

If You Decide to Share a Message with Someone Else

If you're getting a message that seems persistent and feels as though it's intended to be shared with someone else, you might be asking yourself whether or not you should say something. This is a call you have to make for yourself in the moment, and if you're new to sharing, it can feel like crossing a very scary line. If you think you might be ready to take that leap and trust your intuition, whatever you do, let it be on the other person's terms. In addition to keeping your actions ethical, this also eliminates the burden of deciding whether or not to share and puts it back on the other person and those who may be trying to connect with them.

How do you follow through and make sure a message is shared on the other person's terms? *You ask permission.* This is a clear and blatant inquiry that you make with the other person. If you tend to pick up things before doing some type of healing session, you might say before the session even begins, "Sometimes I get intuitive information during sessions. Would you like me to share that with you if it comes up?" Or if you're just picking it up outside of a reading or any type of session, you could say, "Sometimes I pick up on intuitive information. If I ever get anything that seems to be meant for you, would you like me to share that with you?" If they say no, leave it at that. If they say yes, then you can move ahead with sharing. Let them know you picked up on something and ask them when might be a good time for you to share that with them.

If they're open to hearing the information, it's your call on how you share it. For example, if you're connecting with a spirit guide or some other being but you aren't sure the person you're sharing with would be open to that part of it, you could skip that bit of information. Instead of talking about a guide or spirit that you're seeing, you can just pass along the main message. Ask the spirit what the message is that they want to be shared.

"Give what you get" is the rule that some people follow when sharing information, because the more detail you provide, the more likely it is that something will end up making sense and help to connect the dots of all the other details. By sharing everything you're getting, there's more chance that it will "hit" and strongly connect. But if you're only comfortable sharing certain details right now, go with your comfort level.

Alternately, if you're randomly picking up on a message that someone in spirit wants you to share with someone, you can put up boundaries and let them know, "Right now isn't the time, but you can come back and share your message when I'm actually in a session with this person. If you need to get a message to them through me, I'm placing the responsibility on you to make the arrangements for them to come to me for a session." Once again, this takes the burden off your shoulders and puts it on those in spirit and the other person for whom the message is intended. If it's meant to be, Spirit will find a way to make it happen but within the terms of your healthy boundaries.

PRACTICE
Healing Past Energetic Trauma

Before you begin this practice, note that this and all other practices in the book are not a replacement for mental health care. If you find this triggers you even further, stop and seek professional care to help you resolve the trauma.

If you've experienced a spontaneous recall of energetic trauma and are wondering if it's really real or if maybe you're just imagining it, I defer to the wisdom of past life regressionist Shelley Kaehr, who clarifies that, essentially, it doesn't matter.[32] You don't need to fact-check the details to figure out if it's a historically accurate past life. You don't need to question your family line to figure out if it's a trauma that was lived by one of your relatives. You don't have to wrack your brain trying to remember if this was

---

32. Shelley A. Kaehr, *Meet Your Karma: The Healing Power of Past Life Memories* (Woodbury, MN: Llewellyn, 2020), 145.

an event from earlier in this life that has long been buried. In the end, it doesn't matter if it was real or not. Maybe it was real, maybe it was symbolic. Regardless, the awareness came to you in the way it did for a reason: as a chance to heal an energetic imprint. Go from there as a starting point and try not to ruminate over the questions from your critical mind, asking, "Should I believe it? Was it true?" If nothing else, assume there is truth within the energy behind the message.

In this life I've gone through PTSD from both emotional and physical trauma. I know how crippling, repetitive, and unforgiving it can be. But I also know that with work, you can get to the other side of it. Whether from this life, a past life, your immediate experience, or something that's been passed down to you, the energy of trauma registers the same. Tools that help relieve one form of trauma can also help with the other forms. There are so many different ways to potentially address trauma, and you might be aware of other modalities that you're inclined to integrate here. Do what works for you. The tools I've found the most support with have been talk therapy, EMDR (eye movement desensitization and reprocessing), dreamwork, visualization, neural rewiring, and physical therapy. In this practice I've incorporated some things that I've learned from those types of methods. They appear here as steps 1–5, but first I'll share some additional notes so you're aware of these details before you dive in.

Move Your Body

While you're doing this practice, you don't necessarily have to be sitting in a meditative state. You could be moving your body to further move all the energy around, especially in step 5 when you're trying to raise your energy level. One of my favorite ways to do this is to turn on electro music, which is impossible not to move to. It gets me jumping and dancing around every time. Try it! Stomp out the old and raise up new positive vibes.

Jumping to Various Events

Especially in step 4, you might notice that you're mind is jumping around to various events. If that happens, follow them and make a note when you're done. You might see an obvious thread after the fact.

In past life regression, a lot of times when people are being regressed, before they dive into a past life they begin in the present life and jump to a past memory within the current lifetime, then they jump back even further to events within this current life, and continue to move backward. Sometimes they will then experience the time in between lives before finally moving to a past life.

Jumping around is also a part of EMDR, a practice that's proven very effective for PTSD. You begin by first deciding on a starting trigger event, then you go into a relaxed state where you allow your mind to reveal whatever it will. In my experience, I would jump from one memory to another, to another, and another, etc. Eventually the therapist would pull me out of this relaxed state and ask what I noticed. I would summarize what I saw, and usually we would see a thread that linked all the memories together. I would go back in and follow where the memories continued to lead, and so on. Through this modality, I learned that with the mind, what seems random often has a purpose. Unrelated memories would suddenly have a very obvious connection, and I realized that this mental jumping, of having your mind show you one image or situation only to jump to another and then another, is usually purposeful. While it can seem random, just like with symbolic and synchronistic messages of intuition, when you string the notes of the message together, you can begin to understand what's trying to be revealed.

I say this because when you're working with energetic trauma, you might notice that it's not all linear. While it might seem like you're only working on one memory, you're actually working with that memory trauma *and all other trauma that resonates at that same frequency.* This is part of why when one memory is being worked on, you might have other different memories bubble up as well. They may all seem unrelated and be a confusing jumble, but just trust that from an energetic standpoint, it makes sense. As long as you aren't feeling re-traumatized, know that it's okay to keep going.

Even when you're done with the practice itself, you might notice that things that used to trigger you don't pull at you like they used to. Or you might still notice the same types of triggers, but now, instead of being carried away by them, you're very consciously aware, to the point that you immediately see that something is a trigger, but you can stop it from raising your emotions in a negative way. You become more mindful and can play an active role in how you respond instead of passively having things pull you along.

Step 1: Breathe

First and foremost, remember to breathe, and that means breathe all the way into your belly. Do a breath check. Notice whether you're holding your breath or whether your breathing is really shallow and staying all the way up in your chest. Your breath hooks into your nervous system and is your best tool to immediately start calming stress patterns that are triggered by trauma and fear. Take several more deep breaths and feel your body begin to relax.

Step 2: Break Fear with a Statement, Affirmation, and Physical Action

To break the cycle of fearful thinking, create a statement that you can use whenever you become triggered by this trauma energy and pair it with some kind of physical movement. This is something that's commonly done in neural rewiring programs like the Dynamic Neural Retraining System (DNRS), Gupta Program Brain Retraining, the work of Joe Dispenza, and others.[33] When you're triggered by something, these types of practices help you emphasize alternate neural pathways to get the brain out of unhealthy programming. These practices are sometimes very involved, with many steps. For our purposes, you don't need to get that detailed. Simply come up with the following:

----

33. For more information about these programs, see the "Brain Retraining/Neural Rewiring" section in the recommended resources.

1. A brief statement that tells your mind to stop
2. A brief affirmation that tells your mind you're safe now
3. A simple physical movement

Your statement-affirmation-physical action combo could be something like "Pause now! I'm safe," with arm movements of putting your hands in front of you like you're signaling someone to stop, or "Silence! I'm here now," with your arms wrapped around you in a self-hug. Write down the phrasing and movement you've decided to use. Practice it now, repeating your statement-affirmation-physical action combo ten times out loud to solidify it in your mind.

Put this combo into action whenever you sense trauma energy or have negative thoughts that are repeating in your mind. After following this step regularly for a few months, you might notice that whenever you're triggered, even before thinking of what to do, your brain will immediately start repeating these words, cutting off the looping cycle of trauma before it can even really begin to trigger you.

Step 3: Break Fear by Counting Your Surroundings

If you need even more support in breaking through fight-or-flight mode, bring yourself into the present moment by counting things in your surroundings. Notice what you see, smell, feel, etc., as in "I see green things: (1) curtain, (2) painting, (3) houseplant, (4) pillows, (5) clock…" or "I hear (1) music, (2) my dog chewing on a bone, (3) the whir of the air conditioning, (4) the clock ticking, (5) traffic, (6) wind blowing outside…" This will break you out of dwelling on the past or fantasizing about the future, get you back into your current surroundings, and help you be grounded in the present.

Step 4: Go Back into the Triggering Event

Important note: If it's too much to relive your triggering event, skip this and move on to the next step.

In dreamwork, when you've had a traumatic dream there's a practice you can do where you intentionally go back into it. You do this while you're awake in order to actively process the dream's message, resolve distressing emotion, and dissolve the trauma that it triggered. In his book *Dreamworking*, Dr. Christopher Sowton calls this "re-enter and explore." [34] We'll do a form of this type of thing here. There are a few ways you can go about it.

- Ask your guide to be with you now to help you through this practice. See yourself and your guide as just witnessing and standing outside of the past trauma. Allow the details of the story to unfold for you. Notice what stands out the most. Focus in on the most triggering detail and ask it what it's trying to reveal to you. You might hear a message or see it transform into a different detail or an entirely new scene that plays out for you. Follow where the details lead. If you start to feel like you're going astray and the practice is becoming unfocused, bring yourself back to the original starting point and focus again on a detail that you'd like explained.

- Another thing you can do is focus on that detail, give it light, and envision it transforming into something neutral or positive, like a poisonous snake that turns into a flower or an attacker that turns into a snowman.

- You can also try adding in vocalization. This is a key aspect of talk therapy. I think of it as turning on the faucet of your throat chakra and allowing the buried well of your heart chakra to rise up and spill open. You might be surprised at how much this addition alone taps into and helps to release deeply buried emotions. As you go through playing out the details of the trauma, speak out loud to move that energy. Say what you're seeing or experiencing. If speaking to yourself feels too odd, ask your spirit helper to participate here with you. Say to them what you're noticing as the details play out, talking out the trauma with them as you go through it.

----

34. Dr. Christopher Sowton, *Dreamworking: How to Listen to the Inner Guidance of Your Dreams* (Woodbury, MN: Llewellyn, 2017), 92.

Step 5: Move into Higher Emotion

Imagination and emotion are two very powerful tools, and we bring them together in this step. Positive thinking is great and all, but instead of working only with thought, getting yourself directly into the feeling of a euphoric emotion is so much more powerful. Instead of thinking positive about the home you're hoping for, you imagine being in that home, see all the details of the space, and really tune in to what it feels like to be there *now*.

What you focus on for this practice can really be anything you want it to be. You could envision hugging and playing with your dog or cat. Get into the details. See them curled up by you, so cozy and warm under a blanket that you're sharing. Feel their soft fur, their wet kisses, the tickle of their whiskers, their wet nose. Maybe they make you laugh by nibbling at your hair or tickling your ear as they sniff at you. If you have a hard time finding something that gets you into that higher level of positive emotion, think of past memories that have been amazing or just make something up. The goal is to be grinning from ear to ear. You might even find yourself crying from happiness. It can be that powerful.

This step finalizes your movement away from the trauma energy and into a new positive state. You're feeling heightened emotion connected to a certain event in real time, which also sets you up for that kind of positive experience moving forward.

°⋖ᴅ.ᴏ⋗°

CHAPTER 5

How to Integrate Your Spiritual Experience

Integrating your subtle experience and revealing your spiritual truth can feel as though you're opening your journal to allow someone else to read it. Knowing where to begin to find validation, acceptance, and community can feel elusive. Finding ways to test the waters in taking things to the next level and beginning to share your truth with others can be important steps for continued development. These are some of the things we'll look at in this chapter.

In order to prepare to emerge safely from your hidden space, you might first need to allow yourself to further explore your interests, build confidence through practice and confirmation of your abilities, and gain an understanding of who you're becoming by examining long-held beliefs. Once you've established this foundation, the natural next step will be opening yourself up to connect with a trusted confidant. But there's no rush on this journey. Take things one step at a time, always tuning in to your inner guidance for where to go next.

Have the Courage to Move Through Your Fear

The fact that you've made it this far in the book tells me one crystal-clear thing: you have courage. Maybe you don't feel that way, but waking up to your true self means setting aside fears that would otherwise have held you back. And even if those fears are still present, you're continuing to follow your inner calling anyway. "Waking up" is the experience of recognizing a part of you that has previously gone unacknowledged and allowing that side to unfold and be accepted. As author Kris Franken puts it, "Waking up can happen at any time. For some, it's an overnight wake-up call. For others, it's a slow, organic process, sped up a little by children, partners, illness, grief, career change, or other transitions. Waking up happens for many reasons. Mostly, it's your mind and body aligning to your Highest Self and responding to the pull of your Soul." [35] She goes on to list some signs that indicate you're going through an awakening, including:

- You're questioning everything.
- You're more often trusting yourself first, and following your heart instead of your head.
- You're recognizing that happiness comes to you from within and not externally.
- You're setting boundaries to feel safe and protected.
- You're feeling a connection to oneness/Spirit/something bigger than yourself.

Fear can be one of the biggest obstacles to this waking-up process, hindering connection with your subtle nature and spiritual self. As Franken notes, these fears can have a wide range, including: "Fear of the unknown. Fear of your own greatness. Fear of what other people will think. Fear of releasing attachments to all you have and know." [36] Thankfully, becoming more familiar with your intuitive makeup helps to break down fear that has a hold of you. Practicing those intuitive skills, strengthening your abilities, and becoming more familiar with the workings of your subtle side provides a light of understanding that casts out shadows of doubt and insecurity.

As you know by now, much of this education initially unfolds in secret, but as your confidence builds and as you connect even more with who you truly are, that embracing of self eventually tends to spill into the less pri-

---

35. Kris Franken, *The Call of Intuition: How to Recognize & Honor Your Intuition, Instinct & Insight* (Woodbury, MN: Llewellyn, 2020), 70.
36. Franken, *The Call of Intuition*, 70.

vate areas of your life, to the point where you simply don't want to hide any longer. When you find yourself at this point, working through fear can become an ever more important issue to address. The discussion and practices in this chapter will help you do just that.

Give Yourself Permission to Seek What You Desire

An important detail of integrating your spiritual experience is giving yourself permission to follow your inner calling, seek what you desire, and access your hidden interests. Even if you believe you have poor access to instruction or resources, you don't have the money to pursue your passion, or whatever it may be, honing in on what you desire is the first step. Allowing yourself to receive opportunities to take action on that is the next step. I'll share my story to help you understand what I mean.

At the time when I was beginning my own spiritual exploration, my interests weren't as accepted in the mainstream as they are today. I had a religious upbringing, and because of its teachings and the subtle and sometimes blatant messages of those around me, I didn't believe I would be accepted if I revealed my authentic self. There weren't any options for exploration that I knew of in my area, and I didn't know of anyone else who had the same interests as me, so I turned to books. I read and I read and I read some more.

During my teenage years, I devoured everything I could find in the local library until I discovered interlibrary loan, which gave me access to even more material. I dove into books on intuition, psychic development, dream interpretation, near death experiences, past lives, spirit communication, the afterlife, energy healing, and more. I signed up for an Asian studies class in high school, where I devoured everything I could about Buddhism and Hinduism. By the time I was in college, my pull toward spiritual studies was so strong that I often wondered if I'd taken the wrong direction in pursuing a liberal arts degree. Even though I was married by that point, the idea of devoting myself to spiritual studies in a monastery somewhere nagged at the back of my mind. I wondered if I'd been meant to be a nun, studying in an ashram, or practicing as an interfaith minister of some sort.

Or perhaps I was actually meant to be a hospital chaplain. It felt like my spiritual life was an all-or-nothing proposition, as though complete devotion was the only way I would be able to integrate it into my world. I was left with a sense of lack.

When signing up for each semester, I would review the available classes and deeply wish I could take the courses on comparative religions, death and dying, and anthropology, where I could learn more about the rituals and traditions of different cultures. But again, the rules of life got in the way. I didn't meet the required prerequisites. I didn't even have extra time in my schedule to just sit in or audit those classes. I felt torn. I wanted to delve into the worlds of mystery, spirituality, and healing, but I was already living a life that seemed to be taking me in another direction.

After graduating college, I moved to a new state and was still getting my bearings at the job I'd moved for, a job that I greatly appreciated but that I also knew within the first week wasn't where I belonged. I felt trapped and lost. Out wandering one day, I was in a bookstore that I'd never been in before. Drifting among the aisles, I intuitively called out to Spirit, "Lead me to the book I'm meant to read." I felt myself nudged in one direction, and I averted my eyes so that I wasn't unintentionally led by the signs or books around me. Following the push of guidance, I moved down one aisle, then another. Eventually, the movement slowed and I lifted my hand, brushing my fingers across the spines of so many books. Still, I kept by eyes down and tuned in to the energy I was feeling. Suddenly it stopped, and so did I. I grasped the edge of the book I had landed on and pulled it from the shelf. I felt a thrill run up my spine as I saw that it was a book on psychic development and energy work. I flipped it over and gasped out loud when I saw that the author lived and taught classes in the very same city as the bookstore where I was currently standing.

This bookstore moment seemed to be screaming at me, "Follow your desire." While online courses at that time were minimal, even if they had been more available, I'd strongly felt a need to study in person as a way to ground what often felt out of this world. With this book in hand and an instructor so close, my dream felt within reach. Still, being fresh out of college, I was deeply in debt from the loans I'd taken out as a full-time student, along with costs from my recent move. My ingrained belief was that I didn't have the money to put toward my passions.

Soon after, I attended a psychic gallery reading where people gathered to hear a professional psychic speak and give mini readings for members of the audience. I was singled out for a message and was told point-blank that my belief around a lack of money was something I needed to get over in order to allow myself to pursue my passions, and that I shouldn't allow this belief to hold me back.

I hadn't talked much about these "side interests" even to my husband, but after this event I finally brought up how much it would mean for me to take a class here and there. We worked on our budget and found a small portion that we could reserve for some classes. I was thrilled and, bursting with excitement, started taking classes with the author of that book in spiritual development, intuition, and energy healing.

This was a *huge* demand, as I'd felt insecure about money all my life, and still do in fact. But I had my passion and obstacle clearly defined. From there, I could figure out how to get past the barrier and reach my goals. Those beginning classes led to further exploration and certification in Reiki, which then opened me up to committing to a more long-term healing program, which led to massage classes. If I had restricted the exploration that I felt driven toward, none of that would have happened, which means I wouldn't have volunteered in hospice, offering energy work. I wouldn't have worked in recognized spas and healing centers, where I offered massage and energy work. And I wouldn't have found myself working as an acquiring editor for a mind-body-spirit publisher, which had been my ultimate dream. And I wouldn't have gained the skill and awareness that has allowed me to be here now writing this book, another huge life goal of mine. As I continue to follow my inner calling, who knows where else it might lead.

I want you to see yourself realizing the wildest dreams of your inner calling too. To get started, try the following practice.

PRACTICE
Define Your Underlying Desire

If someone asked you directly, "What are you most passionate about?" or "What desire do you most wish you could act on?" you might find it hard to pin down. A lot of little things are probably pointing at what that is for you, but it can still be hard to feel out the edges and clearly put it into words.

I can recall one specific moment that helped me put my underlying desire into words. Luke and I were taking a walk one summer evening to get out of an apartment that didn't quite feel like home. We were working hard to build a life together, but sometimes it felt as if we'd never quite arrive at the next level. As we walked, we would admire houses, dreaming of the day when we'd finally be able to buy our own. Already in that dreamy mode of imagination, I asked him, "If you won the lottery and didn't have to worry about money, what would you do?"

He took a second and then responded, "I'd get a workshop and make toys to donate." He is a creative person and very skilled with tools. I could definitely see this dream unfolding. When he asked me the same, I said, "I'd study energy medicine and volunteer in hospitals and healing centers."

This was one of those magnified moments where as I was saying the words, time seemed to slow and it was as if someone was feeding me the line. I was left with the thought, *Why can't I do that anyway without winning the lottery?* A seed had been planted. While this passion wasn't an end goal, it was one strong desire I had that ended up leading to another, and another, and another, opening doors that I couldn't have even imagined at that point. Yet looking back, all those doors were indeed things that I had dreamed of. What you find in this practice is likely to do the same for you, leading you to at least a starting point you can consider.

Step 1: Respond to the Question

Have paper and pen ready to take notes so you don't forget what comes out of this practice. Now it's your turn. Settle in, take some deep breaths, and relax.

Tune in and ask yourself, "What would I do if I won the lottery and didn't have to worry about money?" Really sit with that question and imagine yourself in that situation. An answer might present itself right away, but if it doesn't, just follow your train of thought like a daydream and see where it leads. Follow what's pulling you and discover the source of what it is you're being drawn to learn and practice.

Step 2: Imagine That Future
As you gain some insight into what your response to this question is, let your imagination take hold of your underlying desire. Ask it to show you a future where you're living out that passion. Pay attention to the details. Notice where you are and what you're doing. Who are you with? Pay attention to what the space around you looks like. Do you get a certain feeling when you tune in to these other details? Once again, just follow along as though you're daydreaming and see what is revealed to you.

Step 3: Identify the Obstacles
The last step is to pin down the obstacles that might keep you from attaining this goal. Ask yourself, "What are the key obstacles that I need to be aware of related to this goal?" As with step 1, an answer might present itself right away, but if it doesn't, just follow your train of thought like a daydream and see where it leads.

Once you've intuited the obstacles, take some time to think about what you can do to address them. Write down at least one step you'll take so that you continue to align yourself with your passions.

When you've completed all of these steps, write down what you noticed and put a date on it. One day you may be able to look back and say, "Wow, I remember when I felt this desire, and now I've made it my reality!"

Find the Instruction That Makes Sense for You

You might find that you come to a point when you need a place where you can practice with other people, whether in person or at a distance virtually. For me it felt important to begin my training in person, because I knew it would make what was subtle feel even more set within the real world. But virtual can work just as well and might end up being a much easier way to find resources without having to worry about location. As more instruction has become available online, I've taken excellent courses that way as well.

How much of a commitment you decide to make is up to you, of course. The route I went was individual classes to start (not such a monetary and time investment), then I dove into an ordination program (much more of an investment). If you want to test the waters first, try specific classes before committing to a full program. That way you can also make sure you're a good match with that particular instructor before making a bigger commitment.

As you're searching for classes and programs, if you still have reservation about using the word *psychic*, just know that the term *psychic development* is most likely the language that will be used for the type of instruction you're looking for. Try doing a search for your area and see what comes up nearby. Also look for New Age and metaphysical stores around you, as they usually offer classes. Yoga studios sometimes provide the kind of classes that might interest you as well. And finally, do a search for spiritual centers around you. Even if you aren't looking for an organized service or church, searching for "Spiritualist church near me" or "spiritual community" might give you leads for good resources in your area. (Even if you don't find one that is local, many now offer remote online learning, so that's an option as well.) Once you find shops or centers in your area, you can sign up for their emails. That way you'll be notified regularly about things that you might be interested in participating in.

It's also worth checking in to see what community classes are being held in your area. The topics that drew you to this book are becoming much more accepted in the mainstream, and you might be able to find someone teaching in just such a venue. A couple of examples of how to search for such classes could be doing an internet search for "community classes near me" or "community education in (name of your town)." You can then review the classes that are available now or in the near future. If an internet search doesn't bring you luck, try calling your local school district and asking them how you can obtain information on local community classes.

If you aren't concerned about finding classes you can attend in person, you could look at the books you've read and loved on these topics. Look at who the author is and check out their website to see if they're offering any classes.

Keep an eye out for metaphysical, holistic, wellness, mind-body-spirit, spirituality, and psychic fairs and expos. They seem to happen most often in the spring and fall but really occur all year round. The Body Mind Spirit Directory is my favorite resource for finding events. It lists them by location throughout the world, or you can view the complete list of events by date. Check out the recommended resources section in this book for more information, including a web link to this directory.

Continue Building Confidence Through Confirmation

As you continue on, keep demanding that your subtle abilities and incoming messages prove themselves to you. Look for confirmation. The more proof you receive, the greater your confidence will become.

This search for validation requires a balancing act. On one hand you need to live with one foot in grounded reality and be discerning as to what is actually true information that you're receiving through your subtle skills. On the other hand you need to allow yourself to be receptive to a more innocent and trusting side that allows you to perceive what lies beyond all that sturdy logic. This can feel a bit like whiplash. One second you believe, and the next you're doubting, denying, and dismissing.

You need to find the middle road between being level-headed enough to determine what is truly a message and what is actually coincidence or fantasy. Back in chapter 2, we covered how to know whether you're interpreting a message correctly. For the full list of indicators, jump back to page 64. As a brief reminder, we can boil that list down to a couple of things that can help you find this balance:

- Noticing repeated messages and synchronicity and using them as a guide to confirm subtle information and messages
- Having intuition and messages validated by external sources

Watch for your subtle perceptions to repeat in different ways. Have the messages prove themselves to you. Some of the stories I've shared in this book have demonstrated finding verification through synchronicity and confirming intuition by demanding additional information. I'll share a few more examples here of when I demanded that intuitive messages I was receiving be validated by feedback that came from outside of myself.

These stories emphasize the culmination of this book's purpose by demonstrating moments of acknowledging our extraordinary perceptions; of moving beyond secrecy to begin sharing those insights and abilities with others; of using things like psychic vision, psychic hearing, and external confirmation to build confidence; and of keeping your feet in both the physical world and the subtle world at once.

Pennies and the Movie Ghost

This first story goes back to my previous mention of pennies showing up as messages from my sister. A few weeks after she passed, my dad came home one day and declared that after dinner we were going to watch the movie *Ghost*. Before we started watching the movie, I was talking with my mom on the phone.

"What was the significance of pennies to Amy?" she was asking. We were wracking our brains trying to figure it out. "She would always say, 'I found a penny from Grandpa today!'" Amy found them all the time: in her jeep, in her laundry, on the bed. It was always in weird places, like someone was setting them there as a joke for her. Her superstition had been passed on to many other people, but while I took some notice, I was never as steadfast in my belief as she was.

"She always mentioned it to me, too," I said, "but I can't remember how it started. I swear, though, I've been finding them like crazy since she died."

"Me too!" said my mom.

In fact, I'd told everyone they had to keep track of their change, because if I found a penny, I wanted to be able to trust that it was from Amy and not just someone with a hole in their pocket.

"Dad had one fall out of the truck when he got to the memorial service," I said. "And I had the craziest one last week! Just before going to bed, I told Luke to keep track of his change because I was going bonkers wondering if all the random pennies I was finding were from her. I had just picked up the house a little, so I had it under control. The next morning when I was getting ready for work, I opened my makeup drawer and there was a shiny penny staring up at me, right in the front part of the drawer."

"No!" said my mom.

"Yes! I just stood there staring at it, thinking, *No way!* I knew it wasn't there before. I picked it up and saw the date was 1982."

"Your birth year!"

"Yep. It was like she was trying to say as clear as she could, 'This penny is from me and this sign is for you!'"

The meaning went far beyond just a random penny. When Amy was sixteen, I started a yearly penny tradition. The first year, I glued a penny for each year inside a frame, starting at her birth year. Every year following, I sent that year's penny to her to add on. Still, we couldn't figure out how the significance of her pennies had started. Eventually we gave up and I joined Dad for our movie date.

I hadn't seen *Ghost* in years, and it was almost like watching it for the first time. I recalled my first viewing, when Amy and I had been at our friends' house playing "movie theater," where we would pick a movie, set up chairs in a row, put out concessions, and have each other pay to come watch. At the end of the movie, Amy had cried openly. It had stuck with me because we weren't very open emotionally. I knew even at the age of eight how powerful the story must have been for her.

In rewatching the movie, I finally realized where the significance of the pennies had come from. In the story, a man named Sam dies and is trying to reach out to his partner, Molly. He desperately wants to prove that he still exists and that his love still lives on. No matter how he tries, she doubts and eventually rejects each significant sign. He's finally able to convince her through the gift of a penny. When he was alive and they were remodeling their new apartment, they'd found an old penny in a jar and declared it to be for luck. Here he repeated the sentiment by holding a penny in the air and placing it in her hand. Since she couldn't see him, the penny appeared to float magically on its own. With the mystical event and the meaningful connection, she finally trusted what she hadn't allowed herself to believe up until then.

At that time, my own lack of trust in the signs I thought I was receiving from Amy was reflected in Molly's experience. I saw my own concern for remaining grounded in reality and not becoming overly sentimental. I didn't want to unintentionally stretch the clues to fit just because I wanted them to. Maybe they were real, but it was safer to deflect my subtle perceptions and focus on the solid world around me.

When we got to the ending scene where Sam's spirit becomes visible to Molly, I sensed Amy near me. "This is me," I heard her say. "Tell Dad it's me saying this last part!" she urged. He sat across the room from me, unaware of my inner conversation. I sealed my lips, unwilling to put myself out there like that. *This is emotional enough!* I thought. I didn't want to make it look like I was just feeding off the movie and passing along an easy line. As my thoughts fought against the inner request, Sam started backing into the light on-screen.

"It's amazing, Molly," Sam said. "The love inside, you take it with you." [37] I sat quiet but overwhelmed as he continued to move backward and into the waiting arms of those who were welcoming him to his next life.

When the movie ended, I stood, emotionally spent and determined to head straight to bed. I moved out of the living room and into the hall, but at the last second I turned back. I thought that maybe I would read through some of Amy's writings before going to sleep. I was totally wiped, but the urge to search through the words she'd left behind was suddenly overpowering.

....

37. *Ghost*, directed by Jerry Zucker (Paramount Pictures, 1990).

"What are you doing?" Dad called from the other room.

"Looking through Amy's stuff," I replied. Pretty soon he joined me, sitting on the floor amid piles of boxes and papers. We paged through notebooks and journals, looking for those gems that made us laugh or understand better the life that she'd struggled through. Dropping a folder full of random papers, I grabbed a small notebook with a smiling golden retriever pictured on the front.

"Oh!" I gasped after flipping it open.

"What?" Dad said, looking up from the papers.

I stared bleary-eyed at the open notebook page that contained a single message.

"I didn't tell you," I blubbered. "I didn't want to say, because I wasn't sure." The confusion on his face was almost comical in my moment of shock. I laughed, looking down at the page again. "GHOST," it said in all caps, underlined twice. "The love carries with you." I looked up again. "This was her saying it. She wants us to know she's saying it."

The Velveteen Rabbit

This example demonstrates confirmed intuition and messages, synchronicity that acted to also confirm the message, and me sharing the secret side of myself in a way that I'd never done before that moment.

The first time I received an undeniable psychic confirmation, it surprised me just as much as the other people who were there to share in the moment. On one of those hopeless midwinter evenings in the Midwest when we'd finally fully resigned ourselves to existing in darkness, I headed out for a Saturday night get-together. It was freezing and I hated to leave my warm apartment, but I was looking forward to girl time at an aunt's house. A family friend I'd met a few times ended up coming too. I didn't know her well, but I was aware of the fact that she was interested in metaphysics. At the time, I was midway through a round of classes on energy healing and intuitive development, and somehow the topic came up.

"Would you be open to trying a reading for me?" Renee asked. I shakily agreed to test the waters outside of the safe boundaries I'd found in class, but I warned her I might hit or miss. I was still learning and there were no guarantees. So far I'd been fine intuiting personal information, but for others in class it hadn't been so easy. Renee was all game and I felt comfortable testing the waters with her.

"Is there anyone in particular you want me to focus on?" I questioned.

"My brother," she said, taking a sip of dark red wine. Her eyes were sad, but the energy around her vibrated with anticipation.

"Okay," I said, shifting in the plush chair to get comfortable. "Don't tell me any more than that for now." I took a second to settle myself and tune in. Acting on a practice I'd used since I was a kid, I imagined a bubble of light around me. Trying not to give in to my ego, I pushed the lower-level thoughts about succeeding, pleasing, and proving beyond the borders of my bubble.

After calming my energy, I turned to my internal vision and thoughts. *Renee's brother, do you have anything you want to share with your sister?*

A figure slowly emerged from the black slate of my mind. I could feel that the energy was male and he stood at a distance, wrapped in a gray haze. My vision had always been foggy in this way, like a dream where you remember seeing a person but you can't focus in on the details of their face. I've always found this to be extremely frustrating, but I watched for anything specific that I could pull out. He presented a daisy, plucked the top off, and pressed the flower in his hands, folding them together like the pages of a book.

"Did your brother press or preserve flowers?" I asked, assuming that this was, in fact, her brother.

"No," she replied patiently. I could see her mind turning, trying to figure out how this information might fit for her somehow. I took a minute to tune back in to her brother. Again, he offered a daisy and plucked it, and this time he clearly pressed it in the pages of a book. I took a different approach.

"Do you like daisies? Or are they significant to you in any way?"

"Yes," she said without offering anything more. *Were daisies her wedding flowers?* I wondered. I didn't ask in the moment, but years after this reading she did actually confirm to me that daisies had always been her favorite flower and she had them in her wedding.

Never having done this before, I finally stepped off the edge and went with what I intuitively felt was being communicated. "He's giving you a daisy to say 'I love you,' and he's pressing it to show that even with his passing and the time that has gone by, that love is preserved." As I spoke the words, I had an overwhelming feeling that they were accurate, as if he were choosing and almost speaking the words for me. I thought the message was a lovely gesture and the energy I felt was wonderful. I wondered if she could feel that too. Even with the positive impression, I couldn't keep my logical mind from kicking in. *Yeah, lovely, but that doesn't prove anything. Anyone can say pretty words.*

"Can you sense how he died?" she asked.

I pushed the negative thoughts beyond the edges of my light bubble and continued on. Looking inward through the muddled fog, I saw a crash and assumed it was a car, but something about it didn't feel quite right. I shared the details with her.

"It was actually a plane crash," she said, tearing up.

The reality of it all hit me at that point. Death. It was so harsh, so heart-wrenchingly dividing. Yet there we were, walking between two worlds. I'd never acted so directly as a medium before this. The weight of it all was trying in its newness. I worried about getting something wrong and not being able to communicate the information she needed to hear. She was already in pain; I could see that. I absolutely did not want to add to it.

"Can you tell me his nickname?" she asked, snapping me out of my anxious stream of thoughts. I tuned in again and saw a white stuffed animal in the form of a bunny. I heard "fuzzy bunny," but like the car accident information, it didn't feel exactly accurate.

"Um, I really don't know if this is right," I said, a bit embarrassed for the long-shot attempt, "but I was always told to give what I get. Even if I think it's off-the-wall, it might really mean something to you." Everyone sat waiting for me to get through my lead-up and spit it out. "Does 'fuzzy bunny' mean anything?"

The confused look on Renee's face was all the answer I needed. Still, the image pressed on as if the solution was right at the tip of my tongue.

Gradually the image I saw offered a bit more detail here and there. It transformed from a stuffed animal into inked lines and watercolor. I was trying to think of the name of the story I was seeing, where the stuffed animal becomes real. I could see the illustrations, but the name just wasn't quite there.

"Oh!" I exclaimed as it finally hit me. Still unsure whether I was wandering aimlessly along my self-generated bunny path or if this was the answer to the nickname question, I again offered what I got. "Does 'Velveteen Rabbit' mean anything to you?"

"Oh my gosh, yes!" She sat stunned for a minute before explaining, "My brother always said he just wanted to be real. A note about the story was passed out at his funeral."

Apparently he didn't care about the question about his nickname and felt that was more important for her to hear. As if in response to my worry, her brother offered something that couldn't be denied. Everyone, including me, sat in a state of surprise for a moment, soaking in the reality of what we were experiencing.

Once again, I passed on words that he seemed to speak through me. "He wants you to understand that you don't need to be dependent on others in order to communicate with him. When you ask, most often he's by your side, and if you trust yourself more to listen, you could begin the communication process on your own."

"But how?"

"Through dreams, 'coincidences,' signs, or even direct communication. You could try meditation. He wants you to be empowered. It seems like it would help with your healing process."

As if to confirm this statement, I received several synchronistic reminders the week after our get-together. Luke rented a movie that really was not very good, but there was a stuffed bunny in it and it was the Velveteen Rabbit. The coincidental theme piqued my interest, especially since it hadn't been hinted at in the previews, on the cover, or in any description we ever came into contact with. It was a minor part of the movie, but at the end the last line was a quote from *The Velveteen Rabbit* storybook: "Real isn't how you are made… It's a thing that happens to you." [38] In the book it then explains that by being *really* loved, this is how you become real.

A couple of days later, Luke and I got lost looking for a concert we were going to. On slushy, snow-covered roads, we wove through streets in the darkness. "I need to turn around," Luke said, pulling into the circle drive of a college campus. As we looped around, my jaw dropped. Beaming from the glow of our headlights was a sign calling out a Velveteen Rabbit show that was being put on. These synchronicities added up to declare it was all very real.

Renee later shared the memorial flyer she'd mentioned during the reading. It included the quote from the story about how becoming real happens to you by being truly loved. It also read, "No doubt some accomplish this in a brief span of years. Others never have it happen at all. Rob did."

A Birthday Message

This final example demonstrates messages coming from nature and the external world via animals and objects, and how synchronicity of events worked to push through a message whose understanding was initially delayed. It also illustrates things like recall of past trauma, the sense of just "knowing," intentionally tuning in to receive a message, and thought and feeling being impressed upon you by a loved one who has passed.

This sequence of events occurred almost ten years after Amy's passing. At the time I'd been in the midst of a situation that was weighing on me heavily and that I absolutely would have leaned on her for if she'd been physically alive. I'd been sending thoughts to her as I drifted off to sleep each night, wishing she was there to help and guide me through it all.

Before I dove into work that day, I opened the front door to let my dogs enjoy the screened porch. I assumed all was normal until…

10:00 a.m. I looked out and noticed the dogs taking turns inspecting something. As I approached, I realized it was a little tree frog. My mind flashed to a memory from when I was a kid and had tried to keep a pet frog. After having it only one night in our screened porch, I woke the next day

---

38. Margery Williams, *The Velveteen Rabbit* (New York: Doubleday, 1991), 5.

to find it had passed away. As a child, the grief from that loss and the sense that I had been the cause of it was huge.

I shooed the dogs away and gently picked up the frog. His skin was still springy, but he didn't make any movement and it was clear he was gone. I held him tenderly while saying an apology as I walked over to a shaded area where I placed his little body to rest. Memories of all the swimming in the pool that Amy and I had done during summers as kids flashed into my mind, and I recalled the joy we'd felt when we often found ourselves in the company of tree frogs scuttling around in the water with us.

I walked back to the house, and these thoughts quickly faded as I got on with my busy day.

11:00 a.m. An hour later, an alarm chimed on my phone's calendar and I realized it was Amy's birthday. Thoughts ran through my mind of past parties from our childhood, many of which were pool parties. Joy and grief mixed. Once again, these thoughts faded as I went back to my work.

12:00 p.m. I heard a twittering from the screened porch and looked out to see the dogs watching a hummingbird that was hovering and looking in at us. While I'd had feeders out all summer, I'd only had a couple of sightings all season and I was elated to have one lingering by us. This reminded me that I needed to clean out the feeders, so, taking a break from work, I went outside and set to the task.

In the middle of rinsing and refilling the containers, I remembered the hummingbird from the vision I'd seen after Amy's death, in which it had seemed to hover right in front of me. It was a detail I'd entirely forgotten until I was going through my old journals while writing this book. I wondered if hummingbirds would be a continued symbol from her now that I'd recalled that detail.

1:00 p.m. I received a message saying a package had been delivered. It was a humorous birthday present for one of my siblings that I'd ordered far ahead of time, and I was so excited to see it. I couldn't wait to give it to them. As I walked down the long driveway on that warm summer day, gravel crunching under my feet and flying grasshoppers fluttering in my wake, I could feel my body tapping into a visceral connection to all of

Amy's birthdays past. With my mind elsewhere, I lifted the lid to the large container where mailed packages were placed. I smiled at the sight of the box sitting there, waiting. As I reached in and pulled it out, a frog unexpectedly dropped from above and landed on the edge of the package. I let out a startled cry and then started laughing. I waited for him to jump away, but he remained fixed to the present.

"Hi, little guy," I cooed. "I'm sorry about your friend," I said, thinking back to the frog from that morning. With the drought we'd experienced that summer, I hadn't seen a single tree frog that year. *How odd that I saw one dead and now one living on the same day*, I thought. I coaxed him into my hand so I could set him down in some grass, but as I reached my hand out to set him free, he very clearly nestled in. It was as if he were saying, "I'm not going anywhere." *Maybe he needs some water*, I thought. I held my hand close to my body and kept him shaded as I trudged back up to the house.

As I ran some water into my hand, the frog still made no move to leave me. My eyes were focused on his vibrant green body and shining copper eyes when suddenly a white butterfly fluttered across my vision in between us. Without time to even think, I immediately started crying. Everything in me knew this was Amy before I could even mentally begin to put it all together.

I sat there crying and looking at this little frog who was now moving from my hand onto my wrist, watching me. For ten minutes he sat with me as I tuned in for whatever Amy wanted to share. I felt her energetically hugging me. "You're stuck with me," she said. I zoomed in on the frog's sticky little toes and smiled. "Even in passing I'm not gone. I'm with you every day, every moment. I know what you're going through and I'm here with you through it."

The experience ended with a very meaningful message as a result of the frogs and butterfly, but it wasn't until I started mapping out all the details to write this story that I identified many more connections. The timing of each event had legitimately landed at the top of each new hour of the day, as if to emphasize Amy's point about being there for every meaningful moment. I realized that the hummingbird my dogs and I saw had indeed been a sign; and my sudden urge to immediately deal with the feeders (something I'd been putting off for weeks), my remembering of the hummingbird vision, and my wondering if hummingbirds were a sign from Amy had all actually been things that she was impressing upon me, not things I was thinking on my own. And it had also been completely lost on me that it was her birthday and I was collecting a *birthday present for a sibling* at the time that I was met by this tree frog.

My point here is that Spirit interacts with us far more than we realize. And the minor instances where we actually put the pieces together and acknowledge those moments are a small slice of the continuous connection that's occurring. This is just one more example of why journaling your experiences can be helpful in clarifying the messages you're receiving from those in spirit.

Addressing Your Long-Held Beliefs vs. Your New Spiritual Experiences

For much of this book you've explored topics within your secret internal world. You might have shared with a select friend or two, but if you've kept a lot of this exploration hidden from the outer world, it's time to consider the space where those worlds come together, and how you can work to continue integrating them even more. The eventual goal is to feel less like you're living two dual lives and more like you're living as your complete self in a way that feels authentic to you.

In integrating your authentic self, it becomes necessary at some point to assess your public self versus your private self. This often translates into looking at who you've been in the past and where you feel you're currently heading. This doesn't mean you're choosing one over the other. It's okay to move between and exist in both worlds. But considering your long-held beliefs versus your new spiritual experience will help you see what pieces from each side of life still fit for you moving forward. This also doesn't mean you have to be completely open with every person about every aspect of who you are. I know a very successful and well-known psychic who uses a pseudonym when interacting with people in certain instances. This isn't an action of denying who she really is, but instead is a way for her to set a healthy boundary. It's perfectly fine to choose when you share and when you don't. The key here is that you're allowing yourself to find the balance that feels authentic to you and makes you happy.

Addressing Religion

Before I expound on the topic of religion, I first want to clarify that if you feel in alignment with your religion, that's great! However, for many people this isn't the case, so it's an important topic for me to cover here. Just know that if you don't feel at odds with your religion as you're exploring your spiritual and psychic side, the rest of this section won't apply to you. I don't want anyone to misunderstand or take the following discussion to mean that you need to distance yourself from your religion. If it feels right to you, honor that.

Religion is a stumbling block for a lot of people when they're coming into their own and trying to honor their authentic self. While some may find that their subtle abilities and spiritual explorations can freely live alongside or be woven into their existing religious practice, others eventually find that the two increasingly separate out from each other, like oil and water. If that rings a bell for you, it's probably the large elephant in your secret space that you just aren't quite sure how to manage.

While there's no doctrine assigned to the use of your subtle skills, and dogma simply isn't a part of it, sometimes as we accept our full abilities and open to our true self, we outgrow traditions that offered us a starting point. Usually religion is something that's been decided for us at the beginning of our lives, and is something we're raised in that others assume we'll continue to be devoted to. Even if you consciously chose your religion, we go through different phases throughout our lives as we learn and grow. Sometimes that means we end up expanding beyond the borders of an organization, system, or tradition that previously sustained us. And this is part of the reason why there are so many! When one no longer fits, we might try on another, or we might decide not to assign ourselves to anything specific and instead live within our own unique spiritual inspiration.

In instances where you begin to feel a sense of unease or as though the religion doesn't feel in total alignment with who you are and what you believe, the internal conflict is very real! It can feel like you're being torn in half or faced with an impossible choice. In many ways it's not a clean and clear separate box that we can see the boundaries of, because our family, community, traditions, routines, and more are all tangled into it. You might feel like if you're not all in, then there is the threat of potentially severe consequences, such as being ostracized by the people you most love.

This is one of the bigger reasons that secret psychics are *secret*. And that is okay. You can explore your inner world for as long as you need to without making outward changes. If it feels like you're just going through the motions and playing a role to appease everyone else around you, eventually you'll probably feel the need to shift things. Until you feel ready to find the space that bridges your inner and outer worlds, make an agreement with yourself that it's okay to keep them separate.

Curating Your World

When you *are* ready to find the middle ground and figure out who you are and what life looks like with both your inner world and your outer world fully integrated as one, that's when some editing might happen. This is when you're figuring out what to keep and what to let go of. You could think of it like decluttering a closet. You find the pieces you're inspired by and let go of the items that no longer fit and leave you feeling uncomfortable. You're curating according to who you are *now*. This doesn't mean you have to throw out everything that brought you to this point in exchange for all things new. Instead, you're holding on to long-adored pieces and bringing in a collection of new items to love, creating a mosaic of past and present for who you are in this very moment and who you see yourself becoming.

Unlike decluttering your closet, this entire process isn't going to happen in a single afternoon. More likely it will unfold over years or decades, or even at different points throughout the rest of your life, so don't put a time limit on it. You needn't feel rushed. You get to choose when and to whom you reveal the pieces of yourself.

It's Not Always Either-Or

Editing out what may no longer serve you doesn't always mean that you need to be looking for things to choose between or let go of. Just because you might currently feel like you're living between two worlds doesn't mean you have to choose which one to make your home moving forward. Part of the transformational experience is learning to live a human life while also reawakening to your spiritual nature. You may feel like you have your feet in two different spaces because *you do*. *We are* living in two different spaces, the physical and the energetic, so learning to take both realms into your heart and integrate them within a single life becomes the end goal.

PRACTICE
What Still Holds Meaning for You?

Take some time now to consider some of the things that still hold meaning for you. Sometimes looking at what we will *keep* is easier than starting with what we will let go of. This is where we'll begin.

When you have some quiet time, grab your journal and pen. Get comfortable. Close your eyes and take some soothing breaths. When you feel ready, connect to the energy in your solar plexus, the third chakra. See it bright yellow, clear like the sun. Now sink deeper into this energy and find the area of discomfort sitting within it. You can see it as a fuzzy gray ball marring the brightness of your central chakra area.

Imagine that you're now holding this energy outside of your body in your hands. This energy represents things that are no longer fully in alignment with who you are. Tune in to what this energy is about. Feel into the emotion and notice if any words or images come up. Is there any person(s), place(s), or thing(s) that comes to mind that's connected to it? Try not to force this, but just allow whatever rises to the surface to come naturally.

If many things came up for you, choose one to focus on. You can come back to this practice to focus on the others later. See this one person/place/ thing as a label on a box in your closet that you now take off the shelf. You set the box on the floor, open it, and unpack everything inside of it. Assess what makes up this person/place/thing and lay those items out individually around the box. You could also go about this as a list, writing the things about the person/place/thing that fill you up (pros) and the things that drain you (cons).

When you're done, see yourself taking those good items and placing them lovingly back into your closet space in a beautiful display. The items left that don't support you any longer are placed back in the box and moved out of your space. As a result, you can see the yellow of your core energy glowing even brighter.

Know that at this point you aren't being asked to let go of this person, place, or thing unless you feel ready to take that step. For now, we're instead intentionally looking at the positives that we can pull out of this energy in order to better see what we're dealing with. In the closet decluttering example, this would be the stage of pulling all items out of the closet and placing them on the floor spread out so that you can see everything you have. This action makes it easier to determine what's wanted and what's no longer needed. Instead of a jumbled mess, you can better see what you're dealing with.

Setting an Intention

If you don't notice anything specifically connected to the muddled energy, set an intention by simply saying the following: "The connection will rise to the surface over the coming days in ways that will help me become consciously aware of it." Pay attention and make note of anything that you notice in the days that follow. Once you have those details noted, you can come back and complete the practice again, this time incorporating the additional details.

An Example

This practice can feel a bit hard to grasp at first but will become progressively easier. The energy and intention you're putting into it will start shifting things until eventually you start naturally manifesting change in your real-world life.

Here's an example in case you need something to help get you started. Since many readers will probably see religion as part of the muddled energy, I'll use that as the sample topic to show what you might find yourself left with. These are some of my positive takeaways, the things that I pulled out and that still hold great meaning for me from the religion I was raised in. Thanks to this religion, I learned the following:

- What it felt like to raise my energy through prayer, contemplation, meditation, song, and ritual
- To feel the raised energy of a group of people
- How belief and thought can lead to euphoric and emotionally moving moments of connection to a universal energy much larger than myself
- How music can raise and unite the individual energies of people
- That ritual and intention can help enhance your spiritual experience
- The significance of connecting with Spirit to share my thoughts/ hopes/worries (This act of prayer was a jumping-off point for the next step in spirit communication, of listening for a response to receive insight.)
- That my connection to the physical world's cycle of the seasons can also impact my spiritual connections, through celebrations and the natural shift in energy from one season to another
- To be mindful of my connection with the earth through these types of seasonal celebrations
- That celebrating life changes and milestones with others to witness and commemorate along with you is important
- The importance of community
- The significance of symbols
- Appreciation for spiritual figures/guides

For a time I lived very happily fully integrated in religion with these positives sustaining me. I'm grateful that being raised in that tradition offered me a strong starting point for my personalized spiritual journey. While I eventually naturally felt ready to step away from it, these things still hold meaning and came along with me, finding various ways to remain. For example, my community is no longer found within the walls of a church, but it's still here nonetheless, made up of family, a core circle of meaningful friends, and others who have similar interests. Ritual through the seasons and holidays, celebrations of milestones, the sharing of music, sacred contemplation, and more are all still very important parts of my world.

Be Open to Opportunities to Connect with a Confidant

My wish for you is that if you don't already, one day you'll have a cherished confidant to share this secret psychic side of yourself with. If you've started taking classes, maybe you've connected with someone by now. I didn't find this friend until much later in my own journey, but when we finally connected, it was so fun. And since I had gone through much spiritual exploration ahead of her, I loved being able to answer many of her questions that I'd also had earlier on. At one point when she was asking about soul retrieval and researching someone to go to for a session, I shared that my own desire was to one day experience a Life Between Lives hypnotherapy session, but that first you have to go to someone for a past life regression.

"What is *that*?" she asked with intrigue.

"Oh my gosh, it's so weird to me when you don't know these things," I said with a laugh.

"Stop giving me new things to research and spend money on!" she declared.

If you also don't know what these various things are all about, that's not a surprise! There are so many different branches of interest and ways to learn about our spiritual selves. My advice is to look to the wide range of modalities and avenues for exploration with excitement. Learning about it all with a friend can provide even more fun and confirmation along the way.

One tip for finding just such a friend is to look for those around you who show signs of interest in the same things. When you find them, see if you can start a discussion on a topic of interest. Ask questions to scout out like-minded people among your family, friends, and acquaintances. These don't have to be risky questions, because they can be framed as hypotheticals and don't have to reveal that they're directly about your situation. Some possible questions offered by psychic medium John Holland in testing the waters are "How do you feel about intuition? Do you think you have it?" and "How do you feel about the afterlife?" If the other person engages and shows interest, perhaps it can be the start of a growing bond and a more regular connection.

When things feel like they need to be kept secret, we tend to miss even obvious opportunities because we're so focused on looking in at our own energy in order to hold it close and not unintentionally reveal ourselves. But if you start paying more attention outwardly, you might notice those opportunities more and more.

Here are some example scenarios of testing the waters:

- A friend brings up their dreams pretty regularly. You strike up a conversation around dream symbols and contemplate their meanings, and soon you find you're talking about signs and synchronicities that you both notice while awake.

- A coworker mentions watching their favorite show and it's something you also watch. One of the characters on the show is psychic, and you bring up an event in a certain episode that focused on that character. You ask your coworker what they thought of it and they light up, sharing that they find that kind of thing fascinating. This leads to more regular chats about intuitive things you both notice in your own lives.

- A family member mentions how they feel that dragonflies are a sign of their deceased mother. You mention how you've always had the same feeling. You both end up sharing your accounts and

your discussion rolls into other experiences of animal symbolism
and spirit communication that you've both had.

In an example from my own life, Amy and I used to tape a daytime talk
show whenever there was the occasional appearance of a popular psychic
medium. While we planned for and watched these episodes together, for
some reason we never talked about it much more beyond that. I wasn't
sure what her level of interest was or whether she took the topic seriously
beyond just being a form of entertainment on a show. At the time, I wasn't
willing to step out of my safe zone enough to ask her more about what she
thought about it, which is a shame because we both lost out on a valuable
connection. It wasn't until years later, when I'd moved away from home and
began taking psychic development classes, that she opened up to me about
her own interests and we finally realized how aligned we were. We began
having regular phone chats about all things metaphysical, and it filled us
both up in the best way.

If even one of us had allowed ourselves to open up sooner, we could
have benefited from support at a time when we both felt very alone in
these interests. Broaching the topic could have come naturally during those
moments when we watched those episodes together. Somehow it surprised
us both that our potential confidant had been living right there in the same
house all along. Just like us, your confidant opportunities could be right
under your nose, so watch out for them!

As you open up to find the "right" people to share with, you'll also find
the people who are not in alignment with you. It's just the nature of things.
By finding the people you do need in your life, you'll also find people who
fall away and eventually may no longer play a key role in your inner circle.
This can be really hard to handle sometimes. Believe me, I know. I hold a lot
of love and also some grief for those who are no longer my close confidants,
but in the end I'm very grateful for the people I still find close to me. I
know that these are the relationships that are feeding me the energy I most
need in my life right now.

It's true that as you open up and find those who most align with you, your community may shift. Instead of fearing this, it can be helpful to think of it as though any loss you experience is opening up space for a stronger alignment to take its place.

PRACTICE
Manifest a Friend

If you're feeling alone in your internal explorations and are hoping to have someone to share your inner world with, try asking Spirit to connect you with a like-minded friend. Get your journal now and write down today's date and the details of your desire to manifest this friend. Include why you're hoping for this to occur. Write this as though you're addressing it to a guide, a loved one, a spiritual figure, or Spirit in general.

Once you've completed writing out the specifics, settle in, take some deep breaths, and relax. Close your eyes and see yourself once again moving down the stone steps toward a door at the bottom of the staircase. Before opening the door, call on whoever you addressed your request to. Ask them to be there waiting for you on the other side. Now open the door and step through.

Take in your surroundings and notice that the spiritual support figure is there waiting for you. Walk toward them and receive whatever greeting they have for you. Let them know you have a request for them. The note you just wrote is folded in a shirt pocket over your heart. Pull it out now and hand it to them. They take it with a smile and it dissolves with their touch. The request is now energetically in motion.

Take some time to receive any further messages that your support figure has for you. Once they're done, bid them farewell and move back through the door and up the stairs. As you reach the top, bring yourself gently back to the present. Jot down any additional details that you want to remember from this practice. Being able to look back at this record might be significant to you in the future when your friend eventually manifests in your life.

I remember doing this practice in my teens and twenties, and while I didn't know it at the time, I was already connected with people who had these interests, like my sister and a friend from high school who I lost touch with but who eventually came back into my life. In both instances, we wouldn't realize the depth of our shared interest until years later. Just because it took that long for me doesn't mean it will for you. No matter how long it takes, though, don't shut yourself in a room and wait for someone to come knocking on your door. Become a participant in manifesting.

Once I put my request out into the universe, I didn't just sit around. I continued to cultivate my interest by reading everything I could get my hands on. I found it easy to make connections online, which is great for two reasons: (1) sometimes it's actually easier to share with strangers because they don't really know anything about you other than your interest in a certain topic, and (2) it offers the potential to develop new friendships with people who are obviously like-minded. Once I finally had the chance, I found in-person classes and made connections there. While I still didn't feel that I'd found my confidant, I continued to follow where my passions led me. Eventually that friendship was realized. Do this practice, but then also continue to take actions that move you toward the life you desire. Keep your eyes and ears open and allow Spirit to guide you.

°◅⟋⟍▹°

Find Moments to Be Intentionally Receptive

The more skilled you become with your subtle abilities, the more you'll find yourself intentionally choosing moments in your everyday life to open yourself up to them. This is in contrast to the last chapter, where we focused on the experience of subtle abilities unexpectedly slipping into everyday life. As you integrate your abilities, instead of them taking you by surprise, you'll find more and more that they are a kind of natural superpower that you can consciously wield when most needed or simply when you're most curious. Maybe you're out in nature and want to connect even deeper, so you tune in to the unseen energy around you. Maybe you're writing in your journal and you decide to have a conversation with your spirit guide to see what insight they have to share with you about a specific dilemma you're facing. Perhaps you're touring a house that you're considering buying and you want to tune in to the vibe of the space as you're in it and hit on whether or not it's the right place for you. Whatever the instance may be, look for those opportunities to consciously engage with your subtle abilities.

One such instance came for me during the passing of my paternal grandpa. This occurrence brought about many of the things we've talked about throughout this book: spirit contact from a deceased family member; communication through the psychic senses of vision, emotion, and hearing; confirmation through external signs and synchronicity; and the clearing of subtle energy. During one of the last visits I had with him, when we finally knew he was going into hospice, I was intentionally psychically open and waiting to find Amy. When I walked into the room where my grandpa was sitting up in a lounge chair, there she was, standing behind and kind of leaning in, as though she was attending to him. There was a glittering shimmer around her and she was beaming with excitement, in contrast to the grief that we as a family were all feeling.

Amy had always been one to be distraught over the passing of someone, anyone, whether close or distant to her. She would read about the death of someone she didn't even know and be left unsettled and unable to shake the despair she felt over the unfathomable loss of life from this world. It rattled her to the core every time. And if she'd been physically standing alongside me in that moment, there's no question that she would have been falling to pieces. But as it was, I could see she was exuberant at having the opportunity to play a new role.

"I get to be the greeter now, to help prepare and welcome," she said. Her curls were tied back and she still wore a white headband, but her previously all-white garb was now broken up with a cute blue jacket. Seeing her here in this way had me thinking about what my dad had said of her passing. Hours before her death, he'd watched her with her eyes locked in a distant gaze, looking at things unknown. "It was like she was watching angels come through the windows," he'd told me. And as if to explain what she was seeing, unbidden she'd pointed past his shoulder and said to him, "They're there, you know."

Now here she was two years later, seeing it all from the other side. Still, I couldn't help but wonder if I was just making it all up. As if to counter that thought, on the way home from our visit, my dad saw that same meaningful license plate for the second time. "There it was under the mud: 'Amy Joy,'" he said, flabbergasted. I thought his choice of words was so symbolically meaningful. Since we had only seen that license plate once before, just after her passing, it was a shocking synchronicity for it to turn up again in that moment. "She must be in town again!" he concluded.

"Oh, she is!" I exclaimed, thinking of seeing her with my grandpa. "I couldn't tell you in the moment because I would have started crying, and I forgot to mention it afterward."

Then it came: another early-morning call relaying loss. But this time we had the chance to say goodbye. Like the last time I'd received a similar call, my body held the same chill from a lack of sleep, the same shock as I stepped out into the cold winter air, and the same deep hollowness in my gut that wasn't a call for food. My husband, siblings, and I drove in quiet darkness together, facing anxious pauses at red lights, all the while hoping there was still time.

Time. To support. To love. To let go.

We ran into the hospital, pulling back glass doors, the clomp of hurried feet in heavy shoes hitting the floor and echoing off sterile walls. Rounding a corner, we saw familiar faces glistening with tears and stricken with grief. We were pulled into hugs and my dad asked to say a prayer. As my grandpa's children all circled round his bed, my siblings and I stood by, arm in arm, keeping each other standing. At the same time we were saying goodbye to our grandpa, it seemed we were simultaneously saying the goodbye we hadn't had the chance to say to our sister as well. My dad's voice filled the space, saying, "I ask that God bring Amy to be here with him, so he has someone he knows to help bring him home."

One by one, everyone took a moment with him. When it was my turn, I sat next to him and rested my hand on his. A strong man with a sharp mind, who fiercely loved his community, family, and most of all his wife, he'd been fighting so hard to stay. There was so much to hold him to us all. "You can go now, Grandpa," I said, rubbing his arm as he took in another shallow breath. His mouth rested open, relaxed. His face wasn't his own, sallow and thin, missing the jovial humor and mischievous smile. I kissed his forehead. His breaths came further apart and I could feel a shift in his energy.

I opened up to energetically offer him whatever might come through. Peace, I hoped. I waited to feel the familiar rush move through me for him to receive, but instead of taking in energy, he released it. Energy moved from him and into my hands, down my arms, through my body, and out the soles of my feet back to the earth. Like an act of confession, he let go of what he wouldn't be carrying with him.

And finally I sensed Amy there. I'd been waiting and wondering, but hadn't felt her until then. While I opened to help release, she opened to accept. "Call me the 'spirit catcher,'" she said with a wink. It was a silver lining in the depths of loss, so odd and wonderful to be with her in this way, to hold sacred space in a dance of give-and-take on opposite sides of the looking glass. It was still not enough, would never be enough while I lived this life, but it was something knowing that no matter what was to come, she would be there holding a space of Joy, ready to catch us all.

Look at How Far You've Come

One day you'll be surprised to find that you've come so much farther than you ever realized. Without knowing it, you've been integrating your inner and outer worlds into a single life more and more each day. In fact, if someone were to ask you how to go about tuning in or receiving intuitive messages, you might actually find it difficult to articulate because your own starting point is suddenly now so far behind you. You may be left wondering how exactly you got here and when you made all this progress. You might even find that if you needed to, you would have difficulty figuring out how to break the process down and even begin to try to explain things to someone else, because it all just seems so natural now. It's a wonderful kind of shock to realize the distance you've gone.

In reflecting on how far you've come, you can also more easily see who you're becoming. Where do you see yourself moving with your subtle and spiritual insights in the future? Maybe your practice becomes putting your insights to use in your personal life. Maybe you go all in and offer psychic readings. Maybe you're a massage therapist and it becomes a part of your energetic practice.

Years after the Velveteen Rabbit reading, my aunt asked me if I practiced mediumship or did readings professionally. When I responded that I didn't, she expressed what a shame that was, because it was such a gift. I understood what she meant—that an ability to connect living and passed-on loved ones is meaningful and shouldn't be withheld. Also in this sentiment I understood that she felt it was rare. But from my perspective, I know that this isn't a rare ability that only I and select others possess. We all have these abilities. As I contemplated where I was headed, I knew at that time that my focus would be on helping others realize those abilities for themselves. Instead of people seeking readings from me, I wanted to help others learn to acquire that subtle information on their own.

I'm still using my skills personally and even professionally. Instead of giving people direct information in a reading, I've been focused on giving them tools so they can do it themselves. I've also aspired to help others teach by assisting professional psychics, mediums, and subtle energy intuitives in sharing their knowledge through their books. Because I have an understanding of the topic through both study and personal experience, I'm able to help them effectively communicate their messages to others.

This is what I was becoming. I was figuring out how to use my subtle skills in ways that felt authentic to me. This meant putting aside the assumption that in order to use your subtle abilities, you must be a professional psychic reader. Instead, my focus has been more on personal application and instruction for others. But in the future, who knows what else I may become.

What are *you* becoming?

Emerge

You've come a long way! Maybe you feel more confident about existing where you are now instead of feeling like you have to throw your life away in order to embrace this secret side of yourself. Maybe you're starting to feel like you have a sturdier footing in both worlds. And maybe you're even feeling ready to emerge from hiding to share your authentic self with others.

Revealing the hidden parts of yourself and sharing your secret spiritual world may not happen until you've been able to subtly confide in someone a bit here and a bit there, establishing a feeling of security over a long period of time. You may not feel ready to fully share things until you have such an astounding experience that you simply can't hold it back. The Velveteen Rabbit reading finally spurred me to share more with my husband, and hearing my sister while watching *Ghost* spurred me to share more with my dad.

If you haven't already realized by now, I'm a big movie watcher, and here is yet another parallel to my point, courtesy of a film. In the 1998 movie *Practical Magic*, Sally grows up cultivating her natural-born magical and intuitive abilities. Some everyday instances of her using these abilities include paying attention to the signs around her for warnings, intuiting who is on the other end of the phone before picking up a call, using ritual to attract and open up to the energy of her desires, and empathically connecting to a loved one from a great distance when they need help. The mainstream community has never accepted her and her family for their differences. All her life, she has wanted nothing more than to be "normal" and live happily like everyone else, without this magical side of herself. She shoves that part of herself aside and pursues an average life. It is only when her deeply loved sister is in grave danger that she finally accepts her magical abilities in order to try to save her, to the point where she opens up about it to others.

She calls a friend, saying, "You know the stuff that everyone's always whispering about me? … Well here's the thing … I'm a witch!"

This friend calls another friend and exclaims, "I've got the best news! Sally. Just. Came. *Out!*"[39]

---

39. *Practical Magic*, directed by Griffin Dunne (Warner Bros., 1998).

"What a *fabulous* affirmation," the second friend says, with a wry smile. It was a moment they'd obviously been waiting for.

The way Sally came out to her friends might be similar to the way you finally declare yourself as intuitive, psychic, or some other preferred phrasing. No matter the language you choose, the thing is, when you finally reveal yourself, your emergence may not be all that surprising to many of those you finally confide in. Often they'll already have noticed who you authentically are, even while you may have been trying your best to hide it. And because it's just naturally who they perceived you to be all along, it's not that big of a deal. While you might be waiting for them to be shocked at whatever you've carefully chosen to reveal in what feels like a hugely significant moment, their response might simply be, "Oh, I already knew that about you," or "That doesn't surprise me about you at all."

In one instance, I was sharing with a coworker how I hear other people's thoughts sometimes, but I usually only realize it when I hear a thought and then immediately the other person says it out loud. Sometimes I do catch on as I'm saying something and I realize that I'm actually speaking out loud the thought that the other person is having. His response was, "Oh yeah, you've totally said things I've been thinking before." Yet another moment of reveal that was already known!

In *Practical Magic*, those whom Sally finally opens up to, even those who had been her "frenemies" for most of her life, celebrate her self-acceptance and the sharing of her authentic self publicly. They welcome the news and are glad to finally get insight into things they'd suspected and been avidly curious about all along. It opens the door for them to finally ask questions and explore that side of themselves, too.

You'll probably find these kinds of instances in your life as well. Follow your intuition, share with those who resonate with you, and feel free to leave others in the dark. Just because you're sharing with select individuals doesn't mean you need to come out with details to everyone. Being discerning is a good thing, because sometimes it's just not worth sharing. But when you *do* finally share and it's with the right people, you might just find them saying, "Now that you mention it, I've experienced something like that before!"

Part 2
Answers from Secret Psychic Mentors

One of the things that helped me the most along my own secret psychic journey was hearing about the insights and experiences of others. The more I learned, the more I realized that the things I was going through weren't unusual, at least not for those who are called to develop these skills. In fact, they were downright *normal*! I found that much of what others talked about were also ways that I perceived things, or were also things that I did without really realizing it until they put it into words for me. By hearing about their experiences, I gained confirmation of my own, and that felt really good. When you start making connections with others who have a similar desire to learn about subtle skills and all things spiritual, I'm confident you'll be able to say the same. As un-normal as you might feel sometimes, believe me, when in secret psychic company, you are totally the norm.

Nothing convinced me of this more than when I began inquiring with those who have made their psychic skills a large focus of their professional lives. Specifically, it was hearing about their starting-point experiences that left me with goose bumps. I was astonished at how often my own start-ing-point experiences aligned exactly with theirs. I'm betting you'll feel the same, and in this section you'll have the chance to see that for yourself.

Here in part 2 are the questions I posed to twelve professional psychics, mediums, and subtle energy intuitives, along with their responses. The questions follow the progression of topics that you found in part 1, which means that they cover these specific categories:

- What it means to be a secret psychic
- Experience with subtle intuition
- Recognizing the natural occurrence of spirit communication
- Noticing when intuitive senses seep into everyday life
- How to integrate your spiritual experience into your daily life

In the following pages you'll see that each section begins with the question that was asked, followed by the answers that were provided by the various contributors. This way you can immediately see the range of perspectives all together to compare how the answers might differ from one person to another.

PRACTICE
Completing the Secret Psychic Questionnaire

Before you move ahead to read others' responses, you might want to take this opportunity to jot down your own answers to the questionnaire. This way, you'll be able to really see how your experience compares to others. You'll also be able to come back to the questionnaire to complete it again in the future and see how your responses might have changed over time.

You can either answer the questions in your journal as you come to them in the following pages before you read the contributors' responses, or jump to appendix 3 to find the questions lumped together in one place. There you can fill out your answers all at once and then come back to read the rest of part 2.

There are a lot of questions! Some of these are things you may not be able to answer if you're just starting out on your secret psychic journey. If that's the case, just skip over those. As I noted to the contributors, feel free to only answer the questions that you feel drawn to. Set aside a chunk of time in a quiet space where you'll really be able to feel into the space of each question. Allow this to be an entertaining exercise in self-exploration.

Introduction to Our Secret Psychic Mentors

I've had the benefit of being mentored by those with greater knowledge than I, and also then being a mentor to others to continue sharing that gained wisdom. A mentor is simply someone who provides guidance and imparts wisdom within a specific area, such as career. We're almost ready to delve into insight from others, but before we do, here is a brief introduction to each of our participants (presented in alphabetical order by last name), or, as I like to think of them, our Secret Psychic Mentors.

Melanie Barnum is a psychic, medium, international author of multiple books, intuitive counselor, life coach, and hypnotist who has been practicing professionally for over twenty years. Melanie helps others connect to their loved ones, discover their own greatness, and dive into their intuitive abilities through individual and group sessions, workshops, and mentoring.

Cyndi Dale is the author of twenty-seven internationally acclaimed books, including *Energy Healing for Trauma, Stress & Chronic Illness*. She has worked with over 65,000 clients and taught workshops worldwide.

Sherrie Dillard is an internationally renowned psychic, medium, and medical intuitive, and a bestselling author. She is an expert at helping others develop and understand their intuitive gifts. She has given over 60,000 readings and has been featured on national television for her work as a psychic detective. Sherrie has an MDiv in metaphysics and New Thought. She has taught intuition and spiritual development worldwide.

Granddaughter Crow (Dr. Joy Gray) is a professional psychic, teacher, and author and is internationally recognized as a medicine woman. She comes from a long lineage of spiritual leaders. As a child, she was fashioned and trained to serve the people through ministry. As a member of the Navajo Nation (Dinè) and a person of Dutch heritage, she is able to provide a sense of integration through life experience.

John Holland is an internationally known psychic medium, author, and spiritual teacher. He is the author of the best-sellers *Bridging Two Realms, Born Knowing, Psychic Navigator, The Psychic Tarot Oracle Deck,* and *The Mediumship Training Deck,* as well as three top-selling apps.

Jodi Livon, The Happy Medium®, has been a corporate psychic and intuitive coach for over three decades and is the author of The Happy Medium book series. She's the resident psychic on a television show airing in the Midwest and is a frequent guest on local and national radio.

Danielle MacKinnon is an animal communicator, psychic, and the Amazon #1 bestselling author of *Soul Contracts: Find Harmony and Unlock Your Brilliance* and *Animal Lessons: Discovering Your Spiritual Connection with Animals.* She has taught the psychic arts to students from more than sixty countries in her Danielle MacKinnon School.

Michael Mayo is an internationally respected medium, astrologer, and spiritual teacher. He brings a practical, grounded, and evidential style to his work. Throughout his fifteen-plus years of working with the spirit world, he has demonstrated his ability to connect with departed loved ones in both public demonstrations and private sittings. By bringing messages of love and hope from the spirit world, his mission is to show that we, like love, are eternal.

Chanda Parkinson has been a professional psychic intuitive and spiritual teacher for over fourteen years. She uses her psychic gifts, tarot, and astrology to assist others through transitions in life with clarity and compassion. As a teacher, she shares knowledge gained over the course of twenty-two years in the fields of intuitive arts, metaphysics, and human potential. Her messages are comforting, healing, supportive, practical, and delivered with great compassion and care.

Troy Parkinson has been offering his services as a medium for over twenty years. He is the author of *Bridge to the Afterlife: A Medium's Message of Hope and Healing*.

Kristy Robinett is a professional psychic medium, psychic detective, author of a dozen books, astrologer, kitchen witch, gardener, cat hugger, dog lover, wife, mom, and grandma.

Jurema Silva is an internationally celebrated intuitive healer, spiritual mentor, speaker, and teacher. She is a gifted and inspirational woman who inherited a range of healing techniques from her native country of Brazil. Jurema has been transforming people's lives in the US and worldwide.

When I initially contacted our Secret Psychic Mentors, they were all so enthusiastic about the focus of this book. They recognized the need for it, and many expressed that this type of resource would have been an immense help to them when they were starting out. Cyndi Dale shared further, saying, "So many of my students have to hide their abilities for a variety of reasons, such as no one around them being similar to them, religion, feeling odd… This is such a common experience." They wanted to help in any way they could, and they delivered by providing a wealth of answers to feed the many questions that any budding secret psychic is sure to have.

The Secret Psychic Questionnaire Q&A

What do you see are the key benefits of engaging with our intuitive and spiritual abilities?

Melanie Barnum: I feel the benefits are infinite! But some of the key benefits are: When we tune in, we are accessing so much more of our natural abilities than when we don't, and we can take advantage of the guidance that using our sixth senses offers. We have an increased layer of wisdom not available to those who ignore their gifts. It makes us feel better and more connected to life in general. We become more relaxed. As we engage, we become more connected to those around us. We understand that we are all connected and we become more compassionate toward others.

Cyndi Dale: I believe intuition is a way of connecting to the invisible or inaudible, the subtle realms that actually dictate much of what occurs in the physical realm. In other words, intuition is a vessel for comprehending what is occurring in the causal. Based on the insights we're able to gather, we can make decisions that can serve ourselves and others to the highest level of goodness.

Sherrie Dillard: Becoming aware of and developing our intuitive and spiritual abilities increases our self-awareness and assists us in moving through our limitations to create a better and happier life. It also provides us with helpful insights into everyday issues and challenges, provides comfort, and illustrates that higher guidance is always available.

Granddaughter Crow (Dr. Joy Gray): I see the biggest benefit as being whole. Connecting the physical, emotional, mental, and spiritual aspects of self allows for a fuller experience here on Mother Earth. Plus, it just makes life so much more magickal.

John Holland: Too many people think of psychic ability as how it's represented in TV and movies, and it's not like that at all. It's not about fortune telling. It's about learning to use these abilities in your everyday life: in your relationship, your work, your career. It's not just about the future. It can help you *now*, in every aspect of this life. It can even help you with your health.

Some people become so sensitive. Their abilities affect their energy centers and they become anxious. When you start to learn psychic ability, you have to quiet your own mind, because how can you know when an intuitive thought comes in when you have so much chatter in your head? If you were to regularly meditate (it could be five to ten minutes of slowing down your mind), it also has wonderful health benefits: you slow your blood pressure down, it slows *you* down, and it helps every organ in your body.

Jodi Livon: Intuition is a free and natural resource. Being alive to it can enhance every area of our life.

Danielle MacKinnon: Being psychic isn't a gift reserved for only special people. I believe we are *all* intuitive and we're meant to discover, engage with, and use those skills to enhance our normal, everyday existence. Imagine how helpful it is to intuitively know which is the best car for you or that you shouldn't trust someone. The key benefits to being intuitive are simply a better, easier life.

Chanda Parkinson: An enhanced sense of self-awareness, greater alignment with the decisions we make in life, to move through life's conundrums with greater ease, and fostering a greater understanding of our connection with all living things.

Troy Parkinson: The benefits of engagement include a new perspective on life, a profound sense of awe and wonderment, an expanded community of like-minded people, and overall balance of spirit, mind, and body.

Kristy Robinett: Trusting your intuition strengthens your life choices. It anchors you to your natural vibration, giving you an advantage in all areas of your life, from love to business.

Jurema Silva: By engaging with our intuitive and spiritual abilities, we gain a sense of protection, enlightenment, confidence, serenity, and awareness of the self. Knowing that we all can tap into our intuition to find answers, guidance, and comfort, especially during times of grief and confusion, is a blessing. Intuition is our naturally inherited tool to communicate with the spiritual world. Through this connection, we can benefit by attaining confidence, trust, and the will to live.

When you first started learning about psychic/intuitive abilities, was it something that life thrust upon you or were you drawn to it with your own natural curiosity?

Melanie Barnum: For me, it was both! I'd always been able to "read" people, but I thought everyone did that. I was always drawn to intuition and psychic abilities and thought it was very cool. But my life really changed when one day, over twenty years ago, it felt like I was hit over the head and I heard the words aloud, "You need to do this work now!" It made absolutely no sense but at the same time made all the sense in the world! Instantly I knew it was inevitable that I would absolutely, eventually, become a professional psychic.

Cyndi Dale: I was naturally intuitive as a child and didn't know there was something unusual about me until my parents started to react. Strong Christians, they soon informed me that I was "playing with matches," if not the devil himself. I was surprised and hurt to be treated like I was doing something wrong when I was simply connecting to the world in my own instinctual way.

Sherrie Dillard: I was intuitive from a young age and saw and communicated with spirits. It felt normal to me.

Granddaughter Crow (Dr. Joy Gray): I was lucky enough to be raised by a long lineage of spiritual leaders. Although some family members are devout Christians, even under their faith I was able to develop certain gifts, such as seeing visions and speaking prophecies when I was a child. However, many people will go through a harsh life event that will lead to an awakening.

John Holland: I was very sensitive as a child and I knew things I couldn't possibly have known. I knew when people were going to visit unexpectedly at the house and I used to pick up other people's thoughts. I was fascinated with magic, ghosts, and religion. So it started very young, but I hid it. An automobile accident when I was thirty awoke the abilities. That's when it came out full blast and I had to study how it was all working. That's when I found my true life. It put me on the path that I needed to be on. It was a wake-up call for me.

Jodi Livon: It was thrust upon me in a big way. At one point, I knew either I would have my intuition or it would have me. Once I surrendered, I fell in love with it.

Danielle MacKinnon: I was always interested in intuition, but I grew up believing it wasn't real. Initially, I opened to it out of necessity. My dog was sick and no one could figure out why. As a last resort, I took her to a pet psychic and it changed my life. If she hadn't been sick, it would have taken me much longer to overcome society's view of the psychic and spiritual world. I'll always be grateful for that experience.

Chanda Parkinson: I was drawn to it naturally out of a space of curiosity after losing several family members in a condensed time frame. I wanted to know what happens to us when we die, and it sparked a yearslong learning and exploring journey.

Troy Parkinson: I was drawn to the work through my own natural curiosity. I had a death in the family and a friend of our family passed away in the same day, and that led me to start exploring psychic, spiritual, and mediumistic websites and training.

Kristy Robinett: I was born with the gift of seeing, feeling, hearing, and knowing. For decades I thought it was a curse. I was raised in a religious household (Lutheran—Missouri Synod) and taught that all I was experiencing was evil and occult, so I thought something was wrong with me. Because I saw the dark side of intuition, I received the dark side of intuition—predictions of death, loss, and despair—and that simply validated my parents' (the church's) teachings.

Jurema Silva: Psychic, intuitive, and healing abilities run in my family. According to my late mother, I started "seeing" spirits when I was three or four years old. I was raised as a Catholic in Brazil. In terms of culture, ethnicity, and religion, Brazil is one of the most diverse countries in the world. It is the perfect environment to be curious about the miscellany of society that my country was offering. I started exploring a variety of religious beliefs, human behavior and energies, cultures, and the meaning of spirituality. Most importantly, I wanted to understand the phenomena of intuition and healing. The fact that I was seeing spirits and could sense energy from other people and places drove me to study and search for explanations. I knew I was different from most teenagers at that time. I also grew up listening to stories from family members and friends of people who could contact the dead and heal diseases. They had intuitive abilities and often made visits to psychics for readings.

In my early twenties I moved to the US and started a successful business that I operated for decades until tragedy changed everything. After the loss of a dear loved one, I experienced a revelation. A veil was completely pulled aside. During that period of pain and awakening, I received several messages with details about my new mission and purpose in this world. Still, it took me two years to completely detach myself from my successful business, and my ego, before I humbly accepted my new journey.

How did you begin learning about your psychic abilities?

Melanie Barnum: I set out to learn everything I could. I took local classes with psychics/mediums who were not well known, some in continuing education classes at local schools and many at Omega, a holistic learning institute. I also devoured every book I could that not only explained psychic abilities but, more importantly for me, was also a memoir, sharing the author's (psychic's) real life and stories from readings they had done.

I became certified in so many modalities, including other healing forms, i.e., reiki, hypnosis, and reflexology, on top of my more specific psychic certifications such as Psychic Detective, Certified Coordinate Remote Viewer, Past Life Facilitator, Psychic Medium, etc. I felt that learning all aspects of energy work helped with my psychic development.

During this time, I began offering free readings by phone, internet, and in person. The internet back then, twenty-plus years, was very slow and I did them in chat rooms. I paid attention to what felt comfortable and right for me personally and then pushed myself to try the other stuff, specifically the different psychic senses.

Cyndi Dale: I shut my intuitive gifts down when I was a young teenager, but I continued reading supernatural books. I was intrigued and fascinated by all things ghosts, ESP, healing, sci-fi, and the like. I then reactivated my abilities when a therapist suggested I was psychic, not only codependent. At that time, in my early twenties, I was traveling a lot and started to observe the healing customs of other cultures, which was refreshing, as everything psychic was hidden away in dark closets in the US. I took my first class in energy healing at twenty-eight and was hooked. Finally, my sense of energy colors, bodies, and fields was validated by people who could explain my reality to myself.

Sherrie Dillard: Reading books gave me an understanding as to what I was experiencing. I also sought out others who were using their gifts and were more advanced than I was.

Granddaughter Crow (Dr. Joy Gray): In my thirties, I opened up to earth-based spirituality and my gifts blew wide open. I learned my gifts through reading, classes, journaling, and finding a support group so I would not feel so crazy with my growing understanding of the unseen world.

John Holland: Growing up, I read any books that I could find on psychic ability. I didn't stop the interest; it was always there right up until my teenage and young adult years. But when the accident happened and the abilities were back even stronger, I needed to know how this was happening, why it was happening, and how to shut it off. I learned about how the mechanics of psychic ability work, like the energy centers (the chakras), breathwork, color, and the three clairs (clairaudience, clairvoyance, clairsentience). I really got into it because I wanted to control it; I didn't want *it* to control me. Then, little by little, the mediumship started happening.

Learning about the energy systems of the body gave me a solid foundation. It seemed to always come down to chakra, meditation, aura, and breath. You are one big psychic antenna. I needed to learn to control that, and now I have the ability to turn it on and turn it off at will, so that I'm not overwhelmed by my surroundings or people around me.

Jodi Livon: I paid attention to my intuitive leads and tracked how they worked or how they didn't and why. I studied patterns.

Danielle MacKinnon: I took a weekend-long pet psychic course and discovered my innate animal communication skills. From that moment on, everything I did was focused on delving in further. I read books, I played with tarot cards, I became a Reiki master... I immersed myself as much as I could. Not everything resonated with me, but the things that did have stuck with me.

Michael Mayo: My introduction to the spirit world was rather unexpected. I stumbled into a mediumship demonstration where a medium gives messages to the audience depending on whose loved one in spirit comes forward. When he came to me, he said that I was a medium and that I needed to begin my development because I would one day do what he was doing.

Shocked by his prophecy, I decided to see if he was correct by attending a psychic development circle taught by a lovely lady named Barbara. She would become my teacher for several years. Before this, I'd had no prior experience with mediumship or psychic awareness. It was through the years of dedicated development that I began cultivating my abilities. I also read many books on the topic and worked on meditation.

Chanda Parkinson: With the help of a mentor, who pointed me in the right areas to explore, I started with Reiki and Tarot and expanded eventually to include my psychic and mediumship abilities.

Troy Parkinson: I started by sitting in a development circle for two years and then continued to work on building my abilities through endless reading and research.

Kristy Robinett: When I began to accept the abilities as a gift, I taught myself in an unconventional way. I read true crime books with a notebook beside me, and I created a secret language between my guides and myself. What would a drowning feel like? A stabbing? Was there one person there or many? Did I see water or woods? I read the books and tested the language, my guides, myself, and my intuition.

What do you wish you'd known when you were first discovering your psychic abilities?

Melanie Barnum: One thing I wish I'd understood more was that everyone receives psychic information in different ways. Although there are many similarities, we are all unique in the way we receive psychic impressions.

Cyndi Dale: That they are normal. That everyone is psychic, whether or not they are aware of it, and that these innate abilities, like any capability, deserve to be explained, trained, honed, and practiced with. Oh, and I also wish that someone would have taught me about psychic boundaries! That we can absorb others' energies and that there are ways to refrain from doing so.

Sherrie Dillard: I didn't fully know the wonderful life that it would help me to create.

Granddaughter Crow (Dr. Joy Gray): The experience of the "ego snapback." Yes, I coined this phrase. The ego snapback is the time after the spiritual experience, and thoughts like, "What just happened?" "Am I crazy?' "Who do I think I am?" come flooding in. I see this as the logical/linear mind challenging a new concept in order to understand it more—it feels harsh with thoughts of doubt, but that is natural too. It does get easier.

Jodi Livon: Boundaries! It would have made a monumental difference to have learned about them early on. It would have saved me from taking on other people's "stuff" so often!

Danielle MacKinnon: Although I didn't discover my psychic abilities until I was thirty, I don't have any regrets. If I had been exposed to this at an earlier age, I wouldn't have been ready to embrace it like I did. Everything happened at the best, more perfect time.

Michael Mayo: I wish I would have known that connecting to your psychic abilities derives from not trying to get information. That passivity and surrender are the keys to accessing information. Contrary to everything else that we do in our lives, mediumship and psychic awareness work best when we don't try to get the information. I wish that I would have understood that if I wanted to get information, I had to cultivate a sense of neutrality about the entire process and get rid of the desire for a specific outcome. The more that you can just describe what you're experiencing without trying to understand the information, the more accurate it will be.

Chanda Parkinson: That no two people receive psychically in the same way. We are all different! I tried hard to be like the psychics I admired, and discovered my gifts opened much more naturally when I let that go and allowed my gifts instead.

Troy Parkinson: I wished I'd known that it is a long game and that there is no "arrival." Development is a lifelong process and will have its ebbs and flows.

Kristy Robinett: I wish I'd recognized that it is a gift rather than a curse. I wasted so much time hiding and trying to conform to what society thought psychic abilities were. It wasn't until I discovered multiple resources (books, social media groups, conferences, workshops, and a beautiful group of like-minded people) that I felt more comfortable blazing my own path instead of attempting to satisfy old, conventional, and outdated ideas.

Jurema Silva: What to do with it. How to serve. Did I have to do anything? Intuition is the best tool to navigate life's challenges. It is a portal that connects us to the spiritual world and facilitates communication from us to them, and vice versa. Intuitive abilities are an innate mechanism. Without noticing it, we use our intuition to various degrees every day. The question of what to do with our intuition is not complicated to answer: We've been using our intuition daily without even realizing it, and we use it for simple, everyday issues. And we can develop this ability even further on our life journey as a way to elevate, enlighten, and guide ourselves, and perhaps others.

What would have helped you most when you began your own spiritual and metaphysical journey?

Melanie Barnum: I had different mentors over the years, but none that I could really call on whenever I had questions—they were more like teachers rather than mentors. I feel that would have helped a lot. I also would have liked to have people in my circle that had the same gifts as me but were better than me. I feel like that would have helped me progress to the next level. I have not found anyone specifically, to this day, that I feel totally comfortable sharing my personal life with. Meaning, there are a lot of people in my area that I don't really vibe with. I feel I am very "normal"—lacrosse mom, coffee with friends, average life. I don't do a lot of gatherings with other psychics. Most of the people I've met that are in this business in my area, unfortunately, are more "woowoo," which to me means they are more in their spiritual self and less grounded on a daily basis. I can't do that. I only turn on my intuition when I'm working (unless, of course, it's personal).

I also wish there were people around me, again, that were better than me but that worked in a similar way. Most people, I've found, that want to hang out with me on a personal level seem to want my help developing their abilities. Not that that's a bad thing—we always learn—but I'd like it to be the other way around! I kind of crave the connections to other psychics who I can vibe with and that are more developed in their practices so I can learn even more. It helps to raise my energy also and I love that.

Cyndi Dale: (1) A clear explanation of *psychic*, (2) a review of all the different cultures that have employed the psychic ability—and how, (3) a quick process for establishing psychic boundaries, (4) easy ways to figure out which gifts I innately have and which I might have shut down, (5) simple processes for practicing the gifts, and (6) people to practice with.

Sherrie Dillard: It would have helped to know that I could trust what was happening and that using intuition is practical and not as "out there" as we may initially think.

Granddaughter Crow (Dr. Joy Gray): I think that it would have been tremendously helpful if someone would have told me, "Relax and remember that this is how you came into the world—it was merely blocked for a number of years by societal influences. You are now remembering who and what you truly are."

John Holland: My journey happened years ago, and the words *psychic* and *intuitive* weren't really around. It was not as much in the public as it is now. Knowing a like-minded person would have been helpful. There was an aunt who was the closest thing to it. She was into dreams and had dream books, and she would use numerology, so it was helpful. I was a child, and little did I know that psychic ability was part of that side of the family. My grandmother had it, but they used to just say, "Grandma knows things." So having like-minded people to talk to would have helped, because even the books back in the sixties were hard to find. I ended up trying to find anything that I could, but there wasn't a lot in those days.

Jodi Livon: Boundaries! Knowing where my space begins and ends would have been priceless. This would have helped me understand how to stay in my own lane and also not give away my energy.

Danielle MacKinnon: When I began my journey to rediscover my intuition, I tried to get my husband to start his journey. I dragged him to classes, I tried educating him, and I signed him up for events. This didn't go over so well, as he had no intention of starting his own journey at that time. Now I know that it works much better to let others have their own path, at their own pace. When I let go of trying to make my husband come along with me, he eventually made the choice to come along with me.

Chanda Parkinson: Focus. I was sort of all over the place in the beginning. It took me years to narrow down the areas that were my strengths.

Kristy Robinett: Like-minded people.

Jurema Silva: It would have helped if I hadn't been so doubtful about my own abilities. At first, I wasn't 100 percent sure if I had any intuitive abilities. It also would have helped if I hadn't had certain expectations about what others would say or think when I revealed my gifts to them. I should have stripped away all these misconceptions and doubts at the beginning of my journey. The first time I truly felt confident and was not self-judgmental about my abilities was when I was at an event and strangers came to me for healing and guidance. It was then that I placed my faith in myself and trusted the Source.

Did you feel you had to keep this part of yourself a secret from others? If so, why?

Melanie Barnum: It's hard to tell people you are a psychic. Some are totally into it and are in awe. Others that haven't experienced it or that are doubting just flat out don't believe it's real and think you are full of it. And, for some, it goes against everything they were raised to believe in, especially if they are religious. People also have a tendency to view you differently after that, until they see you're normal, like them. And still others will thrust their hands in your face and tell you to read their palm and tell them their future. I don't prove my abilities to anyone to get them to believe in what I and so many others do unless they pay me for a session. That is just too exhausting.

Cyndi Dale: Absolutely, even as a small child. Once I was shamed for "making things up" or "doing the devil's work," I stopped talking about my inclinations and insights. Even when I started going to classes in my late twenties, I didn't talk about what I was learning with most of my friends and family. It was too "weird" and "spooky." So I went to my classes and read my New Age books and kept it to myself. When my family did find out, no one would converse with me at events. I was "too strange."

Sherrie Dillard: I didn't feel that I needed to keep this secret. However, I was selective about who I confided in, as I understood that not everyone would accept and believe my experiences.

Granddaughter Crow (Dr. Joy Gray): At first I was open with a small group found at my local metaphysical shop. However, I hid it from the mundane workplace. I was afraid of being misunderstood or labeled as crazy.

John Holland: Yes, because I was the different one in the family. I hid it because I was called names. I was called strange and weird. And when your own family starts saying it to you, then you learn to hide the ability. I hid it or just stopped talking about it until I was many years older. As an adult, some of my friends knew I had this ability.

Jodi Livon: Yes, I had to keep my intuition and mediumistic abilities a secret because my very conservative family was not open to the concept.

It was all wrapped up in my being a super-sensitive child, which was frowned upon. At the time, few understood anything about being sensitive, so my family was not alone.

Danielle MacKinnon: I didn't feel I needed to keep it a secret from others, but I know that some others wish I had kept it a secret.

Chanda Parkinson: No, I didn't keep it a secret, even though I knew others might have certain reactions, and they did. However, this level of transparency about who I really am is more a by-product of my temperament and personality. I had every reason to keep things secret, growing up in a rural North Dakota town. It took a long time for my hometown community to embrace and accept this, and I have definitely lost a lot of friends along the way.

Troy Parkinson: I first developed my abilities in Boston, and when I returned home to Fargo, North Dakota, I thought for sure I would be run out of town if I shared these gifts. Psychic skills and mediumship fall outside the traditional Christian model, and so the pushback from family and community can be challenging. It took me five to six years before I "came out of the psychic closet" publicly.

Kristy Robinett: Absolutely. Being raised Lutheran, attending parochial school, I was taught that heaven was up toward the sky, in the land of the clouds. I was taught that hell was down below, and if you weren't baptized, didn't go to church, or pretty much weren't a Lutheran, that was the place you went. I was taught that purgatory was something Catholics made up in order to give some an out. I was taught that God judged, Satan ruled, and that there wasn't a gray area. Then there I was, seeing, hearing, feeling, sensing, and communicating with spirits who were telling me firsthand accounts of their afterlife, and it was hardly anything like what I had been told. How was a kid supposed to tell an adult anything different?

Jurema Silva: I did keep my gifts from others for some time. First, I wasn't sure, or perhaps I didn't want to know about my potential. Years ago, I felt the need to fit into society, and revealing my gifts opened me up to criticism.

I avoided my gifts for many years, until my personal experience opened the veil between myself and the spiritual world. It is still not clear if everyone in my life knows exactly what I do. Some think that I am just a Reiki practitioner. And that is fine. People who are not involved or do not understand the intuitive arts may not need a deeper explanation.

If you felt you needed to keep your psychic abilities secret, did this lead to an experience of dissociation, as though you were living two different lives? If yes, what was this like for you and how did you handle it, along with any feelings of isolation, sadness, anxiety, etc.?

Melanie Barnum: After all this time and my many published books on psychic abilities, I feel somewhat legit. This sounds humorous but true. I have felt at times that I needed to keep it separate. It is definitely not the first thing I tell people when I meet them, though when asked, I offer the truth. The one thing I've found over the years is that although I don't open up to my daughter's friends or family unless prompted, they brag about me. I didn't realize they did it until quite recently. That makes me feel really good. I don't feel isolated, because I am a normal, average mother, wife, and community member, even though I don't offer up my abilities on the regular. My family and friends believe in me and who I am, and that is the best feeling in the world—along with getting some amazing, life-altering psychic hits during readings!

Cyndi Dale: Until I was about six or so, I didn't feel an immediate need to hide my thoughts, pictures, or senses of things. Once my parents started getting upset, I found that I couldn't just turn off my gifts or insights. They were still there, but I did stop talking about them. That actually left me feeling strange and lonely. Once my family problems intensified, I sometimes relied on my intuition to figure out what was *really* going on but had to dissociate from "reality" because the difference between the intuitive realms and the family patterns confused me. I would shut down. I learned not to share my truth.

Even when I began training in my late twenties, I felt split. There was the me that *so* enjoyed learning *everything* I could about intuition, healing, and energy, and the me that had to show up at family events and speak to others while hiding my inner self. I've talked about this split a lot in therapy, even quite recently—and I'm well beyond my twenties! I brought up an event in which I suddenly felt shameful and shut down. My therapist explained that I was probably picking up on a lot of information that showed "things were not what they seemed" and I reverted to my old behavior of shutting down to stop feeling uncomfortable.

Sherrie Dillard: I felt more guarded with sharing my experiences than dissociated.

Granddaughter Crow (Dr. Joy Gray): I did feel like I had to compartmentalize myself. It was difficult perceiving the world differently than I had before. I even tried to shut it down, to no avail. I felt a little fractured. I journaled *a lot*!

John Holland: People who are sensitive children are usually loners anyways. They're psychically sensitive. I lived in my own world! I was into art. I would draw with a flashlight at night under the covers in my bed. So I was a loner and I've always been a little isolated anyway. Did it isolate me even more? Yes and no. Keeping it hidden kept me a little isolated because there was no one to share it with.

Jodi Livon: I felt like God was the one directing me to move in a certain way, so knew I was doing nothing wrong. I was confused as to why my family didn't trust their own intuition and why they seemed mad at me when I just "knew" things.

Chanda Parkinson: Though I chose not to keep it a secret, I do recall the ongoing feeling of living two separate lives, especially because I was also working a full-time job and doing work as a psychic on the side for some time. It was as if I was patiently waiting for my "real life" to begin, when I would be able to fully step into my gifts and utilize them professionally. At some point, the other things I was doing at some point began to feel inauthentic.

Kristy Robinett: For years I hid the gift and turned my back on my guides. It was as if I had headphones on and they kept lifting the headphones off my spiritual ear and yelling for me to pay attention and yet I pretended I wasn't hearing them. Those with small kids may understand it best by being able to ignore the insistent "Mom, mom, mom, mom!" That's what I tried to do. It was lonely. It was sad. I was filled with anxiety. I wanted so badly to have someone understand what I was experiencing, to tell me it was okay and help explain it to me. Instead, I felt like an alien. I felt weird.

For those who are in the place of secrecy, what advice would you give them?

Melanie Barnum: I would tell them to keep practicing. However, anything you do in life should provide you with some form of pleasure, so if this is causing you more grief than happiness, then don't focus on it now. Leave it alone until it makes you happy. When you become more confident with your abilities, you'll feel more comfortable sharing with others.

Also, know your audience. Not everyone needs to be a part of your psychic life, just like you don't go home and talk to everyone about spreadsheets if you are an accountant. When you're with people you are comfortable with and who respect you, you will be able to share this part of your life. If this is proving difficult, go online to chat groups of other psychics/mediums. You will probably find others there just like you!

Cyndi Dale: Find a place. A person. A class. Even an online class. A community of people devoted to the ethical and joyful use of their intuition or healing abilities. Read books. And take chances. Learn some phrases that can be used in "normal reality" to share your insights, such as "I'm feeling uncomfortable, like something isn't quite lining up," or "I have a different sense of this situation than you might." I make my living as an intuitive and don't go around and say things like "I see this psychic picture" when I'm at a party. Even now, I use code words in "normal" society for psychic, energy, healing, and intuition. I say I'm holistic or spiritual. I speak from my truth and let others speak from their own.

Sherrie Dillard: Accept yourself and your intuition. You are who you need most.

Granddaughter Crow (Dr. Joy Gray): You are not alone. What you are experiencing is natural. Once you get more used to your gifts, they will naturally and organically come out within safe environments. First, get used to how you are perceiving. The rest will come when it is time.

Jodi Livon: It is both a responsibility and a gift. What we do with it is our gift back.

Danielle MacKinnon: As I moved along my spiritual path, the people and the experiences I surrounded myself with changed. Some people left my life, and it turned out that this was a good thing. I didn't realize until after they left that we weren't really a match. The more spiritual and in touch with my own emotions I became, the less tolerance I had for friendships that didn't serve me and the more that the people who *were* showing up were people who didn't demand that I hide my interests. They were accepting of what I was most interested in: my spirituality. There were a couple people along the way who chose to come along with me as well. While I grew and developed my skills, so did they. It all has to do with a person's readiness to grow and evolve—and the method they choose to do so.

Chanda Parkinson: It's okay, especially in the beginning, to be cautious about who you choose to share your gifts with. It is most helpful at the start to share only with those who you know will be open to it or most gently care for and support you. Do the work of fully accepting who you are, and this will make it much easier to share with the world. Psychic and spiritual gifts are a part of you, and so it can seem deeply personal when you feel slighted or attacked for who you are. Take that path as slowly as you need to, but be willing to do the work.

Troy Parkinson: Find like-minded people via social media, etc. Look for your community's Unitarian Church or other progressive organization. I know in small towns it's hard to find community when you might live in a very conservative environment. But you might be surprised to know that by raising your voice, you might find others willing to connect.

Kristy Robinett: Weird is cool. So stay in your weirdness and other true weirdos will find you.

Jurema Silva: It is very hard to let go of social norms and stand up for what we truly believe, and even harder when the subject concerns psychic abilities. Understanding our gifts, knowing that intuition is naturally inherited, and accepting your unique abilities are the first steps to gaining confidence and strength. Once this happens, we can become less fearful of others, since we are confident in ourselves.

What are three tips you would give for others practicing their abilities and evolving on their spiritual journey if they're working at it all alone?

Melanie Barnum: Read books! My books, and so many others, have a plethora of exercises to help you practice and hone your skills, from total beginner to advanced, professional psychic.

Go online to reputable psychics and chat rooms! You'd be amazed at what you can learn by reading articles and information on others' sites. You can also practice, anonymously if you want, through chat rooms and discussions.

Take classes and try to find a mentor! There are classes available all over the world. You can go in person to a one-hour local class, go away for a week and immerse yourself in delectable psychic playtime, or take online workshops and seminars—many of which are available for free!

Cyndi Dale: You can still attend an online class! That will provide a community. Besides that, compose a lesson plan like you are taking yourself seriously and use it. Keep a journal so you can follow your own journey—count yourself as important. Also, know that you can't really share an intuitive insight unless someone wants it. If you have to keep things to yourself, write it down somewhere so you are keeping track.

Sherrie Dillard: There are people who will understand and may be going through a similar experience. Most don't talk about their experiences for fear of being looked at as odd or different. Take the chance and find connection with like-minded individuals. There are online communities that you can be a part of, talk to a friend or someone you trust, or take a class.

Granddaughter Crow (Dr. Joy Gray): (1) Learn how to ground and center, (2) set aside time to meditate and breathe, and (3) journal—record your experiences and begin to spot patterns.

John Holland: People are lucky right now! There are online communities, bookstores—it's everywhere! There are plenty of places now to take a meditation class, so you can know what is and isn't your ability, to know what your mind is. Get to know your own spirit first. People want to run before they walk. Learn the mechanics first.

Go with a group or teacher that you resonate with, because not every group or class is going to be for you and it's important to resonate with the people. Sometimes there's someone in a group or class who may tend to show off. You want to be in a cohesive group. When I started developing, I sat there and listened. You are not there to be a star! You're there to take in the information.

Everybody has the potential for this. Some have more potential that they're born with, and some people have less potential and they just need to work harder on it. If you're beginning, start off with your psychic ability first. That is the foundation of how mediumship works, if you're going to also investigate that. Find your psychic strength and work with that. The rest will grow also.

Jodi Livon: Read, read, read! Ask questions, learn boundaries, meditate, take classes if you find ones that feel right, and absolutely always steer yourself in the direction of the highest good for all.

Danielle MacKinnon: Find a community of others like yourself. This doesn't have to be an in-person community. Today there are many online communities full of sensitive, spiritual people looking for connection.

Read, read, read. There are so many wonderful books available for learning. Even if you can't "practice" the technique with another person, remember that everything is still energy. Just reading about a technique gets you closer to mastering it!

Have fun with yourself. When you are trying out something new, try it in a fun way! So many of my students forget that they're learning to open their intuition because it's enjoyable. The more fun you have, the easier it is to do!

Michael Mayo: The nice thing about the early part of one's development is that it can be done entirely alone. The first steps in your journey are about sensing and feeling your own energy. Learn to sit in the quiet of your own awareness. Train your awareness to not search for meaning in everything that you experience, but rather, be an observer. Don't try to control it. Let it happen to you.

Be okay with getting nothing or getting it wrong. So many times students of this topic feel like they need to get it right or have a visual or obvious experience or otherwise it wasn't valuable. This is not true. A lot of development in your psychic awareness comes from passive experiences—learning to be still and quiet, learning to surrender to what's floating in and out of your awareness, learning to notice, accept, and let it go.

Chanda Parkinson: Guided meditation is a wonderful and consistent way to access greater aspects of your own spiritual gifts and abilities. Explore many different areas of ability and work to get clear on what your gifts and abilities are. Then focus on your strengths and work to build those first. When you have a foundational working practice, you can more easily expand into other areas of intuitive, spiritual, and psychic development. It is also helpful to work with a mentor who can support you in the opening of your gifts and abilities. Finally, get in a spiritual community you feel drawn to, either in person or online. Having a space to explore what's happening to you can continue to assist you in your own understanding of spiritual concepts.

Troy Parkinson: Find online communities to connect to. Create a sacred space in your home to set the stage for your development. Order books and resources to help you in your home.

Kristy Robinett: (1) Trust. Trust in what you are hearing, feeling, seeing, sensing, etc., even if it feels strange or can't be reconciled in the current time and space.

(2) Believe. Believe in yourself. You can't trust yourself if you don't believe in yourself. Negative thoughts of anything, but especially of yourself, will make you trip on your true self.

(3) Practice. If you want to be in the major leagues of anything, you practice. The same goes for psychic abilities.

Jurema Silva: First, self-acceptance, self-value, and self-love. Second, releasing. Let go of self-punishment and self-condemnation. Detach yourself from emotional pain and from past unpleasant experiences. Go deep inside the heart to remove negative energy. It will be more difficult to connect with your higher self without releasing what weighs in your heart.... Third, empathy. When you understand that we all make mistakes, and our mistakes are life lessons and not punishments, you start to forgive not just you but the mistakes and missteps of others, too. Forgiveness and unconditional love will become part of your journey.

After practicing these three steps, you will be ready to touch the deepest realm of your intuition. When we reach the point of self acceptance and forgiveness, intuitive abilities start to develop very quickly.

Where and how did you find support, resources, and community to develop your skills?

Melanie Barnum: I really just started devouring everything I could regarding psychic abilities, from books to classes to readings. I shared my experiences, concerns, and celebrations with like-minded people in classes, though I often kept my professional practice secret because I wanted to be treated like everyone else in the class. I love being part of a practicing class—it raises the energy and the awareness of everyone there.

Cyndi Dale: I first studied internationally, because so many other cultures have long supported the mystical, whereas it's somewhat new in the United States. I also took community education classes (they are inexpensive), went to a spiritual church and joined a book group, and found local healing classes. If you have the time and money, take an online class or attend a workshop!

Sherrie Dillard: I read a lot and went to spiritual development classes.

Granddaughter Crow (Dr. Joy Gray): When the student is ready, the teacher will appear. Follow your curiosity; it will lead you to your next level. The teacher can be YouTube, a book, a local metaphysical shop, or an online group. Trust that whatever it is that gave you this gift will lead you to the type of support you would benefit from the most.

John Holland: I found some of my support by reading. I didn't just read books from John Edward and James Van Praagh; I went back to the classics also. I read a lot about psychic autobiographies like Elieen Garrett and Arthor Ford. I read Yogananda and Edgar Cayce. How did these people lead their lives? For those looking for resources, you should be able to find a spiritualist community where they have open circles that are free and you can come into a well-supported group with like-minded people.

Jodi Livon: I read the most amazing metaphysical books. The books came alive for me and served as beautiful teachers. I also studied religions from all around the world in college and later on my own. And, of course, I trusted in the guidance and love of my deceased paternal grandmother.

Danielle MacKinnon: A lot of the time, that special friend who can explore with you comes through something coincidental. The friend I explored with was my dog walker. She didn't know anything either, so it was a good match, as we were both open-minded.

Michael Mayo: I was lucky enough to find community at the local metaphysical bookstore where I studied for many years under the guidance of my first teacher, Barbara. That allowed me to join in community with other like-minded people. That being said, in today's world, there are a whole host of opportunities online to learn via remote online classes in the comfort of your own home. It is also why I created my own online school, the Oakbridge Institute, as a hub for mediumistic and psychic development. In addition to this, there are plenty of Facebook groups and online courses where you can connect with others in this field. Just make sure you connect with a teacher who is not fear-based in their teaching—that they recognize that there is nothing to fear from the spirit world, and they create a safe, comforting, and supportive environment for their students. Mediumship is developed best in a harmonious setting.

Chanda Parkinson: My library was an entire wall for many years. As an avid reader, and in the days before so much information could be found on the internet, I found tremendous learning support in books. I have pared back greatly as I've moved on from some areas of interest. I would choose books I was drawn to, on topics I was working on. I also spent a good deal of time speaking with my partner, Troy, who was also interested in and working on his own gifts and abilities. I found it super helpful to have a partner, friend, or buddy to develop and explore topics with.

Troy Parkinson: I found a Spiritualist church in Boston that had development classes. Then I went to the library and checked out as many books on mediumship as I could find. In the social media world, finding Facebook pages, websites, and YouTube and Instagram teachers is the first route. When you find someone you like, follow their work and get a sense of their style and work.

Kristy Robinett: I set my intention that I needed to find like-minded people, and within a few months I began to attract like-minded people.

Jurema Silva: Learning from others is very important when embarking on this journey. Knowledgeable teachers can share their experiences with navigating their own journeys and provide good insight into how you can develop your intuitive abilities. I also read as much as possible—books, articles, manuscripts. Reading about the history of psychic abilities and how other cultures practice intuition can help to guide you as you discover your path. Seek out others who are on a similar journey and share as much as possible. They might be able to recommend books or workshops that they found helpful in their own quest.

If your subtle abilities were initially something you kept secret, when did you finally begin to feel like this secret side of yourself was something you needed to share with others? What were some cues that indicated you were ready?

Melanie Barnum: At first, I "came out" as a hypnotist and reflexologist and reiki master. I felt that was safer and that there was more science behind it. It scared me less than it would have had I just said "Melanie Barnum, Psychic." I also listed myself as an intuitive counselor as opposed to a psychic or a medium because it seemed less threatening and less scary to put out there to the world. Now I rarely do the other work anymore. It was really just to boost my own confidence and self-esteem. I also began feeling more comfortable when I realized that every reading helped people and that, for the most part, I was usually very accurate. I say that with hesitation because I am still a bit insecure before every session, but that's okay. I feel like that actually helps me do a better reading—it kind of keeps me on my toes. When I started getting constant validation, it made it easier to share with the "nonbelievers" and those whom I had no clue as to whether they would think I was crazy or not.

Cyndi Dale: I didn't really feel ready but was sort of forced into coming clean. I heard spiritual guidance that told me to quit my job and start a business doing intuitive readings. It was a loud voice and one that I trusted—what I call God. I made business cards... they were pink with a rose on them... and was picking them up at the printing shop when I was suddenly filled with fear. I vowed I'd take my five hundred cards home and hide them. A woman at the store saw my box of cards, though, and said, "Wow, I'd love to get a reading!" She was a hairdresser and took a handful of cards, which she apparently passed out, and I started to get calls. I was in business and I didn't really even want to be!

Sherrie Dillard: Intuition and medium communication was such a significant part of my life that I readily opened up to others who I felt would be able to accept and understand what I was experiencing.

Granddaughter Crow (Dr. Joy Gray): Mundane people would give me a sideways look and say, "How did you know that?" I would simply smile—because I thought the things I saw/knew were obvious. I did not offer others unsolicited exchanges. People started coming to me with situations and asking me what I thought. It was natural.

Jodi Livon: I was pregnant with my second son and had a strong sense that it was time I step ever so tenderly out of the psychic closet. I had been working professionally as a psychic for hand-picked business owners but rarely referred to myself as a psychic. My husband's support pushed me over the edge, so out of the closet I stepped. I wrote a book called *The Happy Medium*, and it instantly cast me into the wonderful world of media. I've been the resident psychic and a regular guest on a fabulous television show airing in the Midwest, *Twin Cities Live*, since my first book launched. (I wrote another Happy Medium book as well!)

Chanda Parkinson: I remember a time when I woke up day after day clear that this was my path forward, that it wasn't going away, and that it was just a matter of time before I started sharing my gifts freely. I had this undeniable and inescapable pull toward this work. When I tried to deny or resist it, something would happen to bring my gifts and the impulse to do this work even more strongly. I was so fortunate that I discovered so many supportive, loving souls around me who were eager to see me go public with my gifts. I had spent months doing practice readings with others and securing feedback, which I am so grateful for.

Troy Parkinson: I received strong encouragement from my wife to share my work more actively. I started by creating my own development circles and then began to hold workshops. Ultimately, I left my full-time position to pursue my work as a medium.

Kristy Robinett: To a degree, I think I continue to keep my abilities quiet although maybe not secret. I remember years ago I read for an Oscar Award–winning actor. He gave me two points of wisdom. The first was never to read your reviews. The second was never to tell anyone what you do for a living while at a dinner party, because you'll never be able to eat your dinner while warm. A professional baseball player doesn't go around telling everyone he's a professional baseball player unless asked what he does for a living. Why do psychics or light workers feel they need to tell everyone what or who they are? They don't. It doesn't mean lack of self. I also firmly believe everyone has the psychic muscle; it just depends on if it's developed or not.

Jurema Silva: The intensity and frequency of signs, messages, and perceptions is one of the clues that can indicate a person is ready. It is almost as if your heart is trying to communicate with you in a very subtle way. The more messages you receive, signs you see, and visions you are able to perceive, the stronger your intuition has become. As soon as you feel that something very special and extraordinary is happening to you, seek out others to help guide you on your new journey.

Do you feel that the call to develop and work with our intuitive abilities is part of a spiritual experience and/or an awakening of the authentic self? Why or why not?

Melanie Barnum: To me, it feels like it is a natural progression of our lives. It's almost as though we have always had these gifts, but it is becoming more prevalent and more accepted so we talk about it more. It is definitely part of our authentic selves—whether it is an awakening or not depends upon each person's experience. For me, it was kind of a call to action. I knew from the moment I heard the initial words "You have to do this work now" that I was about to open to a whole new world. And I liked it. It has not been a tremendously "spiritual experience" for me, but I feel like that is just the way I work. I am a lot more casual, not needing the accoutrements or accessories that many others use. I don't feel the need to have candles lit or incense burning or to specifically say a prayer before each session. I do, however, do a quick meditation to open my chakras to positive energy before I begin.

I feel this is for sure my authentic self, and without the work I do I would feel I was missing a huge part of something in my life, even if I wasn't able to put my finger on what that part was.

Cyndi Dale: Yes. Our intuition is a communication between our everyday self, our soul, and the subtle realms. How can we understand our inner self unless we can intuitively connect to it? How can we know how to be in the world unless we can accurately assess what's really happening "out there"? Our authentic self is intuitive, but knowledgeably so, and is able to manage the ability, instead of having it manage us.

Sherrie Dillard: Intuition is the voice of our soul, our most authentic self.

Granddaughter Crow (Dr. Joy Gray): Yes, I do. I see the spiritual expression is just as unique and important as an emotional expression or a mental expression or a physical expression. It is the expression of complete authenticity.

John Holland: Yes, it's part of awakening and it's part of who you are. Why do we want to discover or awaken these abilities when it makes us more sensitive? Because it's a part of you! You're a soul that comes with the body. We're physical and spiritual beings. To develop only one side of you is living a life half-lived.

I've noticed the word *empathic* is big now, as a lot of people are getting more sensitive than usual, and I'm seeing people are connecting to the other side more. So is the consciousness of humankind changing? Or is the veil on the other side getting thinner? I think it's a little bit of both. I think the consciousness of humankind is changing right now. Whether it's because of technology or something else, something is happening and we're quickening. It's making us more sensitive, so you might as well learn how to control and use it!

Jodi Livon: Yes, I do. When we embrace our spiritual self, we embrace our soul-self!

Chanda Parkinson: I feel as if this greatly depends on the person, their belief systems, and a willingness to be open. This was a resounding yes for me. The magnetic pull toward this work continued to grow as a part of my own awakening.

Troy Parkinson: I believe any spiritual experience/awakening is a call to your authentic self. I've met so many people who are not self-expressed in sharing their spiritual lives, and it limits their fulfillment. The essence of who you are and why you are here is core to being human. Developing your spiritual life is part of being human.

Kristy Robinett: Absolutely. We've all heard the saying "Live your truth." It can be raw and scary, vulnerable and frightening, but also freeing and fulfilling.

Jurema Silva: It is definitely part of a spiritual experience. Better yet, intuitive abilities are part of our spiritual and personal ascension and evolution. When you develop or practice your intuitive skills, you begin to experience a wonderful world of unconditional love and peace. Your intuitive abilities give you a sense of security, comfort, and awareness of your own self and the numerous energies around you. The development of your intuition is the beginning of a transformative part of your life.

What intuitive abilities are strongest for you? How do you usually experience them?

Melanie Barnum: I utilize all of my abilities. I don't really focus or concentrate on one over the others. I just allow them to flow together to give me a fuller picture of what I am tuning in to. I see and hear things symbolically quite often, which also helps me to interpret the messages I receive.

Cyndi Dale: I'm a bit different at work versus in my personal life. When working intuitively with people, I'm primarily a clairvoyant; I get a lot of colorful images and pictures. I'm also quite clairaudient, and words simply speak into my mind or flow out of my mouth. I also use the various forms of clairempathy at work, sensing what others are, did, or will go through. In my personal life, I receive a lot of messages while sleeping, such as through visions and visitations. While awake, however, I really rely on my empathic abilities. I sense and feel what suits me and what doesn't, whom to trust and whom not to. I don't probe for a lot of data; I merely accept my sensations as true for myself and follow them.

Sherrie Dillard: There is no one that is the strongest. I use them in combination with one another. When I began to experience phenomena, it was mostly through clairvoyance, the ability to "see" energy information.

Granddaughter Crow (Dr. Joy Gray): I will say my empathic nature, as it helps me to pick up the subtleties within energetic fields. I have developed what I call my "personal psychic dictionary." Spirits are able to communicate with me through our agreed-upon language based on numbers, colors, symbols, sensations, etc.

John Holland: Clairsentience and clairaudience are strongest for me. When I'm working mediumistically, I'll feel whether it's a mother or a father, young or old, and how they passed. Clairaudience can be confusing because it comes in as your own thought. Some people think you're going to hear a mother's voice, but that isn't necessarily the case. I may feel a mother, but I hear her voice in my voice. I know intuitively if it's female or if it's male, if it's a child or if it's older.

Danielle MacKinnon: Although all of my psychic senses are open, knowing is my strongest ability. I think it's because now that I trust the intuitive data coming in, knowing is the least work. I don't have to wait to "see" something or "hear" something; I can just start speaking—without any preparation beforehand. Knowing is probably the hardest sense for my students to trust, though, as there isn't a tangible thing to grab on to. It feels safer to say "I see a red ball" than "Your brain works like an architect's." But once you can trust your knowing, it's really fun.

Chanda Parkinson: Clairaudience and clairvoyance, followed by clairsentience. I hear, see, and sense messages and information for my clients and for myself.

Troy Parkinson: Clairvoyance; my ability to see spirit is my strongest. I see images and flashes like pictures in my mind. I feel spirit through clairsentience. So I will "feel" what may have been their aliment or how they lost their lives.

Kristy Robinett: I see. I see spirits from the other side, guides, and those who haven't passed over as physical beings standing next to me. I also see images and pictures in my mind's eye. I have dreams, visions, and precognitions. I hear. I hear messages, words, whispers, noises, buzzing, etc., in my ear. I feel. I can feel another's emotional or physical pain on or in my body. I can smell and taste things that are in the spiritual world. If a man who died smoked, I will smell that smoke. If grandma loved making sugar cookies, I will taste the cookies (and likely smell them too). I know. I'll simply get a "do this" or "don't do this" message.

Jurema Silva: My strongest abilities are seeing (visions) such as past lives and the future. I also experience clairvoyance (seeing past lives, past, present, future); clairaudience (hearing or listening); clairsentience (sensing or feeling); claircognizance (knowing or inner knowing); clairgustance (tasting); clairolfaction (smells); psychometry (sensing energies by touching objects); mediumship (connecting with departed loved ones—humans and animals); and spiritual or astral travel (visiting other spiritual realms).

What is one exercise you would recommend for someone newly exploring their psychic ability? Please share the exercise here.

Melanie Barnum: I feel learning to recognize your natural abilities is a great place to start. One of the first things I always tell my students is to pay attention to how they describe something. Do you say "I feel," "I see," "I heard," "I know," etc.? Listen to the words they use to talk. Usually, they will utilize their more natural gifts. For example, "I feel" is about clairsentience, or clear intuitive feeling, whereas "I see" leans more toward clairvoyance, or clear psychic sight.

Then I ask them a question, I have them listen to their answers. Try this! Think about going out to dinner with a friend—not a dinner you've already had, but one that you imagine. Where are you? What does it look like? Do you hear anything? Who are you with? What do you each order? Are there other people there? When you get your meal, what does it taste like? How do you feel being there?

Once you've answered all of the questions, think about how you experienced those answers. Did you "see" the restaurant or place where you were going for dinner? Or did you "hear" the name? Did you just "know" who you were with, or did you "see" them? There are so many different questions you can ask to help you explore how you receive information and what gifts are more prevalent. This helps you practice understanding your own abilities and how you can tune in by using your intuition.

Cyndi Dale: I use an exercise I call "Spirit-to-Spirit." I affirm my own essential or deep spiritual self. Then I acknowledge others' higher selves. This includes the visible or present beings as well as invisible ones. Then I turn a situation over to the Greater Spirit and put it in charge of an undertaking.

Sherrie Dillard: I would advise meditation and quiet listening within. Keep a journal of your experiences and dreams. Make time as often as possible to simply listen, and don't try to understand and give meaning to everything you experience. Let it unfold in its own time, as it is a process.

Granddaughter Crow (Dr. Joy Gray): There are so many ways to pick up psychic information, so the key is to learn how you are picking it up. Take a moment, relax, and close your eyes. Walk down five steps in your mind's eye. There is a door. Open the door and find yourself in a meadow. Move into the meadow. A bird flies overhead. It calls to you— note it. Next, you find an orange on a branch. Pick the orange, smell the orange, peel and taste the orange. When you are ready, find the door again, walk through it and close the door behind you. Walk up the five steps and return to the present. Journal… how did you perceive the activity? Did you see the meadow or simply know it was there? Did you hear the call of the bird? Did you feel the orange in your hand? How easy was it for you to smell and taste the orange? Did your mouth water? If you saw things—clairvoyant. If you simply knew things—claircognizant. If you heard things—clairaudient. If you felt things—clairsentient. If you smelled things—clairalience. If you taste things—clairgustance. Now pay attention to your strongest one and develop it.

Jodi Livon: When making any decision, follow your heart, trust your gut, and use your head.

Michael Mayo: I would suggest the practice of "Sitting in the Power." In this meditative exercise, you learn to quiet and still your mind, become passive and receptive, and just notice what is occurring in your energy.

Sitting in the Power

Begin by closing your eyes and taking a few deep breaths.

After these breaths, allow your breath to breathe you. Don't control its movement, but rather observe it.

Do this for several minutes until you start to feel the mind chatter beginning to subside. This can take anywhere from a few minutes to as long as ten minutes.

Then allow yourself to begin to feel into your own inner being. Imagine where you feel that the core part of your being resides within you— somewhere between the heart and the solar plexus for most people. As you feel into that space, just allow yourself to breathe into it.

Intend that when it's ready, it will begin to open up and that your own energy and aura will begin to expand outward to fill the body. Then, when it's ready, it might expand further to move beyond the body, and finally, move out into the room in which you sit, expanding to fill it, from corner to corner.

Offer to the spirit world that this is their time and allow yourself to just sense and feel the sensations you feel in your body and in the air around you. You may begin to feel things like tingling, warmth, buzzing, and more. Let yourself notice these sensations, accept them, and let them go. Allow yourself to just relax into the energetic sensations and totally let go.

Then, after anywhere from twenty to sixty minutes, you can return. Let yourself naturally reconnect with the breath. You will feel it when it's time to come back.

Using Oracle Cards

Before you begin, say a prayer to your helpers in Spirit, asking them to help you by bringing you what is needed for you right now using the cards. Using your favorite oracle card or tarot deck, allow yourself to begin to shuffle the cards. Don't worry how long or how many times, just do it until you "feel" like they are shuffled correctly. While you do this, think of a question that you're interested in finding out about—nothing too serious, but something that you will be able to see the outcome of at some point in the near future.

When you feel ready, pull three cards from the top of the deck and place them from left to right, side by side.

These will represent (from left to right) the past, the present, and the future.

Do not pull out the booklet that tells you the meaning of the cards. Allow yourself to feel into the meaning of the cards. What stands out to you in the imagery? Do you get a sense of an emotion or energy as you look at each one? What emotions, images, or ideas are inspired within you as you look at these cards? Then allow yourself to see the story in the cards. They should accurately describe the situation in the past and present as it relates to the question you asked while you were shuffling. If this is correct, then you can look to the future card and see what it says. Then take note of the sense you got and write it down. You can do this about many different questions and see what ends up coming true and how accurate your interpretation was of the card. If it was not, were there things that you misunderstood or misinterpreted that you either experienced or saw in the cards? This would indicate the issue wasn't the cards themselves, but rather your interpretation of what experience was showing you. This will teach you to distinguish between what's coming from your mind and what's coming from your intuition.

Chanda Parkinson: Guided meditation is an excellent way to grow and develop psychic abilities. Breathe and ground your energies, and invite spiritual support and protection. Next, go to a sacred space in your mind's eye, for example, some place in nature. Observe the symbols, animals, flowers, and plants all around you. Symbols in psychic experiences carry meaning, which over time can develop into messages.

Troy Parkinson: Basic meditation is the best place to start. I have beginning meditations in my book *Bridge to the Afterlife*.

Kristy Robinett: A very basic exercise is "Red Light/Green Light." Red light is your no. It's stop. Green light is yes or go. You can either see the lights in your mind's eye or feel the no or yes in your body. I feel my no in my gut and my yes as an airy feeling. You first begin thinking of a question that you know will be your red light and a question that will be your green light, and you practice with the known answers. After a while, you move to the questions you are contemplating and you ask your guides, "Is it a red light or a green light?" and you follow through accordingly, even if you don't like the answer.

Jurema Silva: Meditation. Daily meditation helps us to connect with spirit helpers. If you cannot get any feedback during this process, ask your guardian angel to help. Through a meditative state, our minds can reach the subtle energies around us, capturing the vibrational energies of angels, spirit mentors, and guides. A very close departed loved one may be able to help at the beginning of the process, only if the soul is well advanced and if the help offered comes from the heart. For instance, grandparents tend to give extra attention to their grandchildren. Most grandparents when in spirit continue caring for their loved ones. Perhaps your departed grandmother may be able to help at the start of your journey. Receiving assistance from a loved one provides a sense of security and trust as you continue exploring your potential. Focus on connecting with a close relative or a friend who passed away, and see what happens. Knowing who is assisting you makes you feel more comfortable and confident during the process.

What advice do you have for decoding and discovering your own spiritual language and interpreting symbols in visions and dreams? Especially as a beginner, how do you know when to rely on your own interpretations, when to refer to external resources, or when to ask for input from others?

Melanie Barnum: Sometimes it's hard to know when to do what, but my best advice would be to utilize all of the above. When you begin to acknowledge and recognize your symbolic messages, you can create a symbolic journal. If you have a vision that you understand is something that feels stronger than just your imagination, or it feels like there is a meaning behind it but you don't know what it means, refer to books or other teaching materials to help you interpret the messages. You can write those meanings in your journal and also pay attention to what you intuit it means. As you continue on your journey, you will add to your journal and discover that often you will receive the same symbolic imagery to guide you or help you answer questions because you can resonate with the symbols.

For example, when I see two rocking chairs on a porch after someone asks me if they will be together with their mate for a long time, that is my symbol that they will. Alternatively, if I see a wedding ring dropped on the floor, it tells me their relationship may not last. These are simple yet powerful images I use in my readings. It doesn't mean they will have the same meaning for you, nor does it mean this would be the imagery you would be receiving symbolically. But knowing you have references and can create your own journal in addition to that gives you options and helps you to figure out what resonates with you.

Cyndi Dale: I think you have to mix and match insights from others versus trusting the self. And the category of "others" includes spiritual guides and the Spirit. You can also use practical resources such as websites. For instance, I recently had a dream with a tiger in it. Then I saw a cougar near my dog park. I did an internet search for "spiritual meaning of tiger" to check what tiger signifies to others, but the description didn't totally fit, so I also employed my own sense of the tiger to arrive at the intuitive message. In the end, we all have our own particulars in regard to intuitive insights and interpretations. For instance, I know that when I psychically smell a "bad aroma" when someone asks me to do something, I ought not do it. If I smell flowers, I will do it.

Early on in your journey, I suggest that you keep a journal to figure out your own particulars. For instance, early on I figured out that messages I hear psychically in my right ear are from God. In my left ear, from spiritual guides.

Sherrie Dillard: Meditate on the symbols and listen within. Consult books that offer interpretations and insights. However, trust your intuitive sense of the meaning of what you have received.

Granddaughter Crow (Dr. Joy Gray): Start to build your personal psychic dictionary—a personal agreement between you and the unseen world. Journal as you go. When you have an experience, write it down. Test it using the scientific method. If it holds true, you got it. If it does not, keep digging deeper till it does. In the beginning, it is helpful to have a good mentor to bounce things off. However, the goal is to understand how it works for you—developing self-trust takes time.

John Holland: Our dreams are filled with symbols, and studying those symbols and dreams will help when it comes time to use symbol work as part of your psychic abilities. *The Best Dream Book Ever* by Kevin Todeschi is a great book for studying symbol meanings.

Jodi Livon: Know that your intuition and your guides are positive, kind guiding forces. If something feels right, it often is. Our intuition exists to help, not hurt. Experience is the best teacher.

Michael Mayo: Ultimately, all experiences derive from our own awareness. What's most important is how we are inspired by a symbol in the moment and within the context of the situation or question at hand. Part of the way we learn to know what's coming from our mind or from the spirit world is by practicing reading others. This gives us an in-the-moment validation of whether or not what we are getting is accurate. It is just as important to get no's as it is to get yes's. We learn discernment by getting it wrong versus getting it right, so never be afraid to get it wrong.

Symbols can have many meanings in any given situation. A baseball, for example, can mean that someone likes baseball, watched baseball on TV, just enjoys sports in general, used to play baseball, or even hates baseball altogether! It just depends on the context of what we feel is happening when we are giving the reading. This is why I don't teach my students to use any hard or constant symbol to mean any one specific thing. What's important is how that symbol makes you feel in the moment it appears. Also, if you don't know right away what it means, let go of that image or symbol and let the next impression come, which may (or may not) give more context to your first symbol. Don't try to interpret it, just describe your experience as it unfolds. Through this process, you will begin to learn how to work with symbols and what they mean for you in any given situation.

Chanda Parkinson: Over time, you will begin to see patterns in the symbols, signs, and messages, and with a stronger understanding about why you are receiving those and what to do with them. That's why it's important not to rush your development, and allow it to be a process that unfolds over time. Checking books and online resources and decoding the spiritual language working through you as you go is great, and sometimes you simply won't know for some time what is coming through to you.

Kristy Robinett: I created my language when I was a child, so I don't really remember how I did it other than I just did it. It came natural. It has developed a bit over time, but mostly it remains "stupid and simple." Take seasons, for instance—say someone wants to know if they will get pregnant, wants to know the sex, and wants to know when the baby will be born. I'll see a loved one on the other side handing me a baby—or not handing me a baby. I'll see pink for a girl and blue for a boy. (I know— very gender-biased.) I'll see hot summer sun for summer, tulips or lilies for spring, a Christmas tree and snow for winter, and pumpkins and autumn leaves for fall. I have symbolism for all my senses for each season.

I'll smell cinnamon for autumn. I'll feel the cold for winter. I'll taste cold lemonade for summer, etc.

Jurema Silva: One can interpret many different signs, but some signs are particular to the person who is starting to develop intuitive abilities or who is already practicing it. Many symbols and geometric signs can only be interpreted by the person who is receiving them. On the other end, receiving a feather as a sign is much easier to interpret. I still receive the same or similar signs as decades ago, yet I continue to receive many new signs with different meanings for every situation. As I advance personally and spiritually, signs of all types are going to be part of my evolution as an intuitive person. The same should be for the ones who are willing to accept and welcome their gifts.

How much of our spiritual language do you feel is universal versus individual?

Melanie Barnum: I feel there are many universal symbols, but there are also some that are very personal. Your guides and loved ones from the other side, as well as your own intuition, will give you symbols in a way you can understand. Sometimes those symbols will be universal, and sometimes they are more individualized. A stop sign, for instance, is a universal way of saying, "Stop what you're doing right away!" But you may also have a more personal symbol, such as (and I'm making this up) the time you were debating whether to continue on your hike and you took another step and twisted your ankle. It's quite possible your symbol to stop would be a flash of your swollen ankle, which would not resonate with anyone but you.

Cyndi Dale: I think a lot of our spiritual language is universal but takes a bit of twisting to figure out. Snakes, serpents, dragons, lizards… different cultures will work with different forms of the same type of creature. No matter the culture, these "beings" all represent power, passion, transmutation, and the like. In one culture, God might appear as Jesus. In another, as Allah. In yet another, as the Mother Goddess. The key is to not affix that a spiritual icon is *the* only way to work with Spirit. Does it matter if God appears like Jesus to one person and Allah to another? Not to me.

Granddaughter Crow (Dr. Joy Gray): I believe that there is a large universal spiritual language, such as numbers, symbols, colors, etc. This only gets you started—a base. But in order to develop your personal language, allow your intuition to expand and personalize it more. For example, I speak English, but the choice of words and order that I work with English reveals my authenticity.

John Holland: Every sign or symbol pertains to the person who sees or feels that. For example, I'll say to someone, "What does Niagara Falls mean to you?" and they might say, "Power, generator, honeymoon," while to me it means Upstate New York or Canada. Know that some symbols are just for you.

I don't really work in the way of universal symbols. I can only speak to what some symbols mean to *me*. For example, because my grandmother and my sister are both named Rose, rose means the flower or the name, never something like a funeral. Yet when I feel a single rose, I might intuitively know a different message and say to the person, "You still have the rose from your mother's casket." So it's totally different depending on who the client is in front of me. When I see elephants, for me that means India, for you it might mean good luck, and for someone else it might mean circus animals.

Danielle MacKinnon: I've found that intuition from spirit guides and from animals uses whatever we have in our heads to get information through. For example, I have a heavy '80s movies knowledge, so my guides will use a particular scene from a movie I know well to make their point. Someone else's guides may make the exact same point with a different person using totally different intuitive data. The point with intuition is to make sure that the data that comes through is something we can understand. If you know a lot about cars, your intuition may come through with pictures and sounds of cars or experiences with cars. Basically, whatever is going to make sure you're going to get it is how your info will come through.

Michael Mayo: I believe it is a balance of these two things. I believe that there is a universal language of energy and color; however, I believe that how that is interpreted will depend on one's belief systems, culture, and mental space. This is why it is very important to cultivate neutrality within your mindset when you are doing a reading. Let go of any judgment, ideas about people, or behaviors, and allow yourself to just notice objectively what is occurring. Through this cultivation of neutrality and indifference to your experience, you can better notice what the actual stimulus or experience is showing you, rather than it being colored by your belief system.

Chanda Parkinson: This also depends on the person, because it often is an inside-out process that takes time to understand. Allowing time to genuinely understand your own spiritual language and how spirit will best work with you is crucial. However, there are also many psychic symbols that over the course of time have become fairly universal. It's okay to learn and use those as well.

Troy Parkinson: I believe there is a universal language for spirit, because I've been able to receive messages from individuals who didn't speak English. And there is an individual filter we all bring to messages that allows us to decipher the communication in a way that makes sense to us.

Kristy Robinett: I think most of it is individual, and it has to be individual for each person to get their information. One size does not fit all.

Jurema Silva: I believe the language is universal. At the same time, this language caters to each individual's needs. My guidance to clients is not one size fits all. The language is universal in a sense of compassion and non-judgment, yet it is customized for different situations. My spirit guides and mentors have more like a private language or way of communicating with me that can be very different than when I am channeling messages to clients.

What is one key way that you personally embrace your subtle intuition and messages from Spirit in your daily life?

Melanie Barnum: One way I embrace my intuition is to pay attention to the external signs or synchronicities. I kind of turn down my intuition when I'm not working, so I don't find myself reading others when I don't want to. The signs or synchronistic events kind of push the intuitive nudges to the forefront of my mind so I don't ignore them. Also, if I do tune in, I ask for spirit to send me answers to specific problems or questions I have and then see how my body reacts. If I feel heavy, it is usually a negative response, but if I feel light or goose-bumpy, it is more positive.

Cyndi Dale: I conduct my Spirit-to-Spirit exercise (shared in a previous response) and then remain open for my inner soul and guides to send me messages. And then I observe and pay attention. For instance, if I see three eagles in a short amount of time, I know that the natural world is reaching through and I interpret the meaning. If three clients bring up the same topic, I pay attention. If I trigger into a "negative" feeling or reaction, I stop and meditate quickly, and perform cleaning and clearing, using my intuition to help me pinpoint what's occurring and what to do about it.

Sherrie Dillard: I take time to intuitively listen within on a daily basis. Then I trust and act on what I receive, even if I have no proof or overwhelming evidence in outcomes. This will help you to more quickly become aware of what is intuition and what is self-generated information.

Granddaughter Crow (Dr. Joy Gray): Some of my guides are very practical. For example, I have a spirit guide named Betty. Betty keeps my schedule. Like a personal assistant, she books my schedule and reminds me of tasks that I need to do. She comes as a thought in my mind. I love my guide Betty. Ask for a guide that helps you in a practical way—and see what comes.

John Holland: When I have important decisions and choices in front of me in my personal life, whether it's family, career, or even traveling, I will stop and see how I *feel* about the choice or decisions I am pondering. But sometimes I forget that I even have these abilities. I get caught up in the physical world and I may get worried and a little anxious because I didn't take time to slow down, stop, and tap in. When that happens there are usually issues or drawbacks that might have been avoided. When I explain this to people, many say, "But you do this for a career!" My response: I'm still human. Often, we make decisions way too fast without thinking. Try to remember *before* you make those important decisions to *pause* and *ask* before you *act*.

There will be mistakes, but as you develop, there are going to be more yes's than no's when it comes to intuitive hits. I try to honor them every day.

I'm a big advocate of meditation, but I don't do it every day. I try to get outside in nature. Luckily I have a dog, so I try to get into my intuitive ability when I'm outdoors in nature on "intuitive walks" where you're not just in your head thinking—but you're allowing your intuitive awareness to flow throughout your body—instead of being in your analytical left side of your brain. I advise everyone to look up information on "intuitive walking," also known as "meditation in motion."

Danielle MacKinnon: I leave my psychic abilities on and open (to a degree) all the time so that I can receive psychic data whenever I need to. This allows me to easily receive whatever I'm supposed to receive without having to try very hard. I call it being accidentally psychic—and it just means I picked up something intuitive without asking for it. This is different, though, from leaving myself all the way open all the time. That would make me tired, and it would also make it difficult to receive reliable intuitive data. I simply leave my intuition a little bit on all the time.

Michael Mayo: One key way that I personally embrace my subtle intuition in my life is by learning to listen and be present. The way I was developed as a medium was to learn to never go after information, but rather to let it come to me. Therefore, in my day-to-day life, I am never looking for signs or messages from the other world. Instead, I trust that when the moment is right, I will be given a subtle nudge or sense of moving in the right direction. But again, this only comes when it is needed, not all the time. It's learning to trust that if you need to know something, the spirit will make you aware of it if you're meant to know it.

Chanda Parkinson: I incorporate a tarot reading daily to understand what I need to know from day to day, and I also walk in nature and take in messages from nature spirits and animals around me.

Troy Parkinson: I immerse myself in nature, watch the sunset, and look up at the stars daily. Over the years, I've found the strongest way for me to feel most connected to spirit is to be surrounded by the wonderment of nature.

Jurema Silva: My relationship with my spirit helpers is something I'm aware of on a daily basis. During my morning meditation and prayers, I sense their presence as if we were meditating and praying for others together. I feel their presence throughout the day everywhere I go, and their assistance is amazingly effective. Talking to them is enlightening and powerful. My daily morning connection with my inner self and the spirits is my personal source of love, peace, and strength to face a new day.

How can you intuit whether communication is coming from a positive source versus when it might be best for you to create a boundary to break communication with a certain source?

Melanie Barnum: One of the best ways to know if you're communicating with something positive is to notice whether it is either an attack on or a boost to your ego specifically. Usually, positive spirit communication does not play on your ego at all; rather, it will be gentle and kind but present you with honest, even if not immediately clear or recognized, messages. If you experience a negative energy, tell them to leave. They have no power over you or your own spirit. Tell them they are not welcome. I have had to do this, and I can tell you it may take a minute or two to remember to do this, but that's okay. You can do it at any time.

Cyndi Dale: The distinction is going to differ depending on the person, but I use my clairempathy skills. If a source makes me feel dirty, scared, sick, or "off," I don't trust it and I'll dismiss it. If it feels uplifting, light, and "right," I pay attention.

Sherrie Dillard: I always invoke protective light energy before interacting and receiving intuitive information. If what you receive is negative or makes you uncomfortable or feel violated in any way, it's best to no longer communicate and move on.

Granddaughter Crow (Dr. Joy Gray): Always set your intention first. In setting your intention, banish negative sources and draw in positive. It is your party, so invite who you wish and make the party "by invitation only." Your body will constrict if it is a negative source—listen to your body.

Danielle MacKinnon: I believe that if I am managing my energy and am in a place of balance, there is no need to protect myself from any source of intuitive data. My job, as a human being, is to manage my energy well— that's the best taking care of myself I can do.

Michael Mayo: All sources that come from the spirit world are positive sources. There are no sources that will try to trick you, deceive you, or lie to you. This stems from a misunderstanding of where the spirit comes from. If you ever do experience anything that seems scary, negative, or bad, it is coming from the mind of the medium. Check in with yourself and see if you have fear-based beliefs around working with the spirit world—or even fear around the unknown. An honest reflection will invariably lead to the answer. That being said, it is important to acknowledge that if you receive information from someone else claiming it is coming from the spirit and it makes you feel fearful, powerless, or a victim, do not accept it. That is coming from the mind of the medium, not from the spirit world. The spirit brings forward love, support, peace, and harmony. These are hallmarks of true spirit communication. Remember that you are always in control of your spiritual experiences and that if there's anything that you don't like or that causes concern, check to see if there is a mundane explanation first before attributing it to a supernatural cause.

Chanda Parkinson: It is all in the way the insights feel. If they make me feel good and are energy-feeding, then I know they are coming from a pure source. If the insights make me feel bad, fearful, or anxious, I try to pause and clear myself from those and ask again.

Troy Parkinson: I always encourage individuals to create a positive environment when building their abilities, because your setting helps lay the foundation for communication. Open with light and love and close with light and love and do the work in a place and time that is comfortable for you. Trying to connect at 2:00 a.m. around candles in a haunted house probably won't attract the energy you are looking for.

Jurema Silva: I learned many years ago when still living in Brazil that the ideal is to know who is helping you. Know your spirit helper (or angel) by name. Be familiar with their energy, personality, and the way their particular style of communication flows. You should be in touch with the same spirit(s) always.

A good example that I teach my students is when you answer the phone and can recognize the voice of your best friend without looking at the caller ID. How can that be possible? Because you are very familiar with the tone of their voice and the way your friend communicates with you—from the sound of your friend's laughter or the way you can sense stress or sadness in each other's voices. You automatically know who is on the phone with you and how they are feeling. It should be the same with your spirit helper. It is a matter of practicing communication—through receiving and sending messages or signs—and learning how to stay attuned to (or bond with) your spirit through the energy you share. Other spirits, who I call "players," might try to impersonate your spirit guide, or even your guardian angel, just for the enjoyment of manipulation and deception. When you build a strong bond and friendship with your spirit guide, you will know right away that there is sudden interference that is not familiar to you, just as you will know if the person calling you is your best friend or a stranger.

What is your opinion on the use of spirit boards? Yay or nay?

Melanie Barnum: I feel like it depends on what you're doing and what your intentions are. If you are going to practice with a board, you are opening yourself and your energy up to anything that may be out there. However, you can set your intention that you will only allow positive energy and spirit with only the highest of positive intentions to come through. If something doesn't feel right or makes you uncomfortable, tell them to leave and cut off the communication immediately.

Cyndi Dale: Personally I don't like them. I find them very dense and believe that because of this, they attract dense or more negative spirits. I think that some people are naturally positive in their use of a board, however, and for them it's a supportive mechanism.

Sherrie Dillard: I don't advise spirit boards, as they are too easy to be influenced by lower-vibration energy. Invoking light protective energy ensures that you are connecting with higher divine source energy.

Granddaughter Crow (Dr. Joy Gray): I see spirit boards as merely a gateway, a type of divination tool; learn how the tool works before working with the tool. If you would like to work with any tool, set an intention first. It is your party, so send out the guest list and make it "by invitation only." Open up the space with a set intention and close the space when you are done. You wouldn't fall asleep with your front door open, so close the spirit board door, too.

John Holland: There's a lot of myth about them. The old-school thought is that you're opening yourself up to *anybody*. I'm not a big advocate of the idea of entities and evil spirits, but what you put out, you attract. Why use a board when your body is your own board? I don't feel you should play with it, because then you're playing with your own system and your own psychic ability without being grounded. If you were doing it with an experienced psychic or medium, then okay, but even then, why use a board when you have your own equipment inside of you?

Michael Mayo: Spirit boards are a completely benign form of communication with the spirit world. That being said, I offer caution when using them, but not for the reason you may think. I do not believe anything bad will come to you from using them. I have used them plenty of times with friends and I have never had a bad or scary experience. However, my issue with them is that they are so easy to accidentally influence. The subtle movements of the hands or the minds of the people moving the planchette can very easily influence its movement, and therefore the information coming through is often inconsistent, inaccurate, or influenced by groupthink. If you do manage to get genuine spirit connection, test the spirit. Ask them questions that you may or may not already know the answer to. If they are claiming to be your loved one, ask them questions no one else in the group would know the answer to. It is never offensive or rude to question a spirit on a board, and they will likely happily do their best to answer. This way, you know that you're getting genuine spirit communication and evidence. If anything negative, scary, or bad comes through, it's the influence of the users, not the spirit world.

Chanda Parkinson: I don't have any hard-and-fast rules about the use of games or psychic tools. With any tool or practice, the state of mind and heart you're in when you use them matters most. Spirit boards have gotten a negative rap, but if your heart and mind are in the right place, it can be a wonderful experience to share with others. I wouldn't use them if you're in a negative emotional space, or if those with you are using it for entertainment or to "test" spirit. That is terribly disrespectful, and this is typically why it's met with negative results. Intention matters.

Troy Parkinson: If used in the right setting, they can be important tools, but you don't need them and they bring with them a lower energy.

Jurema Silva: Some people prefer to use tools to access messages from spirit. I in particular use a pendulum. In my opinion, boards are games that shouldn't be played for the purpose of divination. We should all respect the benevolent spirits who are around us to help, teach, and enlighten us on our journeys. Board games for divination purposes can attract negative spirits or lost souls who create fear and confusion.

Do you have any tips for when intuitive senses seep into everyday life? For example:

- Hearing other people's thoughts, feeling others' feelings, or experiencing spontaneous visions
- Unexpected energy, like a cold spot in a space, or some other indicator of a spirit or imprint of spirit energy
- Spirit "pop-ins"—hearing messages at random from those on the other side

Melanie Barnum: The best tip I can offer is just to pay attention. If it's something you want to explore or something you are excited to understand, then go with it. Tune in and discover what it is that you are trying to intuit, but always do it with the highest integrity. Don't invade others.

If you don't want it to happen or you are trying to control when you receive intuitive messages, you should set a protective barrier around you. Imagine a bubble of protective energy all around you that allows only positive energy in and keeps negative energy away. You can set your "limit" with this as well. For instance, if you only want to allow intuitive messages that you need rather than random communications or messages, you can say that. This is the quickest and easiest way to keep unwanted or invasive energy from coming in.

Sherrie Dillard: I advise people to make time daily or weekly to listen within and journal your intuitive insights and impressions. Make the intent that you will not receive intuitive information unless you have asked for it. We have dominion over what energy we engage with and the responsibility to set the intention and the boundary to receive only what is in our highest good.

Granddaughter Crow (Dr. Joy Gray): I think of it like this: Physically I can see, hear, and touch the world around me, yet that does not mean that everything I see, hear, or touch needs my attention. I do not walk up to every stranger on the street and talk with them. I do not add my two cents to a conversation that I overheard. The same goes for my gifts:

Just because I see something does not cause me to engage. I wait to be invited. Additionally, I have a rule… if a spirit from the other side wants me to relay a message, I tell them that they must figure out a way to bring the person to me. That rule saves a lot of time and energy.

John Holland: Every once in a while this will happen to me, but I wouldn't walk up to people. That's very important. *Do not just walk up to people.*

When it happens randomly in a store or something, first of all I have to realize whether these are my thoughts or whether I am really receiving something. Sometimes you may get a thought, like if I'm going through my house I may get the thought, "I should really change the battery on my smoke alarms." And I have to stop and think, "Wait a minute, is that me?" And then sure enough, I realize it was a psychic thought that I didn't pay attention to, because two days later the smoke alarms start going off and my dog is freaking out.

If you were to act on every thought you have, you'd go crazy. But if it happens out of the blue, usually I know it's an intuitive hit. If it happens randomly, I will acknowledge it and let it go. If it's a spirit and I get a pop-in, I don't give a message just like that; it depends on who I'm with. It happens once in a while, but it's very rare. I could be at a restaurant and get something for somebody at the table beside me, but I wouldn't just walk up to the person. I put the responsibility on the spirit and say, "You want me to talk to your sister or mother or child? *You* figure out how that's going to happen."

Jodi Livon: Other people's thoughts are none of your business, nor is how they feel—that is, unless someone invites you to share in their experience.

Spirit energy is alive and is pretty much everywhere. It's okay to acknowledge awareness of spirit energy and then tighten your boundaries and keep moving.

If you are with someone close to you and they agree to receive a spirit message, it's okay to share it. If you do this constantly, however, you will be completely depleted over time. It's wise to have on and off hours!

Danielle MacKinnon: All of these happen when you leave your intuition too open. A lot of my students want to be psychic so badly that they walk around every day all the way open. I advise them instead to turn the volume of their intuition up or down, based on their needs. You have less of a need for intuitive information at the grocery store than you do when you're searching the web for a new job, for example.

Michael Mayo: Our intuitive senses are a natural part of who and what we are. It is completely normal to occasionally have some bleed over into our daily life. However, it should *not* be a regular occurrence. If this is happening, then we need to become aware of boundaries within ourselves and learn how to turn off our awareness. How do we do this? By being present and physical with the here and now. Our intuitive awareness opens when we are in a passive and receptive state or even just by talking about the topic of spirituality. Also, some people are more prone to being sensitive to the energy of those around them due, most times, to trauma in early life where their ability to sense the feelings and intentions of those around them was vital to their safety.

Troy Parkinson: I usually encourage people to open up and close down to communication so that it doesn't occur spontaneously. Unexpected energy can occur spontaneously, and has for me. I encourage people to pause and acknowledge the connection. Listen and see what you sense. Send love and continue on with your day. I recommend people create boundaries for themselves so "pop-ins" don't happen.

Jurema Silva: Sensing people's energies or perceiving energies in a room or in public places is very common to me. Visions are also part of the process, and they can come out of nowhere during a conversation. It is important to hold the vision—or even feelings—and ask for more clarification. Remember, our energy field system is constantly picking up frequencies from others, even when we are not aware of it. Establishing communication with your spirit helper will assist you in discerning your visions that come to you suddenly, or the feelings you picked up from someone else. The spirits helping us don't want us to be in the dark. Asking for more details and explanations is very important in the process of developing and understanding how your intuition works.

A cold spot could mean the presence of a soul who is in limbo (lost) or a negative energy. If you ever experience cold energy, do not panic. Invoke your guardian angel or your spirit guide and ask, "What does that mean?" Sensing is the strongest component of our intuition.

Spirits on the other side usually sense and sometimes look for the ones who carry mediumship powers or who are emphatic, or a person with very strong psychic abilities. If a spirit shows up to you at random, it is usually because it needs your help. It means your vibrational frequency is strong enough for a spirit to perceive and try to communicate with, and perhaps bring a message through you. If a spirit is trying to deliver a message to you, just listen and see what you are able to do with the message.

As a follow-up to the previous questions, how do you decide when to engage and when to let things be? How can you tell if you're supposed to "do" something with what you've just received or if it was just a "bleed-through" moment where you experienced energy that isn't really important for you to engage with? For example, with hearing, feeling, or seeing, do you just clear and ground? Do you engage and offer the message? For unexpected energy, do you try to clear it or just acknowledge and leave it be?

Melanie Barnum: I try never to engage and offer unsolicited messages. To me, that is more invasive. The only time I could feel myself doing that would be if someone was about to get hurt or be in a dangerous situation. On the other hand, if I feel it is a message trying to get to me for me, I pay attention.

Cyndi Dale: This is such an important issue. I *always* "check into" my body and, if I need to, the Higher Spirit. For instance, I might glean an understanding about someone and know I'm right, but that doesn't mean I should point it out. For instance, let's say that I sense that someone isn't going to like a class they are signing up for. Just because I know a truth doesn't mean it's mine to offer. So I check into my body. Do I feel uplifted or lighter at the thought of sharing my perception? Or heavier and darker? Even if I have a sense that the message coming to me would be good to state, I still ask the person, "Say, I have a sense about your class. Do you want to hear it?"

I'll also simply ask the Spirit directly: "Should I share this observation or not?" I might get a word or picture pop into my head or an uplifting or downshifted feeling in my body, and I follow the dictate provided.

Sherrie Dillard: Acknowledge it, let go, and direct your attention away from any phenomenon that is uncomfortable. I don't work with energy that I have not invoked or asked for. It can be helpful to ground your energy and clear your space if you are uncomfortable with what you are receiving. Energy cleanse a room or your home, go outdoors and allow the earth and sun to absorb the energy you are uncomfortable with, or take a hot essential oil or salt bath.

Granddaughter Crow (Dr. Joy Gray): Great question! Think about how you decide when to engage in your day-to-day life as a regular human being. In life, I answer questions only when asked, etc.… Take your answer and apply it to your spiritual life. Feel free to set up healthy boundaries with spirits so that you do not get overloaded.

John Holland: I act on intuitive information depending on where I'm at and who I'm with. Other people have their own faith, religious beliefs, and belief system. I have to feel it out and ask, "Is this proper to give this information?" I also have to ask myself, "Is this *my* thought or is this an intuitive thought? Is this coming *to* me or *from* me?"

An imaginative thought will come in and go away, whereas an intuitive hit will keep coming back. For instance, say you have a relative living out of state and in your head you hear, "Call your sister," and you think, "Oh, I just talked to her a month ago. She's okay. I'll call her another time." The next day you hear again, "Call your sister," and you think, "Oh, okay. I'll call her on the weekend." Then you hear it again, or you see it or feel it. That means *call your sister.* That's not an imaginative thought. If a hit keeps coming back, that's how you know it's something to follow through with.

Jodi Livon: More often than not, it is best to acknowledge it and leave it be. Your guides will lead you in the best direction. Just because we pick up on something does not mean it is meant for us. Getting involved when it is wise not to do so is a huge mistake, and one that psychics make often. Not out of bad intent, of course—it's a boundary thing.

Michael Mayo: Just because you are aware of something doesn't mean you have to engage it. If we get a sense that there is a spirit around us, we can acknowledge it or ignore it. Contrary to the media's portrayal of mediumship, there is no obligation that you have to act on the experience— and in most instances it would often be inappropriate to do it. You must have the consent of those whom you are picking up before offering a message to them. I will sometimes hear people say that "the spirit won't leave me alone" as a reason for them having to give the information. I would offer this alternative solution and perspective. It isn't that the spirit won't leave you alone, it's that you won't stop checking to see if it's there! Every time we go to check if the spirit is present, we are reconnecting to their spirit. It is important to recognize that where attention goes, energy flows. So each time you're checking in to see if they are still there, you are reconnecting to them. The spirit exists in a place of no time and no singular space. They're always there for us to connect with. So the sooner you let go of checking in, the sooner you can return to whatever mundane task was happening. To connect is a choice.

Troy Parkinson: Here are five steps I recommend: pause, acknowledge, send love, determine action, let it be. I never recommend giving unsolicited messages, because you might rock someone's foundation if suddenly you jump in and give them a message. Always seek to ask permission before giving a message.

Jurema Silva: I do engage with most of what I receive through my intuitive powers. If my intuition is sending signals, I always pay attention to them. I learned the hard way once when I ignored the sign and found myself in trouble. Our intuition is the best tool to help us navigate throughout our journey in this world. If intuition is kicking in, most likely something is happening or is about to happen. For that matter, I am always attentive to messages, signs, and visions that I receive. If anything is not clear, I connect with the Light and try to stay inside a bubble of protection.

What is one bit of advice you would give to someone who feels like they are living in the gap of who they used to be and who they are becoming on their spiritual journey? How can they begin to integrate their past/who they have been with their new understanding of who they are becoming?

Melanie Barnum: It is always exciting to me to read for someone who is at the edge of the precipice, ready to jump in but not sure what they're jumping into or how to jump. I prepare them for the energy they are going to experience. I also want them to know that this is their life and their journey. As long as they are not putting others down or judging others for not being in the same place as them, then they can share their journey with whoever they want. It's their own personal journey, and it's up to them to decide who they want to take with them and who should be left behind, for now at least. In order to process their experiences, they need to embrace them without totally letting go of everything else.

Cyndi Dale: Know that the past has led you to this point. Intuition often borrows information and memories from our past to make a point. For instance, I might be trying to figure out if it's smart to make a connection with a certain person or not. I might then psychically picture my second grade teacher, who I really disliked. There is my answer!

In practical, everyday life, start finding places or ways to share your new awarenesses or activated gifts. Find out who is safe and who isn't. Maybe you bring up the fact that you've had a dream. If the person shuts down or says that's weird, they aren't a person you want to share your newfound interest with. If someone is open or receptive, keep sharing. There is an old rule about being safe: you can only be yourself to the extent that someone else is being themself. If someone won't go deep or talk psychic or is scared of the supernatural, you can't dig into those subjects deeper than they are willing to.

Another point: gifts don't suddenly appear. They have always been inside of you, perhaps more or less available, depending on life circumstances. Perform a review of how your intuition assisted you when you were younger. I think you'll discover that these abilities have always been with you.

Sherrie Dillard: Take time to be with people from the past and engage in activities that have brought you joy. Give yourself time to become more at ease and confident with new experiences and be patient. Look for supportive groups or individuals who can understand what you are going through.

Granddaughter Crow (Dr. Joy Gray): It truly is a birthing process, so be gentle with yourself. Oddly enough, I have found that getting a new hairstyle, or changing up my wardrobe to something that feels more like the current me, is really helpful. It is baby steps to manifesting the current version of you.

Jodi Livon: There is a sweet flow to life. Everything is always changing; we are all part of the cycle. There is no need to justify or explain how or why we have changed. Be at peace with the flow and most people will respond in kind. Appreciate and embrace it all and don't expect other people to approve. Make sure you are not force-feeding your newfound insight to them.

Danielle MacKinnon: I don't think it's about "doing" anything in particular, but more about accepting that you're in the in-between space. It simply takes time (sometimes) for the universe to catch up energetically to the changes you're making at the soul level. Just wait, as the universe *will* catch up.

Troy Parkinson: Honor your whole experience and remember that as you journal your spiritual moments in life, you might discover you've had glimmers of them your whole life. When I reflected on my life, I could see the BIG moment that might have catapulted me to a new awareness, but when I sat down to do an assessment of my own spiritual journey, I could see the signposts that were guiding me all along.

Kristy Robinett: Know that you aren't losing pieces of you; you are putting the puzzle of yourself together.

Jurema Silva: Work slowly and with lots of patience. Do not rush. Start your spiritual journey with no expectations at all. Learn how to accept your gifts, and be humble during this process.

You will find out that every day is a learning day. Jumping too high right away will not help you. It will cause stress, and it may push you backward. Remember, life is a journey of learning and transformation. Developing your intuition is a learning process. In school, you start from the beginning as a young child, learning and growing, until you graduate at a certain age. Learning about your inner powers of intuition also takes stages. Gradually you will notice the transformation of the spirit and consciousness. The process takes time and effort.

Also, don't compare yourself with others. You may learn from books, workshops, or classes, but in the end you will develop your own style, skills, and abilities according to your own purpose in this world, soul experience, and especially in relation to your own spirit guides' knowledge.

Is there any practice or action you would recommend that would support someone as they begin to fully integrate their intuitive and spiritual side as part of the whole self?

Melanie Barnum: I would say do what makes you comfortable. If you're like me, you will still live a "normal" (for lack of a better word) life. I have not given up the rest of me, but I have added to my life. I think letting go of what no longer serves you or doesn't make you feel good helps to fully integrate and create space for what does—in this case, it's your intuition and spirituality.

Cyndi Dale: I think it's important to check yourself for triggered issues. As we're growing, the places that hid our shadowed selves become lit. Developing our intuition and spirituality goes hand in hand with self-healing; with feeling and releasing old issues, emotions, and the like.

Sherrie Dillard: Practice self-love. Don't judge yourself or allow thoughts that undermine your sense of self and confidence to take hold within. Be compassionate and take time away from the supernatural to have fun. In the context of intuitive development, self-love can be accepting the changes and being aware of negative self-talk or judgment. It can be helpful to meditate on opening the heart, breathing and receiving love.

Granddaughter Crow (Dr. Joy Gray): I would recommend a journal. Writing in a journal is a great way to bear witness to your personal growth process and to celebrate small victories.

John Holland: I'm a big advocate of meditation. For the people who say, "I don't have time to meditate," I ask, "How many times did you scroll through Facebook today?" That could be meditation time.

I think technology and social media pulls us away from our inner selves. It's teaching us to look outside. A lot of people are on their phone all time. They might sleep with their phone beside them. Even before their foot touches the floor, they're already on Facebook, Instagram, or Twitter and looking at messages. Their soul was just on the other side in a beautiful place recharging itself, and they wake up, look at the phone, and they're already into the physical really fast.

Instead, when you wake, take a moment to put your hands on your heart and say, "I am a soul," and start your day with one word that's going to set the word for the day, like *intuitive, peace, prosperity,* or *healing*. Instead of reaching for your outer technology, reach for your inner technology.

Jodi Livon: Stay in your own lane! Meaning, mind your boundaries. It makes all the difference!

Troy Parkinson: Meditation and finding a spiritual group or book club to share experiences.

Jurema Silva: Practice being with yourself daily. Get used to being with you. When you start appreciating who you truly are, you begin accepting not just your incredible self but also your gifts of intuition. Practicing being silent for a few minutes daily will increase your intuitive powers, and you will eventually feel much closer to the Source. During a few minutes of silence, you are able to hear, see, and sense your energy and understand the whispering that comes from your inner self.

What are some tips for sorting through instilled beliefs in order to move forward with your own authentic spiritual experience?

Melanie Barnum: Realize that not everything you've been taught is right or correct. Understand that life is fluid and what you believed previously may not ring true anymore. Be open to and embrace what makes you happy and what makes you feel good, and let go of anything you've been taught that makes you feel guilty or bad or wrong about who you are, authentically.

Cyndi Dale: Know that beliefs are simply opinions that you've turned into fact. Understand that you decided to hold those opinions as true because they served you—helped you survive—at one level. Think about what beliefs you'd rather know as true. Simplistically, the beliefs that can be actual *truths* instill a sense of wholeness and connection. The ones that are eventually revealed as untrue lead to separation and loneliness.

Sherrie Dillard: Be aware of when self-doubt creeps in, and remind yourself that you don't have to know and figure out everything. Look for the gift in what you are experiencing, even if it doesn't seem that there is one. Choosing to grow and change is always a bit scary. Have gratitude that you are strong enough to move forward.

Granddaughter Crow (Dr. Joy Gray): Give yourself permission to question the beliefs. Give yourself permission to explore other beliefs. Give yourself permission to adjust or release beliefs that keep you away from your authenticity.

Chanda Parkinson: You must be willing to face and challenge what you've been conditioned to believe in your home and community as an impressionable child. The beauty is that you can have it all. You don't have to reject things, but be willing to expand to include other beliefs. They can coexist, no matter what anyone tells you. I personally could no longer be a part of any religious or spiritual community that preached that psychic gifts are bad. However, I could continue to embrace many of the things I was raised to believe in a new light and make peace with it all. A common pitfall is that we have to choose parts of ourselves. You don't have to reject something to embrace something else. It can all coexist.

Troy Parkinson: Follow the light. Trust your gut. Build community.

Jurema Silva: Let go of fear and self-punishment. Be your authentic self and do not fear judgment from others. All human beings have intuitive abilities in various levels. You have no reason to fear what is God's gift to humanity. Having faith in your own potential is an important part of the process. You might start disagreeing with traditional religious norms and begin looking for more answers, but that doesn't mean you will have to ignore your base beliefs and culture. As long as you feel free and determined to begin this journey, old beliefs will eventually melt away over the years. Your spiritual transformation and enlightenment are the primary purposes.

Did you experience a feeling of loss or death of your previous self as you were exploring your metaphysical interests? If so, what was this like for you and how did you handle this? What tips would you give to others who are going through the same thing?

Melanie Barnum: I personally did not. However, I did realize that over time I moved away from many old relationships. My beliefs do not have to be totally synchronous with my friends, but I do think they have to be open to or at least respect my gifts/thoughts/feelings. I have still found it hard to connect with other people who have the same metaphysical interests, because I don't feel like I fit with most I've connected with. So, to this end, I want to say don't get discouraged if you feel disconnected to your new or old lives. Sometimes letting go of what you had as well as letting go of expectations can make room for greater things to come.

Cyndi Dale: Absolutely. I was sad to take a trek that made me appear and feel even more different than I already did. I was sad because the person I was closest to when I started taking classes thought the metaphysical was crazy. I was scared to be rejected by my family, and ultimately was for a while, because they thought I was too weird. I went to therapy and received support from Al-Anon and other places that helped me accept myself for who I am.

Sherrie Dillard: I felt spiritual/psychic growth to be a positive experience. I knew I was connecting with a powerful inner me and I was ready to let go of the old.

Granddaughter Crow (Dr. Joy Gray): With the excitement of becoming authentic, I continued my journey. The hardest thing for me to let go was those who did not understand the new me—or rejected the new me. I had to let some old friends go—that was hard. But this too shall pass. I am surrounded with wonderful people now.

John Holland: No, because it was always there. A lot of people ask if I was nervous as a kid seeing spirit people in my bedroom. How could I be nervous of something that was always there? It's part of me. It's a part that I ignored for a long time, until I had that wake-up call and I couldn't ignore it anymore. Your soul tries to pull toward what it needs to grow and what it wants while it's here. Some of us ignore it. When it became more prominent, I had more clarity of who I was and why I'm here.

Chanda Parkinson: I felt a constant surge of a sense of freedom and liberation as I continued to explore and open my gifts and abilities. The only death or grief I experienced was realizing that the life I had planned and created for myself wasn't the one I was going to live into. I had professional career goals that didn't include utilizing my psychic abilities. Switching tracks for me was incredibly difficult at times, especially since I didn't really know where all of this was going to take me. As is quite common, the plans I had didn't quite match where I felt led to go. I encourage each person to continue to surrender the need to control the process and the outcome, and allow it as a part of the greater unfolding of their own evolution, no matter what comes of it.

Kristy Robinett: I never felt a sense of loss. Instead, I felt a sense of rebirth.

Do you have any other guidance for how we can let go of pieces of who we used to be in order to avoid resisting the transition?

Melanie Barnum: I feel the most important thing is to be true to yourself. If something or someone no longer resonates with you, let it go, gently, with no harsh judgments.

Cyndi Dale: Don't shame those aspects of self or who you've been. We don't shame a one-year-old because they struggle with walking. We don't look down at a first grader because they can't read quickly. Be nurturing and kind and find the silver lining in what we've been.

Sherrie Dillard: A sense of adventure and humor are helpful.

Granddaughter Crow (Dr. Joy Gray): The approach we take toward the authentic self has a lot to do with how we transition into our true self. The hardest thing is the pressures that we may feel from family members, friends, and sometimes a partner. Approach it all with curiosity—you will find your way.

Jurema Silva: Embracing your intuitive powers and using your connection with the spiritual world on a daily basis is an evolution and advancement of the self and the soul. You will naturally let go of parts of the self and experiences that do not serve you or do not bring joy to your life anymore. There are no secrets or tricks for this to happen. The transformation of the self happens intuitively. Pieces of your own self will be discharged slowly, and usually this process is not even noticed. You will realize that change is not immediate, but it happens over time, perhaps over the course of years. I call this process a total awareness and liberation of the self.

How did you build confidence and gain validation in your ability and spiritual guidance? In terms of validation, what ways do you get "confirmation" for intuition or messages that you receive? For example, if I'm critical of a message, I'll ask for it to prove itself in the form of synchronicity.

Melanie Barnum: The more aha moments I was able to give others, the more my confidence grew. Validation, for me, usually comes from my clients. But if I need validation for messages that are more personal, I usually pay attention to how they feel in my body. Also, because it's often hard to be sure, I will use cards or a pendulum for confirmation. And I will be open to signs or synchronicities for confirmation.

Cyndi Dale: I stay aware. I follow my intuitive glimpses and insights and then watch to find out if they were accurate. Did that warning actually pay off? Did it seem smart to go to "this" movie instead of "that" movie? It's also helpful to practice with other people and get their feedback.

Sherrie Dillard: In my books, I recommend asking for an outer synchronicity to confirm an intuitive message. It also helps to be patient if you are unsure as to the significance of what you are experiencing. Put your concerns and confusion aside and the intuitive information and confirmation you seek will come back in a different form when you least expect it.

Granddaughter Crow (Dr. Joy Gray): Feel the liberty of being a partner with the energy, not a slave to it. You are allowed to question it and ask for proof until you are comfortable. Ask for a sign: "If this be true, show me _____ [insert a random item, i.e., a blue butterfly, a banana, or a man on a horse]." Make it fun!

John Holland: I always got the confirmation from people. I was bartending in Los Angeles when I moved to California, and after the accident, stuff would come out of my mouth like, "You're a nurse?" or "Your dog just died?" and the person getting their drink would be like, "Yeah, how did you know that?" I was getting confirmation from my customers and the people from the hotel, but I had to stop that, because it's not ethical and the hotel even asked me to stop for that reason. I tell my students not to give out information unsolicited.

A psychic development class can really help. Sitting in a practice circle and giving off information can be a good way to build confidence as well. Or practice with a friend. You already know a lot about a friend, so you could practice with someone you don't know, like a friend of a friend. Psychometry is the best place to start, holding an item belonging to someone who is living. If someone hands you a grandma's ring of someone you don't know, how are you going to validate the information? Try to work with keys, jewelry, and anything metal. This practice helps you with the foundation of psychic ability—the clairs—and learning which psychic strengths you have.

Jodi Livon: Asking for a sign to validate an intuitive insight is a marvelous idea! It is important not to be tied to the outcome. Maintaining neutrality is powerful. The universe nearly always provides validation.

Troy Parkinson: As an evidential medium, my confirmation comes for the people I sit with. When they can validate the evidence, it showcases the strength of the connection.

Kristy Robinett: I've stopped trying to connect all the dots, knowing that the dots present themselves in the perfect pattern, in the perfect timing.

Jurema Silva: There are times that I ask my spirit guides for confirmation or more explanation of certain subjects coming through messages. The line of communication between a person and the spirit world should be free of doubts and interferences. Do not assume anything if a message is not clear. Just ask for confirmation. Spirits do not get upset when we do not understand a message. They are always willing to help clarify doubts. You can also set an intention up front. One of the conditions I asked for decades ago before embarking on my professional spiritual journey was that there be clarity, transparency, and distinct and direct messages.

How did you go about sharing this part of yourself with others? Do you have any tips for those who are feeling at the point where they really want to begin sharing this side of themselves with others but don't know how? By that point it can feel so big, as though you're about to drop a huge secret in someone else's lap. It's a "coming out of the closet" for those on a spiritual/ intuitive journey. How can you do this in a way that feels safe to you and hopefully unintimidating to the person you've chosen to share with?

Melanie Barnum: The best advice I have is to share it with other like-minded people. Also, beyond that, share it with people who love you and whom you have a good relationship with. I find it best to share your abilities in a nonthreatening way and without too much ego. It's okay to feel proud of your newly developed gifts and it's definitely great to be excited, but I wouldn't approach it with an "I'm better than you are" kind of attitude. Everyone develops at their own pace, and the people you're sharing with may not have gotten as far along in their particular journey as you.

Cyndi Dale: Go slow and test people out! Also take classes at which you know people interested in the topic will appear.

Sherrie Dillard: It's always a leap to share, even if you've been doing it a long time. There's no easy way. Choose open-minded people and give them time to take in what you are expressing. Know that people are responding from their personal belief system. Ultimately, self-acceptance and believing in yourself are essential.

Granddaughter Crow (Dr. Joy Gray): I would open the conversation with, "Have you ever experienced synchronicity or the feeling that you just knew something was about to happen and it did?" Most people can relate to this. Then explain that this occurrence is happening more and more with you. See where the conversation goes.

John Holland: Ask the people around you certain questions and then you'll get a feel for where the person's thoughts are coming from. I'll be doing readings for people and a relative may come through and I'll ask the person, "Can you talk about this session with anybody?" and some people can and some can't. If someone coming through is linked to a relative of a friend, that person may not be interested in hearing about it. I tell the person I'm reading for to ask that linked person something like, "How do you feel about the afterlife?" Trust me, you're going to get a response! The intention is to ask a general question off the cuff, like "How do you feel about intuition? Do you think you have it?" You don't have to let the person know it pertains to you or them. You're just feeling out their level of interest and openness to the topic.

For example, when it came to customers, if I had someone come up to me at the bar, instead of saying "nurse" right away, I would say, "Hey, how you doing? Nice weather. Are you from here? I live on the East Coast. I'm so excited! I just heard my brother passed the nursing exam." And the person might then say, "I'm a nurse!" It's trying to get a validation without freaking someone out.

Troy Parkinson: Find psychic fairs or expos to begin to share your work. Ask close friends to gather and share messages with them. Read all you can on development circles, and if you don't have one in your area, create one.

Jurema Silva: If you are concerned about scaring or intimidating your friends, or if you are apprehensive about judgment from others, perhaps you want to share with a trustworthy friend that you just read a book about spirituality that has brought you another perspective on life and your purpose. Or perhaps tell a good friend or two that you went to a seminar about spirituality and intuition and it made you feel much better about yourself and helped to balance your emotions. Tell a friend that you watched a video on the internet about intuition, that you learned a lot from it, and that you are not afraid anymore.

Introducing small amounts of information about your new journey makes everything so much easier. People around you will get used to your new ideas and points of view, especially if they clearly see some positive changes in you. Over time, close friends and family members will get used to the "new you," and criticism or judgment will dissipate.

Try to give people just a taste of your discoveries or what you are becoming. Sometimes you just need to use simple words, such as "I'm very sensitive with energy from others" or "I am learning how to deal with it and accepting it as a gift, not as a curse." You might say, "I had a strange dream the other night that I was going to find a new job, and the dream came true. I decided to learn more about this, and believe it or not, I am starting to love the topic."

Also, do not disregard or isolate people who don't believe in you or who will try to discredit your gifts. Remember that the practice of compassion is part of your new path as an intuitive person. You don't need to accept their reactions, but understand where they come from. Again, over time, little by little, there will be people around you who will welcome who you are becoming.

How can readers protect themselves while also allowing themselves to emerge from their secret space?

Melanie Barnum: Use your protective energy, your bubble of light. And then, be honest. You will probably come across people who don't believe in what you do or who you've become, but there's really no need to challenge their beliefs. Allow them to continue on their own path while you continue on yours. Protecting yourself sometimes means distancing yourself from those who seek to belittle you or put you down for emerging into your intuitive self.

Cyndi Dale: Be careful and cautious. Test out situations and people. Don't believe that a spiritual teacher is the correct teacher for you or has good boundaries until you experience it yourself.

Granddaughter Crow (Dr. Joy Gray): Feel free to ask for protection and guidance from Spirit. Ground, center, and visualize a bubble or sphere around you. Inside this sphere is you and the divine as it reveals itself to you. The sphere allows you to move in the world with healthy boundaries and a protective cover.

John Holland: When you start studying psychic ability, you're raising your consciousness. Like attracts like. Like-minded people will be attracted to one another. Say you're in the supply room at your office and you're already studying psychic ability. Another person in the room asks how you're doing and suddenly you're talking about a crazy dream they had, and it opens the door to deeper discussion. You'll start noticing people around you who are also attracted to the subject. You could be working with someone for two years who is going to demonstrations or psychic classes that you never even knew about, but once *you* start, you begin to resonate on the same wavelength and notice things you didn't before.

You cannot force this subject of spirituality on others. Everyone is exactly where they're supposed to be. Someone may take a psychic class and then come home and try to push it on other people, but it's your path, your journey. Do not push the subject on other people. And it's okay.

Someone might see that your life's a little better, they see you're calmer, and they ask you, "What are you doing? You seem to be in a better place." That's an opening to share it.

Jodi Livon: By knowing who they are and how they feel and by remembering that intuition is a gift from the universe, and what we do with it is our gift back. Always stay on the side of the light.

Troy Parkinson: Find a few close friends and confidants that you can count on for support. They will support you through this transition.

Jurema Silva: In most cases, a person will feel protected when confidence and trust grow. When you become more secure regarding your gifts, you most likely will feel an energy of balance, serenity, and joy. The lonely part of your journey, and perhaps a feeling of being odd, eventually will disappear. The more you practice your intuitive abilities, the more powerful and self-reliant you will become.

Conclusion

I hope you've found a wealth of answers here to the burning questions you started with on your secret psychic journey. Maybe by now it's not so secret! Even if it still is, hopefully you can at least end here with a sense that you're not as alone as you felt at the beginning. There are many others secretly (and not so secretly) walking alongside you between two worlds.

With a strong understanding of your own subtle ability and spiritual nature, I trust you're ending here feeling more whole than when you began. Keep in mind, though, that this is a lifelong exploration. As you continue along your path, always remember (1) to breathe and (2) to tune in to the messages of Spirit and your subtle intuition. Magic is waiting there for you, and you never know what it's going to reveal next.

Appendix 1
Sample Release of Liability Form

In chapter 1, I covered some safety tips for your practice. There I mentioned potentially making use of a liability release that you have clients sign before your sessions. Here's one example of what this might look like.

Waiver, Release, and Assumption of Risk Form

This form is an important legal document. It explains the assumption of any and all risks in deciding to follow the advice or insight from intuitive consultant **[YOUR NAME]**, who operates as an advising consultant through **[YOUR BUSINESS NAME]**, or a representative of that Company.

It is critical that you read and understand it completely. After you have done so, please print your name legibly and sign in the spaces provided at the bottom.

Waiver, Informed Consent, and Covenant Not to Sue

I, _____, have volunteered to participate in a paid or unpaid session, workshop, or program with **[YOUR NAME]** to include, but also may not be limited to, any and all services provided, such as energy healing, intuitive coaching, and workshop attendance.

In consideration of the agreement to instruct, assist, advise, or train me, I do here and forever release and discharge and hereby hold harmless **[YOUR NAME]** and their respective agents, heirs, assigns, contractors, and employees from any and all claims, demands, damages, rights of action, or causes of action, present or future, arising out of or connected with my participation in a session or purchase or any program WITHOUT LIMITATION, WHICH MAY OCCUR AS A RESULT OF following advice tendered and released or training rendered or use of facilities during a session or event.

I recognize that in no way does **[YOUR NAME]** provide legal, medical, or therapeutic advice and it is my responsibility to secure such advisement.

I acknowledge and agree that I assume the risks associated with any and all activities and/or programs in which I participate and that any intuitive reading, spiritual counsel, or other guidance is for entertainment purposes only.

I acknowledge and agree that no warranties or representations have been made to me regarding the results I will achieve from any insight, session, or program. I understand that results are individual and may vary.

I ACKNOWLEDGE THAT I HAVE THOROUGHLY READ THIS WAIVER AND RELEASE AND FULLY UNDERSTAND THAT IT IS A RELEASE OF LIABILITY. BY SIGNING THIS DOCUMENT, I AM WAIVING ANY RIGHT I OR MY SUCCESSORS MIGHT HAVE TO BRING A LEGAL ACTION OR ASSERT A CLAIM AGAINST **[YOUR NAME]** FOR YOUR NEGLIGENCE OR THAT OF YOUR EMPLOYEES, AGENTS, OR CONTRACTORS.

Participant's signature (parent/guardian if under 18)　　　Date

Please print name

Appendix 2
Common Symbols
and Their Meanings

The list that you'll find here includes signs and symbols that our Secret Psychic Mentors indicated as those they would most recommend people become familiar with, because they're likely to appear in your life. This is the same list you saw in the practice Tune In to Your Personal Meaning of Common Symbols (on page 58 in chapter 2), where you were asked to tune in and write down the meanings that came to you for each item. Seeing how others have interpreted these signs can sometimes help you fill in the gaps for your own list, so you'll find my results of that practice here. See what matches up and what you feel could enhance the descriptions that you recorded. On the flip side, since you'll have already tuned in to your personal meanings, you may find that some of the interpretations recorded here don't feel quite right for you personally, and that's perfectly fine! It can all be very individual. Mixed in with my intuitive interpretations are some paraphrased descriptions of popular meanings from other sources, as well as insights from the Secret Psychic Mentors.

Animals

Bear: Power, strength, ferocity. Cubs—mischief, playfulness. Teddy—softness, comfort, tenderness. Hibernation, introspection, self-care. For me this could also be a symbol of my maternal grandpa, for a cherished teddy bear he gave me for Christmas.

Bunny: Spring, fertility, sexuality, luck (i.e., lucky rabbit's foot). For me, if this symbol appears as the Velveteen Rabbit, it will be a sign of a deceased relative trying to make a connection with their loved one to express that they are still "real."

Cat: Independence. Feminine energy. Reserved but loving and loyal. People need to earn their way into your inner circle. Catching rodents—a need for decluttering and being mindful of your space and mental thoughts.

Deer: Innocence, trust, gently being led onto a new path, a caution to be observant.

Dog: Socialization. Masculine energy. Loyalty and true friendship. Enthusiasm. Sniffing out hidden answers. Potentially a sign to check your emotions or be aware of your clairempathy, in the way that one needs to manage strong emotions while training because mood can transfer to the dog. If shown with a service badge, a sign of accepting more support.

Fox: Mischievousness, cunning, playfulness, camouflage. For me this would especially be a sign of family, as my sister loves foxes and my mom has had fun watching fox families around her home.

Horse: Freedom, power, movement, travel. Embarking on a new journey. Reining in a wild spirit.

Snake: Shedding your skin, transmutation, change. Caduceus, healing. While for me this symbol is more likely to be a positive one, it could also refer to the biblical story of the serpent in the Garden of Eden, warning of temptation, evil influence, or taking extra caution with those who are offering you questionable guidance.

Birds

Blue jay: Assertiveness. For me this is a sign of a bully and the need for enhanced boundaries. You may need to rally against someone else's disrespect of you and your space.

Cardinal: Vitality. A rare instance of bright color during winter, this bird is a sign for me of a passed loved one reassuring that they are still around. It may be a precursor to a more detailed message.

Crow: Messenger. Crows are highly intelligent and watchful of other beings and their actions. For me crows are a sign of someone friendly watching over you.

Eagle: While any bird can be a symbol of rising above a situation to see it from a higher perspective, eagles in-particular are that sign for me. They are also a sign for me of Spirit watching over you.

Hummingbird: Wake up to the sweetness of this moment. A reminder to be present, practice gratitude, and be mindful of (and take action toward) what brings you joy. For me they are also a sign of my sister in Spirit.

Parrot: Conversation, finding your voice. Break out of autopilot mode. Stop just repeating what others have taught you to say/be/do. Flaunt your unique colors, creativity, and talent.

Robin: One of the birds that I notice at the return of spring, and who are often hugely pregnant, robins are a sign for me of coming home to family.

Swallow: Protection. May symbolize someone encroaching onto your territory or a need to rally against someone else's aggression. Alternately, it could be a sign to assess your own reactions. Is something or someone triggering you? And is your response excessive in relation to the situation?

Colors

Colors often symbolize a certain emotion or chakra.

Blue: Throat (fifth) chakra, trust, loyalty, relaxation, sadness

Green: Heart (fourth) chakra, health, luck, security, envy

Orange: Sacral (second) chakra, enthusiasm, optimism, creativity

Pink: Heart (fourth) chakra, love, compassion

Purple: Third eye (sixth) chakra, imagination, spirituality

Red: Root (first) chakra, groundedness, passion, anger, caution

White: Crown (seventh) chakra, peace, innocence

Yellow: Solar plexus (third) chakra, happiness, positivity, caution

Flowers

Baby's breath: While this flower is generally a symbol for eternal love, innocence, and beauty, for me it's a symbol of a baby-to-come.

Carnation: Love is commonly associated with this flower, although each color has its own meaning. Because carnations are so often used for parade floats, for me they symbolize the celebration of significant life (and afterlife) events.

Dahlia: Inner strength, being truly happy, finding what lights you up from the inside out, your true joy and passion.

Forget-me-not: This flower symbolizes true love. For me it comes as a message from a deceased loved one communicating that they are still around and haven't forgotten you.

Iris: Hope, wisdom, and royalty are the traditional meanings of this flower. Because I've so often received irises at significant moments and anniversaries, for me they symbolize an upcoming accomplishment, milestones, or a memorial date.

Lily: Traditionally this flower refers to purity, fertility, and rebirth. For me it's a symbol of springtime. I associate it with a children's Easter show where the villain's name was Lily, so it's also a symbol for me of communication and redemption. I also recognize it as a symbol for poison, because lilies are toxic to many animals.

Rose: The meaning of this flower can vary by color. A red rose would typically symbolize romance, love, beauty, and passion. I will usually see someone extending a single red rose, as though they are reaching out to give it to me or whoever I'm with as a greeting and an offering of love from a deceased loved one.

Sunflower: Loyalty and long life. For me, sunflowers represent abundance, joy, and the seasons of summer and early fall.

Geometric Shapes

Circle: Might represent a cycle of life that is ending or is completed.

Diamond: Wealth or a significant romantic relationship.

Oval: I would translate this as "the Oval Office," where the message is trying to communicate a government connection.

Pentagon: I would translate this as "the Pentagon," the headquarters for the US Department of Defense and a symbol of connection to the military.

Rectangle: I would see this as a door or window, a symbol for new opportunity. It may also indicate a recent disappointment, as the closing of one door and the opening of another.

Square: I would see this as a box, potentially meaning a gift to come, change (as in packing boxes to move), or an unpacking of previously hidden things (Pandora's box).

Star: I would see this as a symbol for your dreams, as in wishing upon a star.

Triangle: As the most stable shape, this would be a sign of stability to me.

Insects

Ant: Community, hard work, preparing for the future.

Bee: Busy, fertility, seeking out beauty/joy, finding the sweetness in life.

Butterfly: Joy, going through significant change, a challenging transformation.

Cricket: Conscience, listening to your intuition, luck.

Fly: Annoyance, observing as an outsider.

Grasshopper: Taking action, leaping forward. It's also been associated with being the lazy grasshopper, joyful in the moment but perhaps unmotivated and, as a result, unprepared in the future.

Mosquito: Annoyance, blood-sucker. Are you or is someone else mooching off others or being an energy vampire?

Moth: A need to look for the light, reclaim your joy.

Numbers

0: Wholeness and potential. Infinite possibility. Completion. A universal symbol of beginnings, endings, and Spirit. The universe working with you to help you achieve a goal.

1: Independence and self-reliance. Making a new start.

2: Balance, relationship, being flexible in collaboration.

3: Harmony, good fortune, creativity and expression, higher wisdom, divine trinity, a measure of time (past, present, future).

4: Stability. For me this number is a sign of home.

7: Spiritual insight, learning to trust your intuition.

666: Popularly seen as representing evil and a symbol of the Antichrist or devil. However, in numerology it's actually about idealism, tolerance, and compassion. With the conflict of negative and positive interpretations of this number, for me it ends up symbolizing the need to step back and reassess your automatic assumptions. Perhaps you need to consider a new perspective on a situation.

1111: Wake up to the present moment, your spiritual side, and your intuition. Could be someone in Spirit saying a friendly hello and letting you know you're moving in the right direction.

Other Common Symbols

Aura: If bright: energized and healthy, connecting to your spiritual nature. If dull: fatigued and unwell. Refer to the colors for additional interpretations.

Birth/labor: New beginning. Life transition. If not the literal introduction of a new family member, then perhaps the beginning of a new project or career or a move to a new location.

Cheerleader: Someone is in your corner rooting you on.

Coins: Abundance, wishes, luck. Like "pennies from heaven," a sign that someone in Spirit is trying to get your attention and show that they're around you. Could also be a sign of someone who had a collection.

Cross: Religious association, faith in general, or a universal message of spiritual energy and love.

Door: Opportunity, the choice to face a new direction, opening to the unknown.

Feather: Like coins, a sign that someone in Spirit is trying to get your attention and show that they're around you. The color may represent different messages.

Fire: Dramatic change and personal transformation. Like the phoenix, the end of one phase and rebirth into another.

Fork in the road: A decision needs to be made, or it may mean there are two ways to do something. This could also be shown as just a fork or just a road.

Mirror: Self-assessment, of needing to look at yourself or reassess the situation you're in.

Moon: Feminine energy, the Divine Mother, cycles, fertility, casting light into the shadows to see through the darkness. Changeable nature.

Radio: Guides or loved ones trying to communicate with you.

Rainbow: Hope. The foretelling of good things or resolution after challenge. Reclaiming a sense of wonder, taking a moment to appreciate everyday magic. Could also be a symbol in reference to a popular poem about crossing the rainbow bridge and represent a deceased animal companion trying to make a connection.

Ring: Someone getting married, a recent marriage, or a good relationship. If dropped or seen being removed from the finger, may indicate relationship issues or a divorce.

Stop sign: Stop, take more time to consider the situation.

Sun: Masculine energy, the Divine Father, consciousness, inner power.

Telephone: An important call or a message coming, connecting with the other side.

Water: Emotion, sadness, overwhelm. Things just beyond the surface and out of reach. Purification.

Window: Opportunity and a new direction.

Plants

Aloe vera: Soothing, healing. Being burnt by a person or situation and finding a way to resolve it.

Cactus: Self-protection and thriving amid challenge. Being overly defensive. A prickly situation that you're trying to maneuver. Being resourceful, living minimally or sustainably. A need for good energy management.

Echeveria imbricata 'Blue Rose' succulent: Nicknamed "hens and chicks," this plant for me symbolizes relationship with a mother. It could also represent whimsy, a playful hobby, and not taking things so seriously.

Fern: Gradual unfolding, a slow reveal.

Jade: Friendship and prosperity.

Peace lily: Healthy, thriving. In contrast, when wilting or paired with a stop sign, a sign of poison or a need for attention to the well-being of a human or animal companion.

Shamrock/clover: Luck. Being Irish, I also see this as a symbol that could be a cue about someone's heritage. It could also be a marker for the time of year, as a symbol for March and St. Patrick's Day. Some shamrock plants close and open according to the light, so for me it's also a sign of self-care and aligning with circadian rhythms.

Spider plant: Rejuvenation, reproduction, creativity, manifesting goals and projects, connection to family and friends.

Trees

Trees represent growth, the Tree of Life, the season, or a stage of the life cycle (budding spring, full summer, colors turning fall, bare and slumbering winter).

Balsam fir: Surviving difficult trials, life still existing through winter, December, joyful celebrations through the Yule season and at the Winter Solstice.

Banyan: Immortality. For me this tree would also symbolize stability, travel, and Hawaii.

Birch: Renewal. Because my sister and I used birch bark as play money when we were kids, for me this tree represents childhood nostalgia and play.

Eucalyptus: Because of the use of eucalyptus as essential oil, I associate this tree with a focus on healing and breathing. After seeing rainbow eucalyptus trees in person in a location I thought I'd only ever see in my imagination, this tree has also become a symbol of adventure and taking action to embody your dreams.

Maple: With its beautiful leaves in the fall, this tree symbolizes autumn.

Oak: Safety and protection. With the production of acorns, this tree also symbolizes resourcefulness and preparation for me. I grew up with acorns loudly hitting a skylight window every fall, so this tree can also represent a noise disturbance.

Palm: A warm weather location, arriving at a destination, return from travel, relaxation.

Weeping willow: Grief, sadness, death. My grandparents had a weeping willow that we would swing on when we visited as kids, so for me it's also a symbol of childhood play, nostalgia, and grandparents.

Appendix 3
The Secret Psychic Questionnaire

Here you'll find all the questions that were asked of the Secret Psychic Mentors. Their responses make up part 2 of the book. On page 181 there is a practice (called "Completing the Secret Psychic Questionnaire") that will lead you in answering these questions for insight into your own experience.

What It Means to Be a "Secret Psychic"

- What do you see are the key benefits of engaging with our intuitive and spiritual abilities?
- When you first started learning about psychic/intuitive abilities, was it something that life thrust upon you or were you drawn to it with your own natural curiosity?
- How did you begin learning about your psychic abilities?
- What do you wish you'd known when you were first discovering your psychic abilities?
- What would have helped you most when you began your own spiritual and metaphysical journey?
- Did you feel you had to keep this part of yourself a secret from others? If so, why?
- If you felt you needed to keep your subtle abilities secret, did this lead to an experience of dissociation, as though you were living two different lives? If yes, what was this like for you and how did you handle it, along with any feelings of isolation, sadness, anxiety, etc.?
- For those who are in the place of secrecy, what advice would you give them?

- What are three tips you would give for others practicing their abilities and evolving on their spiritual journey if they're working at it all alone?
- Where and how did you find support, resources, and community to develop your skills?
- If your subtle abilities were initially something you kept secret, when did you finally begin to feel like this secret side of yourself was something you needed to share with others? What were some cues that indicated you were ready?
- Do you feel that the call to develop and work with our intuitive abilities is part of a spiritual experience and/or an awakening of the authentic self? Why or why not?

Subtle Intuition

- What intuitive abilities are strongest for you? How do you usually experience them?
- What is one exercise you would recommend for someone newly exploring their psychic ability? Please share the exercise here.
- What advice do you have for decoding and discovering your own spiritual language and interpreting symbols in visions and dreams? Especially as a beginner, how do you know when to rely on your own interpretations, when to refer to external resources, or when to ask for input from others?
- How much of our spiritual language do you feel is universal versus individual?

Recognize the Natural Occurrence of Spirit Communication

- What is one key way that you personally embrace your subtle intuition and messages from Spirit in your daily life?

- How can you intuit whether communication is coming from a positive source versus when it might be best for you to create a boundary to break communication with a certain source.
- What is your opinion on the use of spirit boards? Yay or nay?

When Intuitive Senses Seep into Everyday Life

- Do you have any tips for when intuitive senses seep into everyday life? For example:
  - ~ Hearing other people's thoughts, feeling others' feelings, or experiencing spontaneous visions
  - ~ Unexpected energy, like a cold spot in a space, or some other indicator of a spirit or imprint of spirit energy
  - ~ Spirit "pop-ins"—hearing messages at random from those on the other side
- As a follow-up to the previous questions, how do you decide when to engage and when to let things be? How can you tell if you're supposed to "do" something with what you've just received or if it was just a "bleed through" moment where you experienced energy that isn't really important for you to engage with? For example, with hearing, feeling, or seeing, do you just clear and ground? Do you engage and offer the message? For unexpected energy, do you try to clear it or just acknowledge and leave it be?

How to Integrate Your Spiritual Experience

- What is one bit of advice you would give to someone who feels like they are living in the gap of who they used to be and who they are becoming on their spiritual journey? How can they begin to integrate their past/who they have been with their new understanding of who they are becoming?
- Is there any practice or action you would recommend that would support someone as they begin to fully integrate their intuitive and spiritual side as part of the whole self?

- What are some tips for sorting through instilled beliefs in order to move forward with your own authentic spiritual experience?

- Did you experience a feeling of loss or death of your previous self as you were exploring your metaphysical interests? If so, what was this like for you and how did you handle this? What tips would you give to others who are going through the same thing?

- Do you have any other guidance for how we can let go of pieces of who we used to be in order to avoid resisting the transition?

- How did you build confidence and gain validation in your ability and spiritual guidance? In terms of validation, what ways do you get "confirmation" for intuition or messages that you receive? For example, if I'm critical of a message, I'll ask for it to prove itself in the form of synchronicity.

- How did you go about sharing this part of yourself with others? Do you have any tips for those who are feeling at the point where they really want to begin sharing this side of themselves with others but don't know how? By that point it can feel so big, as though you're about to drop a huge secret in someone else's lap. It's a "coming out of the closet" for those on a spiritual/intuitive journey. How can you do this in a way that feels safe to you and hopefully unintimidating to the person you've chosen to share with?

- How can readers protect themselves while also allowing themselves to emerge from their secret space?

References and Recommended Resources

There are *so many* excellent resources out there, but for this list I obviously had to narrow them down somehow. I've included some materials by the Secret Psychic Mentors, and I also asked them what their top additional recommendations would be, specifically for those who are secret psychics. Their responses, along with some of my own recommendations (and sources that I cited throughout the book), make up this list.

The Secret Psychic Mentors

You can find out more about the Secret Psychic Mentors and their books, classes, session availability, and more at the following websites.

- Melanie Barnum: www.melaniebarnum.com
- Cyndi Dale: www.cyndidale.com
- Sherrie Dillard: www.sherriedillard.com
- Granddaughter Crow (Dr. Joy Gray): www.granddaughtercrow.com
- John Holland: www.johnholland.com
- Jodi Livon: www.theintuitivecoach.com
- Danielle MacKinnon: www.daniellemackinnon.com
- Michael Mayo: MediumMichaelMayo.com & OakbridgeInstitute.org
- Chanda and Troy Parkinson: www.chandaparkinson.com
- Kristy Robinett: www.kristyrobinett.com
- Jurema Silva: www.juremasilva.com
- Angela A. Wix: www.AngelaAnn.Wix.com/arts

Subtle Energy, Psychic Ability, and Intuition

Barnum, Melanie. *Intuition at Work: Trust Your Gut to Get Ahead in Business and in Life.* Woodbury, MN: Llewellyn, 2020.

Bodine, Echo. *The Gift: Understand and Develop Your Psychic Abilities.* Novato, CA: New World Library, 2003.

Dale, Cyndi. *Llewellyn's Complete Book of Chakras: Your Definitive Source of Energy Center Knowledge for Health, Happiness, and Spiritual Evolution.* Woodbury, MN: Llewellyn, 2016.

Franken, Kris. *The Call of Intuition: How to Recognize & Honor Your Intuition, Instinct & Insight.* Woodbury, MN: Llewellyn, 2020.

Lovelace, Amanda. *Believe in Your Own Magic: A 45-Card Oracle Deck and Guidebook.* Kansas City, MO: Andrews McMeel Publishing, 2020.

Parkinson, Chanda. *Meditations for Psychic Development: Practical Exercises to Awaken Your Sixth Sense.* Woodbury, MN: Llewellyn, 2021.

Dream and Symbol Interpretation

Alvarez, Melissa. *Animal Frequency: Identify, Attune, and Connect to the Energy of Animals.* Woodbury, MN: Llewellyn, 2017.

Andrews, Ted. *Animal Speak: The Spiritual & Magical Powers of Creatures Great & Small.* Woodbury, MN: Llewellyn, 1993.

Barnum, Melanie. *The Book of Psychic Symbols: Interpreting Intuitive Messages.* Woodbury, MN: Llewellyn, 2012.

Dillard, Sherrie. *Sacred Signs & Symbols: Awaken to the Messages & Synchronicities That Surround You.* Woodbury, MN: Llewellyn, 2017.

Lennox, Dr. Michael. *Dream Sight: A Dictionary and Guide for Interpreting Any Dream.* Woodbury, MN: Llewellyn, 2011.

———. *Llewellyn's Complete Dictionary of Dreams: Over 1,000 Dream Symbols and Their Universal Meanings.* Woodbury, MN: Llewellyn, 2015.

Todeschi, Kevin. *The Best Dream Book Ever: Accessing Your Personal Intuition and Guidance.* Virginia Beach, VA: Yazdan, 2013.

Death, Afterlife, and Spirit Communication

Doka, Kenneth J., PhD. *When We Die: Extraordinary Experiences at Life's End.* Woodbury, MN: Llewellyn, 2020.

Holland, John. *Bridging Two Realms: Learn to Communicate with Your Loved Ones on the Other-Side.* Carlsbad, CA: Hay House, 2018.

Livon, Jodi. *The Happy Medium: Awakening to Your Natural Intuition.* Woodbury, MN: Llewellyn, 2009.

Mayo, Michael. *Effortless Mediumship: An Empowering and Evidence-Based Approach to Genuine Spirit Communication.* Woodbury, MN: Llewellyn, 2022. (Tentative title and release date.)

Parkinson, Troy. *Bridge to the Afterlife: A Medium's Message of Hope & Healing.* Woodbury, MN: Llewellyn, 2009.

Robinett, Kristy. *Messages from a Wonderful Afterlife: Signs Loved Ones Send from Beyond.* Woodbury, MN: Llewellyn, 2017.

Steffen, Edith Maria, and Adrian Coyle. "Can 'Sense of Presence' Experiences in Bereavement Be Conceptualised as Spiritual Phenomena?" *Mental Health, Religion & Culture* 13, no. 3 (2010): 273–91. https://www.researchgate.net/publication/233272815_Can_sense_of_presence_experiences_in_bereavement_be_conceptualised_as_spiritual_phenomena.

Van Praagh, James. *Unfinished Business: What the Dead Can Teach Us About Life.* New York: Harper One, 2009.

Animal Intuition and Communication

"Elephants Journey to Pay Respect … But How Did They Know?" All-Creatures.org. February 2013. https://www.all-creatures.org/stories/a-elephants-journey-respect.html.

MacKinnon, Danielle. *Animal Lessons: Discovering Your Spiritual Connection with Animals.* Woodbury, MN: Llewellyn, 2017.

Mitchem, Jim, and Laurie Smithwick, eds. *Gone Dogs: Tales of Dogs We've Loved.* Charlotte, NC: Thomas Woodland, 2019.

Sewall, Katy. "The Girl Who Gets Gifts from Birds." BBC News. February 25, 2015 https://www.bbc.com/news/magazine-31604026.

Sheldrick, Dame Daphne. *Life, Love, and Elephants: An African Love Story.* New York: Farrar, Straus and Giroux, 2012.

Waterworth, Tanya. "Elephants Say Goodbye to the Whisperer." Independent Online. March 10, 2012. https://www.iol.co.za/news/south-africa/kwazulu-natal/elephants-say-goodbye-to-the-whisperer-1253463.

Personal Transformation and Connecting with the Authentic Self

Granddaughter Crow [Joy Gray]. *Belief, Being, and Beyond: Your Journey to Questioning Ideas, Deconstructing Concepts & Healing from Harmful Belief Systems.* Woodbury, MN: Llewellyn, 2022.

Kidd, Sue Monk. *The Dance of the Dissident Daughter: A Woman's Journey from Christian Tradition to the Sacred Feminine.* New York: HarperOne, 1996.

Lesser, Elizabeth. *Broken Open: How Difficult Times Can Help Us Grow.* New York: Villard Books, 2005. New York: HarperOne, 1996.

Mathews, Andrea. *Letting Go of Good: Dispel the Myth of Goodness to Find Your Genuine Self.* Woodbury, MN: Llewellyn, 2017.

Wix, Angela A. *Llewellyn's Little Book of Unicorns.* Woodbury, MN: Llewellyn, 2019.

Dreamwork and Healing Past Trauma

Johnson, Clare. *The Art of Transforming Nightmares: Harness the Creative and Healing Power of Bad Dreams, Sleep Paralysis, and Recurring Nightmares.* Woodbury, MN: Llewellyn, 2020.

Kaehr, Shelley A. *Meet Your Karma: The Healing Power of Past Life Memories.* Woodbury, MN: Llewellyn, 2020.

Sowton, Dr. Christopher. *Dreamworking: How to Listen to the Inner Guidance of Your Dreams.* Woodbury, MN: Llewellyn, 2017.

Brain Retraining/Neural Rewiring

Dynamic Neural Rewiring System (DNRS), https://retrainingthebrain.com.

Gupta Program Brain Retraining, https://www.guptaprogram.com.

Joe Dispenza, https://drjoedispenza.com/collections.

Spina, RJ. *Supercharged Self-Healing: A Revolutionary Guide to Access High-Frequency States of Consciousness That Rejuvenate and Repair.* Woodbury, MN: Llewellyn, 2021.

Searching for Classes and Events

Arthur Findlay College, https://arthurfindlaycollege.org

Body Mind Spirit Directory, https://bodymindspiritdirectory.org

Journey Within Spiritualists' National Union Church, https://journeywithin.org

Spiritualists' National Union, "Find Spiritualism Near You," https://www.snu.org.uk/Pages/Events/Category/churches

National Spiritualist Association of Churches, "Directory of Churches & Camps," https://nsac.org/directory/churches/

You can also refer to the section "Find the Instruction That Makes Sense for You" on page 150 in chapter 5. As a reminder, here is a summary of ideas that were discussed there:

- Classes in person or virtually
- Psychic development classes
- New Age and metaphysical stores around you
- Yoga studios
- Spiritual centers in your area or those at a distance that offer remote programs
- Sign up for email lists
- Community classes in your area
- Look at the books you've read, see who the author is, and check out their website to see if they have classes that they're offering.

Legal Issues Relating to Psychic Ability

Bahkt, Natasha, and Jordan Palmer. "Modern Law, Modern Hammers: Canada's Witchcraft Provision as an Image of Persecution." *Windsor Review of Legal and Social Issues* 35 (December 2015): 123–146. https://papers.ssrn.com/sol3/papers.cfm?abstract_id=2606165.

Dias, Elizabeth. "In the Crystal Ball: More Regulation for Psychics." *TIME,* September 2, 2010. http://content.time.com/time/nation/article/0,8599,2015676,00.html.

Greene, Heather. "Virginia Priestess Raises Concerns Over Discriminatory Town Code." The Wild Hunt. May 11, 2014. https://wildhunt.org/2014/05/virginia-priestess-raises-concerns-over-discriminatory-town-code.html.

Jackson, Andy. "The Persecution of Psychics Throughout History." Psychics Directory. Accessed August 31, 2021. https://www.psychicsdirectory.com/articles/persecution-psychics-history/.

"Penal Law: Article 165.35—Fortune Telling." New York State Law. Accessed August 31, 2021. https://ypdcrime.com/penal.law/article165.php#p165.35.

Legal Resources

Conflict Resolution

American Civil Liberties Union (ACLU), https://www.aclu.org/

Americans United for Separation of Church and State (AUSCS), https://www.au.org/

Lady Liberty League (LLL)—Religious freedom support for Wiccans, Pagans, and other Nature religion practitioners worldwide, https://www.circlesanctuary.org/index.php/lady-liberty-league/lady-liberty-league

Liability Insurance

Associated Bodywork & Massage Professionals (ABMP), "About ABMP: A Massage Therapy Association," https://www.abmp.com/about-abmp

Energy Medicine Professional Association (EMPA), "Professional Liability Insurance for Energy Healers and Holistic Practitioners," https://get .energymedicineprofessionalinsurance.com/empa

Becoming an Ordained Minister

Universal Life Church (ULC), "Become an Ordained Minister," https://www.ulc.org/

Movies

Buck, Chris, and Jennifer Lee, dirs. *Frozen II.* Disney, 2019.

Burton, Tim, dir. *Beetlejuice.* Warner Brothers, 1988.

Dannelly, Brian, dir. *Saved!* United Artists, 2004.

Dunne, Griffin, dir. *Practical Magic.* Warner Bros., 1998.

Koepp, David, dir. *Ghost Town.* DreamWorks Pictures, 2008.

Spielberg, Steven, dir. *E.T. the Extra-Terrestrial.* Universal Pictures, 1982.

Turteltaub, Jon, dir. *Phenomenon.* Touchstone Pictures, 1996.

Waters, Mark, dir. *Just Like Heaven.* DreamWorks Pictures, 2005.

Zucker, Jerry, dir. *Ghost.* Paramount Pictures, 1990.

Additional Cited References

Bible. New International Version (NIV).

Bruno Chikly et al., "Primo Vascular System: A Unique Biological System Shifting a Medical Paradigm." *The Journal of the American Osteopathic Association* 116, no. 1 (January 2016): 12–21. https://www.cecity.com/aoa /jaoa_mag/2016/jan_16/12.pdf.

Liu Chenglin et al. "X-Ray Phase-Contrast CT Imaging of the Acupoints Based on Synchrotron Radiation." *Journal of Electron Spectroscopy and Related Phenomena* 196 (October 2014): 80–84.

Miroslav Stefanov et al. "The Primo Vascular System as a New Anatomical System." *Journal of Acupuncture and Meridian Studies* 6, no. 6 (December 2013): 331–38. https://doi.org/10.1016/j.jams.2013.10.001.

Williams, Margery. *The Velveteen Rabbit.* New York: Doubleday, 1991.

Acknowledgments

The creation of a book is never an independent endeavor and I'm honored for the assistance I've received in making this dream a reality. To be able to share this part of myself, along with stories I started writing down a decade ago (and thought only I would ever see), is such a gift.

Abundant thanks go out to everyone at Llewellyn working behind the scenes who gave me this opportunity and helped it come to fruition. To those I worked with directly: I'm very grateful to Amy Glaser and Andrea Neff for their support in helping me to get the words just right; to Donna Burch-Brown and Christine Ha for their thoughtful attention in developing a beautiful interior design; and to Shira Atakpu for all her care in creating a cover beyond what I'd imagined, that is so meaningful to what this book is about.

My great appreciation is extended to each of the Secret Psychic Mentors who provided their responses to my many questions: Melanie Barnum, Cyndi Dale, Sherrie Dillard, Granddaughter Crow (Dr. Joy Gray), John Holland, Jodi Livon, Danielle MacKinnon, Michael Mayo, Chanda Parkinson, Troy Parkinson, Kristy Robinett, and Jurema Silva. Thank you so much for providing readers with answers and much-needed context for the secret psychic experience. Your support of this project made it feel real, even when it was only an idea in my mind. With every response I received from you, my own experience came into better focus, and I know the same will be true for many others.

Thank you to Echo Bodine, first for being a mentor to me when I finally began stepping more fully into my own subtle abilities. Your guidance filled me with so much joy, as does your foreword to this book. I feel blessed to know you.

To Pam Paulick, I will always be grateful for being placed next to you in dreaded physics class (so close, but so far, from "psychic")! For all your apologies about the many "book-length texts," they became invaluable as I read back through two years of our secret psychic conversations to build the bones of this book. Thank you for being there and allowing me to mine from our friendship and your phoenix-phase of life.

To everyone else who allowed for the inclusion of stories that related to them, you have my profuse gratitude. Each permission to share allowed theory to come alive with true real-world examples and every conversation ensured those stories were recorded accurately. You breathed life into the pages of this book. It truly wouldn't be what it is without you.

To Luke Wix, who never knew he was marrying the secret psychic, thank you for holding the space where I could grow into my interests and be exactly who I truly am. I also appreciate your support as sporadic dictionary, thesaurus, and general wordsmith. While you sometimes help me find the words, there really aren't any that can define exactly what I mean to say, so I'll sum it up by saying *thank you for being my home.*

I also hold great appreciation for the muses in Spirit, known and unknown, who nudged me beyond fretful fits of procrastination and guided me through all the hours of writing.

And finally, to you, Secret Psychic: Thank you for following your inner calling to better understand your authentic self. I know how challenging that can be and hope you've found solace in these pages. In the midst of a search that's often so isolating, I'm deeply honored to have had the chance to connect with you.

Contributor Photo Credits

- Melanie Barnum / © Bryn Mullins
- Cyndi Dale / © Katie Cannon Photography
- Sherrie Dillard / © John Elkins
- Granddaughter Crow (Dr. Joy Gray) / © Tracy Urban,
  ReturntoSelfSanctuary.com
- John Holland / © Laura Wooster
- Jodi Livon / © Jason Rein
- Danielle MacKinnon / © Erica Robinson Photography
- Michael Mayo / © Corey L. Chattman
- Chandra Parkinson / © Troy Parkinson
- Troy Parkinson / © John Borge Studios
- Kristy Robinett / © Kristy Robinett
- Jurema Silva / © Erica Ann Photography, St. Cloud, MN

To Write to the Author

If you wish to contact the author or would like more information about this book, please write to the author in care of Llewellyn Worldwide Ltd. and we will forward your request. Both the author and the publisher appreciate hearing from you and learning of your enjoyment of this book and how it has helped you. Llewellyn Worldwide Ltd. cannot guarantee that every letter written to the author can be answered, but all will be forwarded. Please write to:

Angela A. Wix
℅ Llewellyn Worldwide
2143 Wooddale Drive
Woodbury, MN 55125-2989
Please enclose a self-addressed stamped envelope for reply,
or $1.00 to cover costs. If outside the U.S.A., enclose
an international postal reply coupon.

Many of Llewellyn's authors have websites with additional
information and resources. For more information,
please visit our website at http://www.llewellyn.com.